HONEY TRAP

www.instagram.com/kanikabatra

9781922267443 (Print)
9781922267450 (eBook)

Book production by Noble Books

Cover design by Xoum Publishing Services
Printed and bound in Australia by Ligare

The paper this book is printed on is in accordance with the standards of the Forest Stewardship Council®. The FSC® promotes environmentally responsible, socially beneficial and economically viable management of the world's forests.

HONEY TRAP

KANIKA BATRA

NOBLE

CHAPTER ONE

July 14, 1974

Waiting rooms depress me. Waiting rooms in psychiatrists' offices make me want to blow a hole through my left temple.

There is a woman on the seat opposite me arguing with herself, her voice alternating between a high-pitched squeal and a poor imitation of a man's deep rumble. I suspect she's fashioned her clothes out of an old lampshade. The man beside her has his eyes closed; a light sheen of sweat coats his balding head. His hands are stuffed tightly into the front pockets of his pants, and I'm not too sure if he's dying or napping.

The office is sterile and uninteresting, despite strenuous efforts to make the décor lively. Four brown walls are adorned with pictures of flowers and beaches, a nurse station in a darker shade of the brown, and chesterfield armchairs instead of hard-backed chairs. Five-year-old magazines, presumably a cesspool of dirt and bacteria, are stacked on the mahogany table in the center of the small room. The receptionist today is a petite, bored-looking blonde. She greets patients with a mechanical smile and ushers them into a seat while speaking in a monotone. She has a clipped estuary-English accent and a disproportionately large nose. A stocky nurse approaches Lampshade Woman and offers her a round blue pill and a plastic cup of water.

"Mrs. Patton, it's important you take your medication," she says, the smile still smeared across her wan face.

The woman cocks her head, brow furrowed. "Who's Mrs.Patton?"

I cringe and look away as a nurse forces the pill into the woman's mouth. I feel a little nauseated at the sight of the woman's decaying teeth. When the doctor appears in the doorway, I'm thankful. It's not often that psychiatrists will see patients on Sundays, but this clinic makes exceptions for special cases. I've always been a special case.

"Maris." He smiles at me, holding his clear clipboard to his chest. He's attempted to go for the whole "hip doctor, I'm a friend, not a medical professional" look. Instead of a coat and pants ensemble, he's wearing a striped Ralph Lauren shirt, rolled up at the elbows, tucked into a pair of tan, flared corduroys. His shaggy dark hair is combed back, and he's young for a psychiatrist, probably only mid-thirties at the most. I follow him into his office, smoothing my cut-offs down over my thighs. He closes the door behind us and takes his seat. I perch on the edge of the patient couch, and gingerly place my tan lambskin handbag on my lap.

"How've you been, Maris?" he asks.

"I've been well, Dr. Walsh, how've you been?" I ask, crossing my legs. "The new hair colour looks fantastic, by the way."

"Oh, thank you. I appreciate it. The dark hair has been quite a change." He flicks through his file, looking up to smile at me. "I haven't seen you in three weeks, what's been happening?"

"I've been enjoying my holidays—exams were a nightmare."

"How was Europe?"

"I spent a week in Madrid coked out of my fucking mind. I can't say it wasn't fun. I had some friends from school with me. We had a couple of weeks in Mom's villa in Cannes beforehand to rest up. She wasn't with us for a lot of the time, which was for the best."

I study his tanned, somewhat leathery complexion. His eyes narrow slightly upon hearing my reference to cocaine. He swallows, his Adam's apple bobbing. He's figuring out how to broach the subject without seeming harsh, restrictive, or fatherly. It's obvious he's debating which issue he should discuss first, the apparent mother hate or the illicit drug use. Blinding orange light from the (very rare for Seattle) cloudless sky streams in through a gap in the drapes, dousing the brown room in a sickly glow.

"Is there a reason you've been using cocaine?" The drugs first. Brilliant.

"I was on a holiday. I was with friends. I was done with exams. What can I say? It seemed like the right thing to do." I feel the edges of my lips curling into a smile.

"Maris, I hope you understand the damage you can cause to your body with cocaine. I know you've experimented with lighter drugs before, but no illegal drug is safe, not even in small quantities." His brow furrows from the seriousness of it all.

"To be fair, Dr. Walsh, pharmaceutical drugs aren't exactly safe either. Snorting cocaine can have side effects, but no more than popping a Clonazepam or two. I'm halfway through a medical degree. I may not have all the knowledge you have, but I do know that much." I meet his eyes and see colour creeping into his cheeks. "But hey, it's a lot more fun to be out in a club till 7 AM on cocaine than on Prozac or Mommy's little helper, diazepam." "It appears to be self-destructive behavior. Has everything been alright at home?"

"Things are great at home. Millie is back now too. She stayed in Madrid for a while longer since she didn't have to get back to school."

"How is Millie? Is she working now?"

"If by working you mean sunning herself at Lake Sammamish during the day and drinking herself into a stupor at night, then certainly. I don't know what she's planning on doing with her life, but I know it will involve promiscuity. Millie's tastes are... eccentric."

"What happened? I thought she'd enrolled in university?" "She did, for a week."

"She decided it wasn't for her?"

"Yeah, you could say that." I quash a laugh, and instead run the tip of my tongue along the inside of my bottom lip. "Millie is not...uh, the university type. She thought it was far out until it came to handing in her first essay, then she split."

"That's disappointing. What do your parents think about this?"

"Well, as long as she's not helping herself to the contents of their bank accounts or medicine cabinets, I don't think they give a shit. Father doesn't exactly approve of her lack of ambition, but he certainly doesn't care enough to say anything to her."

"They must be proud of you, though."

"You would think so, wouldn't you? After all, who wouldn't want their child to become a doctor and save lives." I grin. "I'm afraid you'd be wrong, though. My parents would prefer me to enter the hotelier business and help them out. Don't get me wrong. They're not upset by any means—they just want at least one child to be involved in the family trade.

A chain-smoking media princess is more appealing than a studious introvert."

"You're not an introvert, though, are you?"

"I wouldn't describe myself as such, no, but exam season generally does cause social isolation. A socialite doesn't often have to worry about a looming eighty-percent weighted exam and can focus more on furthering brand images."

"You're probably right, there." He chuckles lightly.

His attempts at sycophancy are transparent. It's both amusing and irritating, and it takes me a few moments to respond. I know he thinks he's edging on the precipice of my psyche, a single breath away from unraveling my thoughts. He leans forward on his chair, and focuses on his writing pad. He jots a few words down, his mouth lightly pursed. I can't read what he's writing, despite shifting closer to him.

"Okay, I know this isn't what you'd most like to talk about right now, but how're your eating patterns?"

"That's a pretty complicated issue. I suppose if you mean to ask whether I'm still hunched over a sink every night throwing up a measly dinner, then no."

"How many calories are you consuming per day?" He finally addresses the situation matter-of-factly, and it's not as satisfying as I'd imagined it to be. I feel a nagging sense of annoyance, not particularly invasive, but I'd like him to believe it is. He's always a bit uneasy asking about this sort of stuff. He struggles to broach the subject, so I'm surprised he's managed this time around. He usually doesn't have the stomach for it, pun intended.

"Fifteen hundred," I say evenly. "My recommendation." I suppose this is a half-truth. I do consume 1500 calories, but not over one day, usually two.

"No, Maris, you're five six. Your recommended caloric intake should be nearer to 2000." He frowns and scribbles on the pad again, his gaze still firmly fixed on me.

"I tend to lose track of these things, especially on holidays. I was far more concerned with being able to find enough ecstasy to get me through a twelve-hour stint at Club 66 in Ibiza." I sigh for effect. "It was harder than imagined in the supposed party capital of the world."

He partially chokes on a sip of water while attempting to maintain a façade of composure. "I'm disappointed. I'd thought we'd made more progress."

"We've made plenty of progress. I have far better things to focus on now than how many bites I've taken of an apple. It's alright, Dr. Walsh. It's hard to get through histology on dream or E, so I won't be continuing that."

"I'm glad. I'm starting to worry, however. At our last appointment, things seemed to be flowing smoothly."

"There's nothing to worry about. I was trying to enjoy my vacation. It's nothing alarming. I'm twenty-three years old; there are worse things I could be doing."

I'm growing tired of the dialogue. It's normally a lot more entertaining to wind him up. He reacts quite easily to most things, especially when I mention them as nonchalantly as possible. Some psychiatrists are more difficult to read; their facial expressions do little in the way of revealing their neuroses and thoughts. Dr. Walsh, however, reminds me of a child: easy to decipher and equally easy to mold. I think he thinks I don't realize when his eyes travel across the length of my legs or when his conservatism colors his interpretation of my drug-related stories. He tries very hard to be that cool, far out dude, but his mannerisms scream of upper-middle class, traditionalist grooming. He probably was sent away to boarding school, boys only, at around five, coming home to visit his parents and younger sister several times a year. His first sexual experience was most likely with a gawky, bespectacled girl lacking the confidence and finesse of a natural beauty. I almost feel sorry for him, his marriage seems unfulfilling. There's a picture on his desk of his ten-year-old son and his wife—she's not too rough on the eyes, a waifish brunette with clear, pale skin and large, chestnut-colored eyes. Her argyle sweater and lackluster smile suggest repression, and I doubt her presence does much to prevent him from scouring hardcore porn magazines or fantasizing inappropriately about his less deranged patients. I suppose I shouldn't get this much pleasure from messing with him, but I'm sure he could use the excitement in his mundane life. When I first met him, I kind of thought he was a fruit, but his style is unadventurous, and his wandering eye doesn't violate the bodies of men.

"Well, that's certainly not true," he says, his tone disapproving. "I hope you understand how much harm you're doing to yourself. If you continue this way you may end up hospitalized."

If he's good at anything, it's doling out empty threats. He's been talking about hospitalization for a year now. It wasn't worrying back then, and it certainly isn't now. Mother could never face the humiliation of putting her child in a sanatorium. Heavens, how the clients and newspapers would react.

"I know, that would be a true shame." I cast my eyes downward in pseudo regret. "Things are changing now that I'll have exams and assignments to get to in a couple of months."

"You wouldn't want to jeopardize your health or your future career, would you?"

I'm tempted to give him a scathing response, but my next appointment is well over a month away, and I'd rather not necessitate one sooner. I smile and nod. "You're definitely right about that." The insincerity must be palpable. I stop myself from reaching into my purse for a cigarette.

He sits back in his chair, crossing his legs. He places his chin in his palm. He wants to discuss my mother some more.

Maybe he wants to discuss my father, maybe he wants to find out how deep my potential daddy issues may run.

"Are you still living with your parents, Maris?"

"I think you're aware that I am. I'm too busy with university to find work at the moment."

"But you don't really need to find work, do you?" His voice is bitter.

"Are you suggesting I live off my parents for the rest of my life?"

"No, certainly not. I meant it's not an absolute necessity when your parents are fairly high profile."

"I'm not sure that's the kind of thing I'd expect to hear from a psychiatrist, Dr. Walsh. It's refreshing."

He reaches for his cup of coffee, now half consumed. I feel like retching at the thought of drinking cold, stale coffee. The idea of coffee, in general, makes me ill; I only drink it out of necessity. He slowly sips, making another note on his pad; at this point, I want to rip it out of his hands.

"I'm glad you think so. How was your father's trip to Shanghai?

Is he back now?"

"I'm not actually sure. He possibly is. I haven't seen him around, though. We run on different schedules."

"You don't talk to your father often?" He finds this interesting, although I'm not quite sure why. I know this has been brought up in conversation at least twice on different occasions.

"I probably see him once a week. He likes to arrange a brunch on Sundays if we're all available. He mainly talks about which new hotels he's opened up recently, and Millie and I pretend to care. Millie often has the aid of narcotics to get her through, which is more than I can say for myself. I'm unfortunately quite sober during our interactions."

"You don't enjoy his company?"

"Would you enjoy hearing someone boast about their business acumen for two hours at a time? It's not as simple as me deciding whether I like being around him. He has his moments."

"And your mother?"

"I'd certainly prefer Daddy to her—not by too much, though. I'm more likely to get Cartier from him when I agree to not tell Mother about the plum-colored lipstick on his business shirts that does not belong to her. That colour would do nothing for her skin tone."

I watch as he digests this, his response less than adequate. I'd hoped to get more of a rise out of him; it seemed like a good thing to get him animated. I'm feeling a wave of irritation. I could use that cigarette about now. I haven't smoked since Monday. I'm not a heavy smoker, mainly because my appearance is important to me, but I'll usually smoke a couple of cigarettes a day just to take the edge off.

"Is your mother still involved in the operations of the business?"

"I don't know. I don't really care. I can ask her for you if you like." I glance at my watch. Ten minutes to go. I didn't expect the session to be this dull. I stifle a yawn.

"I was thinking we could arrange a group session: your mother, Millie, and you."

"If you can convince them to take an hour out of a busy schedule of self-medicating, that sounds like a plan."

"I'm thoroughly enjoying your sparkling wit today, Maris." He smiles at me, looking very disingenuous.

"I'm glad, Dr. Walsh. I try."

CHAPTER TWO

Once I'm out of the stuffy office, I head to my car and pull out a Camel cigarette from my purse. I hold it gingerly between my lips as I light it, using the engraved lighter my grandmother gave to my mother on her last visit to our house. I'd found it in the den before I left and having misplaced my own, I tossed it into my bag. I take a long drag, drawing my breath deep into my chest and exhale a thick plume of gray-blue smoke. It's unusually warm. Seattle doesn't have very many days of heat or cloying humidity and rarely does the weather elicit the beads of sweat currently trickling down my spine.

I perch on the bonnet of the 1974 Porsche—a pale blue convertible number, brand new and gifted to me by Father out of guilt on my birthday a month ago. Millie received the same in mint green—and consider my options. My boyfriend is at Lake Sam with a couple of our mutual friends, and from what he told me on the phone this morning, they've managed to score a ton of Valium and dream. I live on the western side of the beach, so the positives include me being able to escape if they're underwhelming company or have lied about the drugs, plus I've already got a bikini on underneath my tie-front blouse. Millie might be at home, so I could hang out with her, but I know Mom wouldn't be too far behind, and I can't imagine anything worse than dealing with her for the rest of the afternoon. There's not much of a debate. I climb into the driver's seat, starting the car as I smoke the last of the cigarette.

The sun hangs low in the sky, beating down on me with merciless intensity. Almost blinded, I reach for my sunglasses and speed out of the parking lot. Traffic is sparse—surprising for this time of the afternoon and I hit the I-90 within minutes. Karen Carpenter's lilting voice sings from the car radio and the wind, cool and mildly salty, whips through my hair.

My happiness wanes when I reach the state park. The entire city seems to have congregated here, buzzing like insects with their loud children and ugly station wagons. I circle the lot multiple times before I find a cramped little space, almost a goddamn mile from the beach.

I strip to my bikini top, stuff my shirt in the dashboard, and light another cigarette as I walk to the usual spot. I see Hunter first, with Susannah, Carol, Dawn, Stephen, and Jack. They're all laid out, melting into the worn picnic blanket.

"Hey, babe," Hunter calls drowsily, pulling me to him. He's already wired from the dope (and I'm guessing with at least two or three Valium pills too—Hunter's mother's stash is almost as vast as my own mother's) and he's smiling, flashing his perfect white teeth. He's one of the most attractive boys in the area. He's lean, and his face has prominent cheekbones, framed by a strong jawline. He's a year younger than I am, and we've been dating since I was barely thirteen. Somehow, I've managed to survive the past decade with him. His conversational skills make me want to saw off his tongue and force it down his throat. I lean in and kiss him hello, offering him a puff of my cigarette.

"You've started without me?" I gesture toward the stash of pills in the center of the picnic blanket.

"It was hard to wait, but I tried," he says. He gives me the once-over, staring at my chest for a few very noticeable seconds. "Well, I'll have to catch up then. Dawn, honey, where's the coke? Please tell me you have coke." I grin at her, and she hugs me tightly from behind, her skin clammy against mine.

"I always deliver," she tells me, folding a little plastic package into my hand.

"You look foxy today." It's Jack. He squints up at me, shielding his face from the sun with one arm.

"Jack, fuck off," says Hunter, throwing his water bottle at him. I start laughing. "Just today?" I kiss him on the cheek and obligatorily do the same with Stephen and the other girls. "Carol, is this your book?" I ask, grabbing a ratty copy of The Secret Woman.

She nods, "Yeah, and yes you can use it for the coke. I'd watch it, though. I've seen the cops about thirty times in the past hour. I think the pigs are having a picnic around here."

"We should stop by and say hello when we're high enough," I say, arranging about a quarter of the cocaine into a neat line. I lean down and tuck my hair behind my ear, using a rolled-up fiver to inhale as much as I can.

"Where were you? We've been waiting for you for hours," says Stephen, who is the only sober one of the bunch. I've never seen him drink or take drugs in public, but I've also seen enough ketamine to kill several horses in his bedroom.

"I had to get some shopping done. What scintillating conversation have I missed out on?"

"Have you been watching the news lately?" asks Susannah, taking my half burned-out cigarette from between my fingers.

"Well, not really, I only got back a week ago. I'm too busy missing the French Riviera. What's going on?"

"Apparently these girls, around our age, maybe a little younger...I'm not sure. Well, they've been disappearing. One disappeared from our university. She lived in the district, on 12th Avenue." She stutters, her speech mildly garbled, presumably from the beer bottle in her hand. "They think it's probably the same guy. Honestly, I don't think I can hitchhike anymore. I haven't even been going out at all without Stephen."

"It's probably no big deal. Things like this happen everywhere. I don't think we need to be changing our behavior because of one lunatic." I shrug, taking a sip of her beer. My insides are buzzing from the coke, which travels rapidly and consumes each part of me until I feel almost breathless.

"He's going after girls like us. I don't know how, but it's scaring me too," chips in Dawn.

I let out a chortle. "What do you mean 'girls like us'? I think you guys need to chill."

"If anyone should be worried, it's you. Slender, beautiful, long dark hair parted in the middle, petite." She rattles off the characteristics one by one, counting on her fingertips.

"Five six is hardly petite, Dawn. I'm not worried, and you shouldn't be either. Can we enjoy this for a while? Hearing about dead girls is killing my vibe. You know I'll protect you if it comes down to it." I flex my non-existent left bicep and she rolls her eyes in response. My body is tingling, and I'm too high to keep a straight face.

"I didn't mention them being dead. Nobody knows yet, I hope they all come back. You're tiny. What are you, ninety pounds? I don't think you'd be a match for any man, let alone a psychotic criminal," says Susannah.

"I'm ninety-five pounds." She's killing my high and part of me wants to sock her in the mouth to make her stop talking.

"Well look, I'm not going to leave the house without at least one of you with me. I'm not taking any chances anymore. I'm too pretty and young to be dead, alright?" says Carol, propping herself up on her elbows.

"I don't know if that'll be safe. Did they specify what this guy looks like? It could be Hunter or Stephen or Jack. It could actually be any of them, and then you're gonna go out with them, thinking you're safe, but really, you'll be screwed." "It's you, isn't it, Jack?" I squeeze his arm.

"Of course it is, look at me, I'm deranged," he says sardonically.

"It's easy for you to laugh it off! You're not going to be the missing girl," says Dawn, smacking his chest.

"Calm down, neither are you."

"That sounds like something the killer would say," her light-hearted tone taking on a paranoid edge. I imagine the reefer is finally frying her mediocre brain. She's been smoking since we were in middle school and started stealing her mother's lorazepam a couple of months later. Her memory is about as comprehensive as my grandmother's was before she died of late-stage Alzheimer's. She begins nibbling on the edge of one of her long, unmanicured fingernails. I don't know whether it's the drugs or the sun that's making my vision bleary, but from whatever sight I have left, I note the dirt caked inside and shudder. She flips her hair over her right arm, baring the abysmally designed dawning sun tattoo on her bony left shoulder. She's not wearing a bikini underneath her ankle-length dress. In fact, I don't think I can see an outline of underwear either. Her parents are very much of the liberal persuasion—well, if I'm to be accurate, I'd say the pink persuasion. I'm surprised no one has reported them to the authorities for being commie sympathizers— they fall only slightly short of the Rosenbergs. Her sisters are named Rain and Chakra. I couldn't make this shit up if I tried.

"I'm kidding, these little princesses probably couldn't even lift a woman. I don't know how they'd abduct one," I say, rolling down onto the blanket and closing my eyes. "No offense, Hunter." I give him a condescending little tap on his thigh.

"Women's lib has gone way too far already," moans Stephen, lying down next to me. "Now they're trying to have opinions."

"Stephen, sweetheart, didn't you find out your IQ was 95? I think you're a little too slow to be a part of this discussion," I tell him coolly. The other girls snicker at his expense. It's not that they're any smarter than he is if I'm honest. I think they all needed to be held back at least a year or two during high school, but Stephen is a smarmy little bastard that often needs to be put in his place. It's easier to do this with other women around to laugh at him. I don't quite care about gender politics; they don't affect me in the slightest. But male chauvinists can be very entertaining. I like getting into (what Stephen considers to be) debates with him because his innate lack of intelligence is unparalleled. It's like shooting caged animals at short-range.

"Don't get into it with her, Steph, you know she'll fry you," says Hunter. He sits up and removes his shirt, flinging it at the wicker picnic basket.

"I think women's lib needs to go much further. I don't think it's safe to allow men like you to have opinions," says Carol, rolling her eyes.

"See, this is why we need this guy out here keeping the girls in line," says Stephen, tartly. His pale skin blooms with color. "Otherwise, you'll all go crazy with power, like those damn fucking feminists on TV."

"So, you think it's alright that some sicko is going around handpicking girls to abduct because they might oppose one of your views?" she presses, leveling her gaze with his.

Her contempt is far from hidden as she clenches her jaw.

"Dude, you really need to mellow," says Jack, sliding his sunglasses on. "Leave the girls alone."

"You'll get your men's lib soon, don't worry," I tell Stephen, running my fingers through his hair. I reach for the Valium and push the little blue pills toward him. "For now, focus on having fun."

"Have some of my drink," says Susannah, handing him a red plastic cup. I'm not quite sure what's in it, but it sure looks more appetizing than the cheap beer I ingested. It must be out of her little flask. She carries it around with her to class sometimes. I suppose if I had her problematic skin, I'd be drinking at 9 AM too. She tilts his chin up with her index finger and kisses him for far longer than is appropriate in a social setting. I resist a gag and instead grab the flask from underneath her.

"I'm taking some too," I say, and not seeing any spare cups around, I drink straight from it.

"I don't know how you deal with him sometimes, Susannah," Carol sighs. She pulls her glossy blonde hair into a chignon and pins it into place with a small butterfly clip.

Stephen takes a pill, uncharacteristically, and washes it down with Susannah's sloshy liquor.

I can't help but stare a little when Jack unbuttons half of his shirt. His chest is slim but defined, without a trace of hair. I suspect he waxes it off, but he's never admitted as such. He's one of Hunter's closest friends and is remarkably similar in nature.

I could argue Hunter is the less bright of the two, but it's a close competition. He's a recent implant from California, and Stephen clearly stings from losing his childhood friend to a guy who doesn't seem to own shoes. Susannah is the only girl who's paid him any attention, so he's clung on to her for dear life. Both their Utahan Mormon parents approve.

"Do any of you want to take a dip?" asks Dawn, stretching.

She pauses and rubs tanning lotion onto her forearms.

"Yeah, I'm fucking dying out here. I don't know how it's this hot in Washington," I say. I wriggle a little as I pull my Levi's makeshift shorts off.

"Thank god you sorry losers never lived in Cali. This is like winter to me," says Jack, particularly smug.

"Then, get in the water, pretty boy," I say. "We'll follow."

"You've got it." He tugs his shirt off and heads toward the lake.

"I'll meet you guys there in two minutes. I'm going to stop by the ladies' room," I say, grabbing Hunter's cigarette. He groans, but I'm up before he can say anything. I drop my sunglasses on his lap.

"We'll be down there, Maris," says Carol, stripping to her one-piece. She points to a relatively child-free area. "Here, Dawn, I brought a bikini for you. I know you tend to go commando." She starts laughing.

"I just think underwear is unnatural, you know?" Dawn's voice fades behind me.

I walk toward the bathrooms barefoot, wishing I'd had the foresight to bring something to tie up my hair. It falls an inch above my navel and is a nightmare to swim with. I readjust my bikini, for which the top is running obscenely tight. I'm pretty sure it's Millie's. She's only a C-cup.

"Hey, I'm so sorry to bother you, but I was wondering if I could get some help."

I look up from my bikini strap to see a guy in tennis whites, with his arm in a sling. He's about six feet and is unnervingly attractive. He grins at me. His eyes are a vibrant blue and his patrician nose culminates in a fine point. He has a light tan, and his chestnut hair is combed into neat, close-cut waves.

I smile back at him. "You're not bothering me. What kind of help do you need?"

He studies me with a deep concentration, hungry, barely blinking. It's a look I understand very well. A look I know he's straining to control. "I'm having trouble unloading my sailboat," he says, glancing down at his bandaged arm. "I would really appreciate it if I could get your help." His charisma is incisive, albeit shallow by the way he stumbles in between certain words as if second-guessing himself.

"Absolutely, I'll help you...but on one condition." I hold his gaze steadily and put a hand on his uninjured arm.

He's puzzled. I'm sure he was expecting a little more resistance. "What's that condition?"

"You have to give me a ride; I never learned how to sail."

"Sure thing, you've got it. My car is down over this way," he says, heading toward the overcrowded lot. "It's so nice of you. I've been somewhat unsuccessful in getting a pretty girl to help." "I wouldn't imagine it to be difficult for you, but I'm more than happy to help. What did you do to your arm?"

"Believe it or not, it's a tennis injury! Sure hurts a hell of a lot, though." He's still watching me, his gaze traveling across the length of my body before squaring in on my face.

"Having played it since I was five, it's definitely believable. The number of sprains I've had over the past eighteen years is astronomical. I didn't get your name, by the way. I'm Maris."

He extends his hand to me. "Oh, that's rude of me. I'm Ted. It's lovely to meet you, Maris."

His accent seems slightly foreign, British, or Canadian, considering the way he rounds his vowels. There's a lack of authenticity in it, though, and I'm not quite sure whether it's merely a performance or not. He continues walking beside me, falling into step.

The asphalt is blisteringly hot, and I'm regretting not wearing my flip-flops. The din of bustling young families and unattractive couples is distinct in the parking vicinity, so

I move in closer to hear him. His refined manner is reminiscent of another time, steeped in politeness and chivalry. He leads me to a beat-up, tan Volkswagen buggy, possibly the '68 model. I look a little closer and notice the passenger seat is missing, and there's no sign of a sailboat either.

"Wait, where's the boat?" I ask, turning to face him. "This is the car, right?"

He's still watching me, eyes bottomless and focused. He pauses for a moment, allowing himself to blink. His beautiful face betrays a certain anxiety, but he soon amends himself, standing up a little straighter, leaning on his car as he clumsily attempts to propose a justification.

"Oh, I'm so sorry. Didn't I mention it's at my parents' place?

It's, ah, up the hill in Issaquah. It'll only take a minute."
"Whereabouts in Issaquah, are they? I ask. "So many of my friends live around there. I'm up in Bellevue." While his persona lends him a certain air of reliability, I know he's lying. He has a nervous twitch in his unaffected arm and his breath quickens briefly before he manages to get it under control, brushing it off with a cool, pleasant smile.

"Ah, it isn't too far up, about a five-minute ride. I promise it'll be worthwhile. You'll love sailing. I'm, uh, sorry I didn't let you know beforehand."

"Where would I ride? You don't seem to have a passenger seat," I ask playfully.

If I weren't attentive, I'd almost miss the colour appearing in his cheeks. It's close to imperceptible, but I do have finely honed instincts. He's been caught out. "Look, Ted, I'd love to help you, but I have to get back to my boyfriend and friends. They'll worry that I've been abducted or something silly like that, you know? I would've enjoyed that sailing lesson. Perhaps if you're here another day. Like I said, I live in Bellevue, so I'm here all the time."

"Oh, right, okay. I'm sorry."

"Sorry that I have a boyfriend? Or sorry you asked?"

"Sorry that you have a boyfriend, of course," he says with a nervous laugh. He scratches the bandaged arm.

"Well, don't go telling him, but I'm pretty flexible with the boyfriend issue. Come say hi if you're here again." I hold his gaze for several seconds. "I hope you feel better soon." I wink at him and then walk backward a few steps, toward the bathrooms. He stands rooted to his position and then waves at me as I turn around. I almost want to hang around and watch as he finds another target, but I'm thirsty and hot as all hell. All I want is some alcohol and a long swim in the lake.

I jog a little, trying not to burn my feet, relieved when I finally hit grass. I drop into the bathroom, fix my bikini strap, and check my hair in the mirror. Women are lining up to wait for one of the two stalls to open. I'm not quite sure how people can bring themselves to use public bathrooms. I, for one, can do without contracting crabs from the unwashed masses. I don't even share bathrooms with my family. Rosa, the daytime housekeeper, is on a short leash, and I make sure to watch while she cleans.

When I leave the bathroom, I notice Ted's not around. I stop by the picnic blanket, where only Stephen remains. "Aren't you coming?" I ask him, grabbing the bottle of SPF 40. I slather it onto my arms, stomach, and legs. I don't particularly need ghastly red patches of sunburn.

"Nah, I want to read in peace for a little while," he tells me.

I don't give a shit, nor do I have the patience to pretend to. I take a long swig from the flask and run toward the water. Hunter, Jack, Susannah, and Dawn are frolicking in the shallow end, only knee-deep. Dawn is splashing Hunter, still wearing her sunglasses. He sees me and pulls me to him by the waist, grinning. I lean into him, pretending to do so to kiss him, and instead shove him into the lake. He's surprised, so the impact alone is enough to topple him. "Get in the deep end, you fucking losers," I say, diving in.

The water is icy, despite the radiating heat from the sun. I stay under for as long as I can, only resurfacing when my lungs begin to ache. I float on my back, and Hunter swims to me.

"I'm going to get you back for that one." His hands find their way to my hips, yanking me down deeper. He grazes my neck with his lips underwater. I grasp his shoulders and kiss him roughly, before kicking him away.

"Are you telling me you can't wait the hour or so until we get back to my house?" I ask once he emerges.

"I don't know. Have you seen yourself in that bikini?"

"You raise a good point," I say, swimming out further. "But I think you can hold off."

"Guys, don't stop on account of me. I'm definitely happy to watch," Jack calls, wiggling his eyebrows.

"Why don't both of you make out, and I'll be the spectator? I think that's an idea we can all get behind, am I right, Susannah?" I grab her by the arm, using her as a temporary floaty.

"Hunter, I love you and all, but that's something I can't ever do," says Jack.

"But you're from San Francisco, Jack," I push. "You must be used to that sort of thing."

"I'm happy to watch," says Susannah, mimicking his voice.

Dawn giggles.

"I'll see you at home, Jack baby," says Hunter. His laughter is forced; I know when he's uncomfortable. He has a rather strong hatred for the queers, which he strives to mask-he's successful in doing so. He's the heir to a candy company, and his public image has to be similar to mine: liberal, but not too liberal, supportive of the queers and blacks and Indians, but always erring on the side of the whites and straights. Quite frankly, I think he has neither the capacity nor the willingness necessary to cultivate that kind of image. The most he is capable of is speaking from improvised cue cards, being prodded by his cold, shrewd mother. While I recognize his absolute lack of ability to lead a company that large, I know that he'll have a lot of weight behind him, should I ever need it. Also, I never tell him, but Carlyle chocolate annihilates Godiva and Hershey's combined. I make sure to swipe some whenever I'm over at his house. His parents are expecting our families to merge at some point soon, so they're very generous with favors. They've planned a wonderful trip to Aspen for Hunter and me in the winter, allowing us the use of their entire chalet. I feel Vail is more enjoyable as it lacks the aspirational-rich, who douse themselves in new money and ill-fitting designer garb, which Aspen is absolutely rife with, but I'm grateful anyway to get the fuck away from my family.

"Where's Stephen?" asks Jack, presumably to Susannah. "He wanted to get some reading done. I don't know, maybe he's licking his wounds. He actually doesn't know how to swim." She pauses, placing a hand on her mouth. "Oops, I probably shouldn't have said that."

"He doesn't even know how to swim? God, he's really got nothing going for him. The least he could do is learn to swim," says Jack, almost in hysterics.

"Not everyone's as blessed as you, Jack. We can't all have green eyes and picture-perfect bodies," I tell him, partially to get a rise out of Hunter.

"Don't worry. I'm available for you any time, Maris."

"I'm glad to hear that. I saw him on the picnic blanket, though. He was reading, so maybe he does want to read and isn't ashamed of his inability to swim," I say. "I'd probably be pretty ashamed about three-year-olds surpassing me, but we're all different."

"Was Carol with you, Maris?" asks Dawn, shielding her face from the sun with a bent hand. "She said she was going to the bathroom and would walk back with you."

"No, I didn't see her. She's probably chilling with Stephen. Maybe she felt sorry for him and wanted to offer him company," I say. I dip underwater again.

Dawn shrugs. "Yeah, you're probably right, she'll get here soon, I'm sure."

"Stephen is definitely sparkling company," Jack says, sarcastic and all, to Susannah's derision.

"You just need to get to know him, he's a wonderful person." Her response is brief but terse, discouraging a continuation.

He mouths "ouch" at me when she can't see, and I hug him, laughing into the crevice between his neck and shoulder. We swim for half a mile and then laze around in the water until I feel myself coming down from the coke. It's a lousy feeling, and it makes me really sickly and anxious. It always helps to have Xanax or Valium around when coming down from a coke or ecstasy high. Ketamine is hell, nothing helps, and I rarely touch anything that requires a needle, so heroin and morphine are mostly out. The sun lowers into a peachy-pink sunset over the lake, and the evening chill is somewhat aiding me as the weariness of the comedown takes hold.

"Do you guys want to head back in?" asks Hunter.

"Yes, thank you! I'm fucking freezing over here," says Dawn, shivering for effect.

"Yeah, I could use a Vallie kicker right about now," I say. I wade toward the shore, my limbs tender and worn out.

Stephen is splayed out across the picnic blanket in a rather effeminate manner, perched on two of the towels the girls brought. I yank one out from under him, giving him a polite little smile when he shoots me a look of irritation. I wrap it around myself, but I'm still trembling from the cold. I wipe off as fast as I can and pull my cut-offs on; they do little to nothing to help. I huddle against Hunter, harvesting as much body heat as I can from him.

"You ready to head home, Stephie boy?" he asks. He looks like he's struggling with a substantial amount of guilt for ditching his loser buddy for two hours.

"Yeah, I managed to get through all my book," Stephen says breezily, but his face is tense and hardened.

"Where's Carol? She said she would be joining us for a swim. I thought she might've decided to sit it out with you," says Dawn. She glances down at Carol's untouched suede Chanel purse. The keys to her Camaro poke out.

"She told me she was going to head to the bathroom. I thought she walked a different way to the water because she didn't stop by." Worry trickles into his facial features, slowly consuming them.

"Maybe she went home?" asks Susannah.

"Her purse and keys are still here. She wouldn't leave without telling us, and she definitely does not live close enough to walk home and back to get her car," says Dawn. She paces back and forth in panic.

"I'll check the bathrooms, maybe she's sick or has sunstroke or something," says Stephen. He jumps to his feet and slips on his flip-flops.

"She wouldn't leave without her purse. I know Carol. She'd never go anywhere without her goddamn purse. She drove me in. I can't drive a stick and my car's still at the mechanic's," says Jack. "Alright, let's not freak yet. I'm sure she's around here somewhere. We all know Carol. She wouldn't leave her stuff and disappear," I say calmly to curb the annoyance in the pit of my stomach. I want to go home, smoke several cigarettes, and knock myself out with some Valium.

"Maris, she said she was going to meet you. Did you not see her?" says Stephen. He's jittery and confused.

"No, I didn't see her. I would've at least passed her if she was near the bathrooms or on her way in."

"Where the fuck is she?" asks Hunter, glancing around the park.

The crowd has dispersed considerably, with the families packing their picnics and children into various station wagons and SUVs. Apart from us, I can only see a handful of other groups, spread out thinly across the grass. I can't imagine she'd have gotten far. She's not exactly athletic, often winded after walking about half a mile. While intelligent, beautiful, and stylish, she has the fitness of a geriatric woman. I notice a few blondes, but none with the same shade of hair as hers. Hers is quite distinct. She is the only natural blonde I know, and the ones here clearly rely on Clairol for their color.

"Alright, Hunter, you check along the lake. Stephen, you stick to the bathrooms. Dawn, check the car park; maybe she's near her car. Maris, you and I can scan the crowd, toward Issaquah and Redmond, a mile or two—you go north, and I'll go south. Susannah, go to the phone booth and call her house phone, maybe she's home. Meet back here in half an hour," says Jack, assertive but flustered.

We scatter according to his directions, and I run along the grass, heading Redmond way. Running has always been one of my strong points, but I'm on empty right now. My body resists, and I'm starting to get cranky with the bitch. I don't know if she's out here, but I hope she's not because I sure will rip her a new one if I see her, for making me go through this bullshit when I just want to be in my bed.

There're barely ten or so small clusters of people left around this side of the park, mostly hippie high school types sharing doobies. It's dusk when I've exhausted my search. I stand still, glancing in all directions. I call her name several times, in varying tones of irritation. No response. She's got to be nearby. She definitely can't walk back from Redmond. I don't have time for this, and I'm starving. My stomach turns in on itself, the hunger wracking my body entirely. I give up and walk back to the blanket. Dawn is chewing her nasty, dirt-filled nails, sobbing. Susannah is hugging her, wrapping a towel around both of them. Jack's shirt is back on, and Stephen's face is flushed.

Even Hunter looks on edge, pacing back and forth. "Nothing?" His tone is grim.

"I called her house, her mother said she hasn't heard from her, then I called her dad's office because it's nearby and maybe she dropped in to see him or something, but no one's seen her," says Susannah, tears rushing down her face. She starts hiccupping.

"How on earth am I meant to drive her car back to her house without her in it? Her mother is freaking so badly. Her car's brand new too. I don't want to scrape it; she'll be so angry," says Jack, on the verge of tears. I'm tempted to slap them all at this point. If there weren't so few of us, I'd have slipped out by now.

"Do we call the police?" Hunter's the voice of reason, and I'm as surprised as the rest of them.

"Yeah, let's let them handle it," I say. Realizing I sound rather cavalier, I add, "I don't think I can do this. I hope Carol's alright." I cry to cement my concern.

"Okay, ah, shit. Look, Stephen, can you drive the girls home in my car? Jack and I should go to Carol's house in her car, so it would be good if you could meet us there. We can call the police when we get there," says Hunter.

"It's alright, I drove here," I say. Maybe I'll get to leave.

"Jack can go with you, then. I'll drive Carol's car alone.

You're her best friend. Maybe her mother will calm down with you there."

"Yeah, I'll take the girls home," says Stephen.

"No, I want to go to Carol's and be there if she turns up," says Susannah, in between sobs.

"Fine, Stephen, drive the girls to Carol's."

CHAPTER THREE

It's a shitshow when we get to Carol's. Her mother is a weeping mess, her bony chest heaving up and down with every sob. We're all crowded into the cramped little sitting room because, apparently, she doesn't see the need for the rest of us to have seats. She's phoned the police and keeps looking up at a framed school portrait of Carol at her graduation. We wait, standing in a little huddle. She hogs the one sofa, and no one knows how to ask to sit. They're all too polite and numb with shock.

"Not my Carol, not my Carol," she repeats.

"Mrs. Greene, I'm sure she's alright. You know Carol. She's always getting herself into little adventures. It's only been a few hours," I say tiredly, for the seventh time.

"Maris, she wasn't with you? You're her closest friend. Why wouldn't she tell you where she was going? Was she talking to other boys?" She barrages me, also for the seventh time, and I brace myself to answer her without snapping.

"I'm sorry, Mrs. Greene, I didn't see her. You know I would tell you. Carol gets into adventures all the time. We should wait for the police." I shiver violently, and my teeth start chattering. "Mrs. Greene, please stop crying."

"She's my only daughter, she's my only daughter." She rocks back and forth, looking like an absolute basket case. "I bought her the Camaro, so she'd be safe. Nothing can happen to my Carol. I begged god for a girl for so many years."

"Mrs. Greene, you know Carol's very careful. I don't think you should panic yet," I say.

I look out to the driveway where the Camaro sits, glossy and empty. She follows my gaze and cries harder. Susannah and Dawn are crying, too, their wailing contributing to an excruciating crescendo. I stand silently, my still-wet hair dripping icy water along my neck and chest. Mrs. Greene stands up and squeezes me, crying into the hollow of my shoulder. I close my eyes and pat her on the shoulder, gently, awkwardly, while I think of an excuse to go home. I offer surface-level concern and mimic her behavior, shedding as many tears as I can until the doorbell finally rings. The cops are plain-clothed and gruff, unaffected by Mrs. Greene's frenzy.

The shorter one speaks first. His hair is slicked back, and I'm not sure if it's gel or sweat that's holding it in place. "Uh, so when did you last see Carol? Has she run away from home before?" His beady eyes dart around the room while he jots down notes. He stares at me for a few seconds before turning back to Mrs. Greene. "No, no, she hasn't run away. She's missing. My Carol never does things like this. She's a very happy girl. Why aren't you there looking for her?"

"Why aren't we where?" This time the taller one speaks. His face is rounded, quite like a manatee.

"Lake Sammamish, where she went missing. Why aren't you looking there?" She sits down again, sobbing hysterically.

"I take it you kids were there with Miss Greene?" He looks at us.

"Yes, sir, we went to Lake Sam for a picnic and a swim.

It was so hot. Carol said she was going to use the bathroom and then meet us at the water's edge, but she never came. We thought she was maybe sitting with Stephen, who was reading on our picnic blanket, but she wasn't around when we came back about an hour and a half later," says Hunter, composing himself. He's still high and very fidgety. He has a real problem around police as if he's about to be arrested for something when usually all he's done is smoke reefer.

"Carol's a very responsible person, and she'd tell us if there was an issue. It's possible she bumped into other friends, nearly everyone we know is at the lake when it's hot out," I say, addressing the short one. He lets me know his name is John.

"I think you all ought to head on home and get some rest so we can talk to Mrs. Greene. We'll call tomorrow to organize meetings with each of you to get your accounts of what happened and everything you remember. Obviously, you're all, uh, kind of affected, and we need you to be alert so we can get the search started. She'll likely return within the next twenty-four hours as most runaways do—" he is curbed abruptly by Mrs. Greene.

"She's not a runaway. She's missing. My daughter is missing." "Alright, well, we're going to do our best to find her, ma'am.

Go on home, kids."

Forlorn and defeated, they fall one by one and acquiesce. Susannah is the first. She dries her tears with the back of her hand, shoulders slumped. Stephen holds her protectively as if she's at risk of facing the same prospects as Carol. His earlier audacity has morphed into cowardice and fear. Hunter holds my hand tight and Jack stays put, immobile.

"Please let us know if you find out anything. I'll likely be awake most of the night. I'm meant to work with my father tomorrow, but if you need me, call me and I'll be there," I say, forcing a tear to slip along my cheek.

"Pardon me if I'm wrong, but you're Maris Caldwell, right? I've seen you in a couple of my wife's magazines. You're Henry Caldwell's daughter?" John eyes me, examining my face to reassure himself. I'm surprised he's managed to snare himself a woman at all, what with the pig snout he's passing off as a nose. "Yes, I'm one of his daughters. Just give me a call if need be. I hope Carol's home soon." I turn to her mother, "Please don't fret, Mrs. Greene, Carol will be terribly upset once she finds out how distraught you've become." I wave, thankful, and ready to bolt. I drag Hunter along, with Stephen and the rest trailing behind us. "Come on, Jack. I'll drop you home," I say when we get to the driveway. "You're right on the way." He lives about two blocks away, and Hunter is an easy twelve-minute walk from my house. That was convenient before I'd learned to drive and was too inept to take my mother's keys when she was out cold from the Klonopin. I always thought she'd wake up in time to see me hightailing her car out of the garage.

"I'll get Susannah and Dawn home," says Stephen.

"Call us when you're all home safe, alright?" I shout, with as much concern as I can muster. It's the best I can do when I'm coming down, and they should be glad I didn't drive home straight from the lake. Hunter and Jack settle into the car, and I strap my seatbelt on. "Are you doing okay, Jack?" I glance at him in the rear-view mirror. I reach into the dashboard for my blouse and ChapStick. My lips are dry as all hell.

"I'm okay. I'm just...I don't know. I don't know where she would've gone without telling me. She's not like that. She's always so cautious."

"I'm sure she's fine. Don't panic too soon. You know worrying does very little in the way of helping," I tell him, rephrasing the line I've been using on her mother all evening.

We drive most of the way in silence, and I have a niggling

suspicion that Jack's crying in the back, but I go out of my way to avoid looking at him. Seeing a man cry is so nauseating. It's in the top five of the ugliest things I've ever seen, second only to excrement. When I reach his house, I pause on the side of the street and wait impatiently for him to peel himself off the leather seat. Jack's walk to the front door is excruciating, and slow to watch. He half-waves and disappears inside.

"You're coming back to my house, aren't you, babe?" I ask, turning to Hunter. I grin. I don't want to drive him home, and I could probably do with a little action while I wait for the benzodiazepines to kick in.

"Yeah, we haven't had much alone time."

"Millicent and my mother will probably be home, but we'll get past them pretty quickly. Just make sure not to mention this whole debacle. I don't want to deal with a fucking press conference, especially since Carol will probably waltz in tomorrow all casual."

"I won't say anything, don't worry. It was hard enough dealing with Carol's mom."

I pull into the excessively long winding driveway. I could swear it's almost a mile to the front door. Renata, the portly night maid, answers the door, taking my purse for me. Hunter offers her a polite, robotic smile and hello. I lead him through the house, down the hallway and vast parlor, to the casual sitting room toward the back where I'll need to give my dutiful greetings to my mother—if she's not drowning in a river of wine and Xanax upstairs.

We encounter Millie first, as I'd expected. She was due to hang out with us earlier, but she's always been quite the flake. I'm older by twenty-three minutes, and almost nobody can tell us apart. We've managed to trip up our parents on many occasions. Looking at her is like looking into a mirror. She's an inch taller, but, other than that and our bra size, there's almost no visible dissimilarity. She has silken jet-black hair.

It falls in a sheath to the small of her back. She boasts full, bee-stung lips, a small, delicate nose, and doe-like aquamarine eyes. She's very slender but has no interest in running or athletics in general, so I'm about five pounds lighter. We both share Mother's Mediterranean tan and high, well-defined cheekbones, and Father's long, naturally black eyelashes. Mother is tiny, barely topping five feet, but she generally has the attention of every male aged twelve to seventy-five in the vicinity. Millie and I take our height from Father, who's closer to about six two. Millie's sitting Indian style on the leather sofa, watching The Mary Tyler Moore Show with wide-eyed joy. It's been her favorite show since it came out four years ago after I initially found it and developed a liking for it, and usually, we watch it together. I love that Mary; she's adorable. Millie is in my silk charmeuse La Perla slip and robe, but I don't have the energy to be annoyed.

"You're watching Mary without me, Millie?" I ask, draping myself around her. I kiss her repeatedly on the cheek. She squeezes me back, grinning.

"I had no idea when you'd be home. It's a new episode, Maris. We were meant to watch it together, but I see you were out with Hunter here." She pulls him down into a hug.

There've been at least six or so occasions we've managed to confuse Hunter into not knowing which of us he's dealing with. It's always good fun, especially if I need an excuse to yell at him about something.

"How are you, Millie?" he asks.

Mother walks in, still in her daily uniform—an elegant but bland Dior square neck dress that ends just above above her knees. Her pearls are around her neck, and the Harry Winston diamonds are embellishing her ears. She is rarely without her heels, even at home. She's perpetually on a diet and won't go a day without this bizarre red Rooibos tea that kind of tastes like dirt.

"Hunter, it's lovely to see you again. Maris, I feel like I haven't seen you all week."

It's most likely because I've been avoiding her for almost the entirety of the past week, leaving before she wakes around noon and coming home when she's in a stupor.

"You, too, Mother—it's great to see you." I peck her quickly. "I'm exhausted and cold, though, so is it alright if I head upstairs to shower?"

I don't wait for an answer. I drag Hunter out of there as fast as I can. I ascend the stairs two at a time despite the dull sting in my thighs. I lead him to my room, but he doesn't need directions. He closes the door behind us and sits on my bed, playing with the twirling silk from the canopy.

"I need a shower, do you?" I ask. I hold his gaze and unbutton my blouse. I undo the strings of the bikini top and let it fall to the floor, along with the cut-offs.

He reaches for my arm and pulls me to him. Sitting down, his eyes are level with my chest, but he looks up to my face, studying me closely. He kisses along my neck before brushing my lips with his.

"You're so beautiful, Maris." His hands press into my waist, and he pushes me onto the plush quilt cover. His kisses become harder, more fervent as he climbs on top, holding himself up with one arm. I can hear footsteps outside my bedroom door. He freezes.

"Are you scared someone's going to walk in on us?" I taunt him, challenging him to push on. "Oh no, what a nightmare that'd be!"

He grabs at my bikini briefs, almost tearing the soft fabric in the process of pulling them off.

I wake around 10 AM. Harsh sunlight streams in through the bay windows. My bedside telephone is ringing incessantly. The Valium and Xanax combination I used last night to knock myself out hasn't worn off yet, consuming my body with an overwhelming sense of lethargy. I fumble for the receiver, squeezing my eyes shut as I border on blindness. I don't know why I keep forgetting to close the goddamn drapes. I hope it's not Father waiting to badger me about not turning up to his new downtown hotel. I'm supposed to be on the advertising team now that I'm on college break.

"Hello?" I'm cranky and my voice rasps from the alcohol and the cocaine nasal drip. I almost regret taking as much coke as I did, but I remember that I didn't pay for any of it and I'm quite pleased.

"Hello, is that Maris Caldwell?" "Uh, yes, this is Maris speaking."

"Hi Maris, it's detective John Simpson, we met last night at Miss Carol Greene's house." His voice is gentler on the phone, with a kindness that seemed entirely absent in person.

"How may I help you, detective?"

"I understand that Mr. Carlyle may be with you, we've attempted to reach him at home with no luck. We'd be very grateful if both of you would come down to the station to discuss Carol's whereabouts yesterday."

"Wait, she hasn't come home yet?"

"No, unfortunately she has not returned, and we're attempting to piece together her movements so we can find out what could've happened."

I shake Hunter forcefully into consciousness. His first instinct is to raise his hand to his face to shield his eyes from the sun. He blinks sleepily, confused. I sit up a little straighter, clearing my throat. "Yes, of course. He's with me. What time would you like us to come by?"

"As soon as you can, Miss Caldwell, your other friends

are giving us statements currently. We have been trying to contact you since about eight this morning, but I'm not sure if your housekeeper understood us."

"Alright, sure, I'll try and be there within the hour."
"Thank you, we appreciate your time and effort."

I place the phone down, sitting dumbfounded. "Carol still hasn't come home, Hunter."

He jerks upright as if prodded by a branding iron. "What the hell, are you kidding me?"

"Clearly not, they want us to come to the station as soon as possible. We need to get dressed." I spring to my feet, heading directly to the bathroom to brush and shower. I'm starving, and I definitely need that time to eat breakfast. I get dressed in a Kelly-green tennis miniskirt, knee-length socks in a matching shade, and a short-sleeved Indian print blouse. I debate between my platforms or patent leather Mary Jane heels and decide on the latter. I'm not usually one for makeup, but I use my Chapstick, eyeliner, and a hint of the baby blue eyeshadow my mother brought me from her last trip to Paris. I brush my hair into place, parting it in the center and combing it over my shoulders and chest. I grab a pocketbook from my closet. "Hunter, you shower, I'll be downstairs in the dining room."

"Maris, how could you forget to tell us that your friend went missing last night?" This is my mother's way of greeting me once I'm in the kitchen.

"How did you find out?" I grab a fresh croissant from the bakery basket. Rosa may be difficult to look at, but her food is the closest a person can get to heaven.

"What do you mean, how did I find out? It's in the newspaper, for god's sake. Maris, what is wrong with you?" Her honey-colored eyes darken in ire. "Poor Carol's disappeared and all you had to say was that you were cold and wanted to shower?"

"It's in the newspaper? Wow, a little bit of an overreaction if you ask me."

"Here, see for yourself." She slides a newspaper at me across the granite benchtop. Two girls have vanished from Lake Sammamish, according to the front page. There's a police sketch of a handsome twentysomething man named "Ted" accompanying the shock-factor headline. They've not captured Ted well by any means. His nose had a better structure and his eyes were larger, very feminine. The sketch makes him out to be a bit of a grungy savage, I can only imagine how annoyed he must be. His whole act attempted to establish the exact opposite.

"There was a second one too? Jesus!" I bite into the croissant. "Damn, Rosa skimped on the butter today, didn't she?"

"I'm not quite sure what to say to you right now," she says, her jaw clenched.

"Well, I have to drop by the police station in about ten minutes, so there's barely any time. You're safe."

"Did you see him? Did you see her going with him?"

"No, I didn't see him. I don't know who he is. The last I saw of Carol was at the picnic blanket. Don't be so dramatic."

"Have you even mentioned it to Millie?"

"Mentioned what to me?" asks Millie, strolling in, dressed in a cotton summer nightgown.

"Millicent, why aren't you dressed yet? It's 10:30 AM," my mother snaps. I'm surprised she's awake herself at this time.

"I don't have anywhere to be just yet."

"Go on, Maris, tell her what's happened."

"Well, Mill, Carol disappeared from Lake Sam yesterday. Why don't you read this newspaper, though? It seems to revel in sensationalism and Mother is clearly a fan," I say calmly as I flip over to the second page. "She'll turn up in a day or two."

"Maris is right, Mother. I don't think there's anything to

be worried about," she says steadfastly. She looks at me. "I don't need to read that crap, I trust you."

"Do you ever say anything contradictory to your sister, Millicent?" Mother is fuming now.

"Why would she need to? She's smart enough to know what to believe. It takes a real moron to fall for salacious stories in newspapers clearly created to profit off gullible readers." I smear a little strawberry jam onto the remaining portion of the croissant, licking the spillage from my pinkie finger. I devour it in two bites and then pour myself a cup of black coffee; I need to stay awake. I could really use a cigarette but, as far as my mother is aware, I don't smoke. While I enjoy irritating her, I don't want to risk being cut out of the will. "Mother dear, you do make the best coffee."

She doesn't know how to use the coffee machine. I don't think she's tried either. Her rage is palpable. She smears on an alarming fake smile when Hunter traipses in.

"Come on, Hunter, we'd better get going." I brush the crumbs from my blouse and grab his hand.

"Bye Mrs. Caldwell, Millie."

I grab my keys from the hallway. "You can get something to eat after," I tell him. Once we're out of earshot, I ask for cigarettes. He always keeps a pack in his jeans, and I could've sworn he tossed it into the dashboard last night. I was high as a kite, so I don't remember exactly, but the vague outline of the trip is in my mind.

They separate us once we're there. Hunter is led into a room on the other end of the hall, and Susannah and Stephen are seated in the waiting area in the center of the office. I'm a little surprised that no one here recalls me. My records were expunged, but I imagined at least someone would remember me. It's all a little too familiar: the vomit-yellow paint on the walls is peeling, and the linoleum flooring is sticky against my shoes. King County PD doesn't seem to have been updated at all.

"Maris, thank you for coming on such short notice—would you like to accompany me to a questioning room? It's up this way," says John. I feign ignorance and follow compliantly. He doesn't know that I've memorized the floor plan for convenience. He and I are alone. He has a cup of coffee at his side. He hesitates for a second and then decides to ask if I'd like a drink, and I decline.

"What would you like to know, detective Simpson?" I clasp my hands together on the desk. I assume it's his. It's a bit of a sty, though, so it could be a communal desk.

"Can you please run down your activity yesterday, from about 2 PM to 7 PM?" He adjusts his grandfather-style rectangular glasses.

"Yes, I certainly can. I arrived at Lake Sam about two, perhaps a little earlier, and looked for parking for half an hour or so. It was a real mess, there were cars and kids everywhere—everybody and their extended families seemed to be congregating. When I managed to get parking, I walked down to where we usually hang out in, near the water and all. They were there, Susannah, Stephen, Dawn, Carol, Jack, and Hunter, I mean. They were on Hunter's ratty old picnic blanket, eating sandwiches that Carol had made. We talked for a while and decided to go swimming, but I had to use the restroom.

When I came back, I went straight for the water and stopped by the picnic blanket to see if anyone was still there—only Stephen was. He'd made a couple of questionable comments, it's very silly, and I won't go into it, it'll only bore you, and I told him I'd be with the rest. We were swimming for an hour or two, and when we went to dry off, Stephen was still the only one there. Carol was quite upset by what he'd said, but I figured she'd have calmed down by then. We searched for her for well over an hour. I headed toward the Redmond end, and Jack looked around the Issaquah end. We ended up going to Carol's house to let her mom know and then she called you guys."

He doesn't interrupt me, listening quietly, patiently, and writing down notes. When I'm finished, he speaks. "I understand it might have been silly, but what exactly did Stephen say to upset Carol?"

"Oh, I don't want to get him into any trouble or anything. It wasn't much of a big deal. They were talking about some girls our age going missing around Seattle, and he said that it was probably for the best—I'm paraphrasing here—because the women's liberation movement was giving women too much power to speak, and someone had to keep them in line. He said that it was good that this man, well, we're assuming he's a man, was essentially putting women in our place. I don't think he was being serious, he's often quite flippant."

"He actually said those things?" He's concerned, brow furrowed, disbelieving. "What a bizarre thing to say." He speaks as if he were alone and talking to himself.

"Stephen is a little peculiar—I don't think he intended to offend anyone. Like I said, it's all very silly."

"Were Stephen and Carol alone at all?"

"I think so. When I went back out to the water from the bathroom, the rest told me that Carol was with Stephen and had to use the bathroom, so she'd be back soon. I think they must've been alone for a little while at least. I wouldn't expect too long. Carol isn't exactly Stephen's biggest fan."

"I see, did they often argue?"

"I guess they were a little quarrelsome, but I don't think there was any bad intent on either of their parts."

He pulls a sheet of paper out of a manila folder. It's the composite sketch of Ted.

"Did you see this man at all while you were at Lake Sam? We've had reports of him speaking to several women outside of the restrooms. His arm was apparently in a bandaged cast."

I study it for his benefit, concentrating really hard. "No, I can't say I saw him. I would've remembered that." Ted needs to remain in the shadows, at least for now.

"Another young woman vanished several hours prior to Carol, in nearly the exact same spot. Are you quite certain you don't remember this man? He approached quite a few young women, much like you."

"No, I absolutely would recall if a man in a cast approached me, detective, with all due respect. I don't think it's something you'd forget, at least not in a 24-hour period."

"Oh, yes, of course. I'm sorry. I didn't intend to imply that." He places his fingertips on the surface of the desk as he thinks—I imagine he's figuring out how to word an accusation against Stephen.

"Do you think Stephen could have anything to do with this? We do have reports of this Ted person, but we're not sure that he's responsible or that his name is, in actuality, Ted."

I hesitate. "Well, uh, I'm not quite sure." I shake my head. "No, no, I don't think Stephen would do anything like that. He's a great guy, a little strange sometimes. I'm sure, I'm sure he wouldn't do that."

"You seem a little undecided. We're not trying to assume here. I want to know a little more about Stephen and his actions on the day. There's no blame as such, I want to make sense of the situation."

"Okay, now I don't want this to be taken the wrong way, but Stephen sometimes enjoys scaring women, like sometimes he'll hide behind our cars and jump out when we try to unlock our doors. It's always a joke. Like I said, he's a bit eccentric. Maybe he tried to scare Carol...Other than that, I honestly wouldn't say he caused her any harm."

"Has he ever tried to, uh, 'scare' you?" He uses air quotes.

"Yeah, he's tried to a couple of times—once he knocked me

into the Yakima River when we were white water rafting." John doesn't need to know it was the other way around. If I'd been the one pushed in, I wouldn't cry like a little bitch like Stephen did.

"Didn't you find that a little strange?"

"I guess I did, but it was just one of his little jokes. Please don't say I mentioned it, I don't want to upset him. I thought it'd be alright to mention it. It was a joke."

"Don't worry, Maris, this is confidential."

I meet his eyes, simulating reluctance, nervously interlocking my fingers. "I don't want him to get into any trouble. I don't think he's responsible for what's happened to Carol, assuming she has actually gone missing and isn't with other friends."

"It's not looking good at the moment. We've released images of both the girls to media outlets, and we should've heard back if they simply were otherwise preoccupied."

"Oh lord, no." I start sobbing quietly. He hands me the Kleenex box but doesn't comfort me. "I can't lose hope—I have faith she'll return. I'll begin praying for her."

"I'm afraid there's only so much prayer can do," he tells me, unmoved. He probably has mothers in here crying daily. "Do you remember Carol saying anything out of character?"

"No, not really, she was her usual self. She was in high spirits.

She's always a very cheery girl."

He makes more notes and then pushes another photo to me, this time of a Bambi-eyed blonde. "This is Janine Warren. She was last seen approximately six hours prior to Carol going missing. Did you by any chance come across her?"

"I wouldn't have reached the lake by then."

"You see, we have quite a problem here. Girls have been going missing since January, and now two have disappeared on the same day, in broad daylight. Are you absolutely positive you didn't see or speak to a man who called himself Ted?"

I'm a little confused. I'm not sure what he's getting at, oscillating so quickly between Ted and Stephen. "No, I did not see a man who looked like Ted, I did not speak to one named Ted either."

"Alright, so we may have to look a little deeper into your friend Stephen. What can you tell me about him?" He's frustrated, shallow crow's feet forming at the corners of his eyes.

"I don't know, there's not much to tell other than what I've already mentioned. We grew up together. He's pretty shy and can be quite awkward. He's never had much luck with women, but he's dating a mutual friend now, Susannah. He's pre-law at UW." "Is there anything else you can remember about yesterday that might be out of the ordinary? I'm sorry to be so pushy, but I'm sure you can understand the gravity of the situation."

"No, detective, nothing. I'll be certain to let you know if I recall anything else—please call me with any updates on the case. I'm so worried about my Carol." I let out another little sniffle.

"Well, if that's all the information you can provide, I think we can wrap things up." His affect is cold, clinical. He gives me a mechanical pat on the shoulder and again offers the box of tissues to me, which I refuse. He ushers me into the hallway where Hunter is sitting dejectedly. His face is drained of color, as is Stephen's. Susannah's gaze is directed to nowhere in particular, and absent. It's looking like a goddamn funeral parlor in here.

"Are you guys done?" I ask, wiping away a non-existent tear from the corner of my eye. "Thanks, detective," I add, turning to John. He smiles and closes the door.

"Did you see that other girl? She was so beautiful," says Stephen. "I can't believe two disappeared on the same day."

"You do have a thing for blondes, don't you?" I say it softly but ensure the taller detective is in earshot. "It's so horrifying that girls are missing, let alone girls we actually know."

"Carol does have friends up in Issaquah and some others near Snoqualmie Pass, maybe she's visiting," says Hunter.

"Don't you think it's a little far-fetched that she'd head up to the Cascades without her car? Even if she did decide to hitchhike, don't you think she'd have left her car at home first?" Stephen doesn't disguise his skepticism.

"Poor Jack must be devastated. I've never seen him so smitten with a girl before," I say, to make conversation. I just want to go back to bed.

Susannah's hand is clammy and trembling when I reach to hold it, jolting her back into reality. Her shoulders are flush against the hard, wooden bench and her legs are crossed, the top one trembling.

"Susannah, honey, are you doing alright?" I ask, sitting down next to her. I embrace her but retract a little when I feel the cooling sweat on her skin. She doesn't answer; instead, rivulets of tears pour down her face.

"No, I think I want to be alone at home for a while," she says. She remains fixed in her seat, though, making no effort to stand up. Her rose-patterned sundress has a rather low neckline, but her lack of a female figure keeps it from looking vulgar in such a conservative setting. Her chest is flat like a child's, and her pale skin is almost translucent. She's fixed her chest-length auburn hair into a ballerina bun and is sitting next to Stephen. I can barely decipher between the two in the shade. I always find it more difficult to accept a red-haired man than a woman, and I harassed Stephen mercilessly about it until about the tenth grade. "We're all wrapped up here, would you like me to drive you home?" Stephen leans toward her, his voice tender. I try to inconspicuously wipe my dampened hand with the Kleenex I'm still holding. I don't want to seem too rude, but I feel it's equally rude to let someone hold your hand when you're sweating like a horse. I walk to the water cooler and pour chilled water into a Styrofoam cup and bring it back for her.

"Here, drink some water and rest for a little while. It's stressful for all of us, but I think it ought to help," I tell her. She takes the cup from me but doesn't drink, almost deriving strength from holding it.

The door for the room I was in opens again and John sticks his head out. "Sorry to bother you guys but, seeing as you're still here, would it be possible to speak to you for another moment, Stephen?"

"Uh, yeah, sure, I guess. I'll just be a minute Sav. Maris, could you please sit with her for a while?" He follows John into the cramped interrogation room without waiting for a response.

She's still sitting there, entirely immobile. While I understand that it's quite a shock to have your friend go missing on a trip to the lake, she's had at least a day to process it, and it's baffling to me that she's still dumbfounded and is not in the least able to take care of herself. I don't even think she and Carol were particularly close. I, on the other hand, have been friends with Carol almost since birth.

Her mother was in my mother's little pregnancy group (in which they discussed the frivolities of giving birth and dressing up their future children, as well as sharing diet recipes so their baby weight wouldn't last for any longer than it had to), and she went into labor about three days or so before Millie and I were born. They organized playdates for us that the nannies attended to. Mother was all about motherhood as long as it didn't involve effort on her part. I spent a lot of time at Carol's house when Father would be opening a new hotel in Barcelona, and Mother would be spending away her supposed stress in Monaco or New York. It was better to be with her and her loo-loo mother than the succession of nannies that were hired to tackle the immense problem that was Millie and me—most quit after a couple of months. I have to give props to a large horsewoman who managed to deal with us for the entire summer back in 1965. I think she's spending time in a sanatorium currently, but I think it's more to do with her lack of equestrian success than her tenure at the Caldwell residence.

I reach into my pocketbook for the rest of Hunter's cigarettes and light one. It's this horrific cheap tobacco that makes the back of my throat burn, but it'll have to do for now. "Susannah, take one. I promise it'll help take the edge off." She agrees, and I light it for her while I scan the place for an ashtray. I stare at the linoleum floor in silence, taking liberal puffs until the cigarette dissolves into ash. Susannah doesn't speak, and Hunter looks like he's been punched in the stomach. He's blue as hell.

I don't want to talk about Carol anymore. I don't want to be with Susannah or Stephen or Hunter. I want to be back in bed so I can regain all the sleep I lost last night due to Hunter's post-sex sobbing about the poor missing girl. I am very aware of social etiquette: I know what to say and when to say it, but that doesn't ease the burden of it. It takes time to develop a persona of empathy and concern, but I'm always there when a friend needs me, tissues and chocolates in hand. I don't understand why people feel the way they do or what makes them attractive to one another, but I fulfill my obligations and my drive doesn't allow me to be mediocre at anything, not even the illusion of compassion. It tires me out to no end. The only person who I understand and who understands me is Millie. If we're not in the company of others we can communicate simply, effectively, without phony pleasantries. She serves many purposes for me, and I know how to placate her. Watching Mary Tyler Moore with my sister, followed by a nap would surely be preferable to this hell.

The fluorescent lights are too bright to agree with my hangover. I shift my gaze to the sketch of Ted that's been tacked to a noticeboard in the center of the station. There's apparently a task force that's been created to track him down. It would help if their depiction looked even faintly like their suspect. King County PD never has been any good with their selection of sketch artists. The drawing of his car depicts a '66 model VW bug, which his does not resemble.

I'm rather impatient, but the one thing Mother always taught us was composure. I know never to tap my foot against the floor or jiggle my leg or express any sort of inconvenience or discomfort. Every move, she taught us, should be deliberate, slow, and purposeful. She'd smack us about the face if we spoke while eating, slouched, disrupted someone's conversation, wore clothes that were not year and style appropriate or used curse words. Crossing your legs at the knee was frowned upon and sitting with them apart was unfathomable. Composure allowed you extra time to decide your course of action and ensure it was entirely fitting. When someone gives you bad news or treats you poorly, you don't jump to anger or insult. Instead, you note it down and file it in your mind for a time that will allow you to react with as much force as possible. Being polite and courteous always works out as it gives you the benefit of the doubt (often when you don't warrant that kind of luxury).

About forty-five minutes later, Stephen walks out, visibly shaken. John must've worked quite a number on him. I knew he'd been holding back.

"Steph, dude, are you alright?" Hunter springs to his feet. "Have a seat, you look a little rickety."

CHAPTER FOUR

I've always found that once you put a lot of effort into something, you don't feel complete until you find a way to preserve it. Once you do it right, you don't want to forget it. Some people like to keep photographs, but I like tangible mementos I can use to calm myself when the aching boredom rises, spreading malignantly from limb to limb, finger to finger, and toe to toe until it consumes me whole. I love a trophy almost as much as I love the hunt. I'm not an idiot. I know better than to cast suspicion on myself by striking too often. My family is perpetually bathed in publicity. Often, we're subjected to intense scrutiny by those who couldn't achieve a tenth of what we have. My mother is the head of damage control. She quashes anything remotely controversial before anyone can pick up the wave of a whisper. I'd prefer the police to an investigation headed by my mother, but I've learned to bypass both. I take a long shower and smoke a cigarette to its last ash. I dress slowly, deliberating between two pairs of shoes—I'm not sure which would look better with my billowing, cobalt Ossie Clark dress. I look to Millie, who's dressed identically.

"Which shoes?" I ask her, taking a seat on the divan.

"Well, last time I came so close to twisting my ankle in those platforms, so I'm leaning toward flats," she tells me, applying the finishing stroke of nail polish to her outstretched pinkie.

"We're going to wear the Valentino ballet flats," I say. The only other shoes that match our dresses are these hideous strappy sandals that should've never left the design studio. I grab Millie by the shoulders and bring her to a standing position. I smooth her hair down and study her face for any discrepancies in makeup. She's taller, but there's little I can do about that with our shoe options. Other than height, it's like looking into a mirror. "Millicent, you need to get your emotions under control, we can't have any repeats."

"I cried for literally less than a minute," she tells me.

"You shouldn't be crying at all. It's so entertaining. I don't know how it upsets you so much, honestly. Remember how the last one peed himself, it was hilarious. Messy but still hilarious." She isn't moved, still bordering on hesitation. She always has reservations. She's too scared of the blood. She's too upset by the screams, and she can't finish the job. She has no desire to have that kind of power. Well, wait, I don't quite think it's that—Millie wants power. She's overcome by the idea of it, but she seeks it by other means. I don't really understand because there's no higher power than being in the position she'll be in within a few hours. She needs to realize that her mediocre fantasies of control are just that—mediocre. Also, I'm no queen of comedy but seeing a man piss himself out of fear is pretty fucking funny.

I grab my eyeshadow palette and dab a little more cobalt on Millie's closed lids. Her hand is trembling, and I hold it for a minute to steady her. "You need to get a grip, alright? You're brilliant, and you won't let this go down like a sinking ship. I need you; you know I can't do it alone." I kiss her on the forehead, making sure not to leave a trace of my cherry ChapStick on her skin.

I can't have her fucking this one up, too, but I need someone to work with me to make it a little easier. Being a five foot six, ninety-five-pound woman has its severe disadvantages, no matter what the women's libbers may tell you. Men do tend to be larger, stronger—that's why I never choose women as prey. I like a challenge. I planned this particular one before I left for Europe. My instincts are animalistic, and I started early, watching as he headed to classes before midday on Mondays and returned from the gym at 5 PM on a Tuesday. He stayed home on Wednesdays and saw his girlfriend every Saturday, like clockwork. He lives on 12th Avenue, in the university district, with three other male roommates. They drink most evenings at Dante's, and one of his roommates leaves the house every weekday morning at 5 AM, presumably because of a job, but I've yet to confirm this. He's doing a Bachelor of Science at UW, and he's in several of my biology classes. We don't have any mutual friends, and though he's made numerous passes at me, I've yet to take him up on any offers. It's Monday, nearing 10 PM.

I drove past his place a couple of times earlier today to confirm he was at home. Since returning from Europe, I needed to ensure his schedule was still the same, as it was important to factor in summer holidays. He was around most of the day, sunbathing on the front lawn with his shirt off. He's one of the liberal types, with wavy, dirty blonde hair brushing his shoulders and a winning smile. His workouts show on his lithe frame and his deep brown eyes are flecked with amber. He seems to spend a lot of time on-campus campaigning against supposed injustices overseas, more time than on his actual degree. He's not particularly wealthy, but he certainly has no need for the socialism he crusades for. I could sleep with him. I could let him take me out on the date he's been trying to organize for a few months now, but there's something so repulsive about a consenting male.

"Get to the car quietly, Millie," I tell her, my voice low. Mother seems to have the supersonic hearing abilities of a bat, despite the tranquilizers she consumes, and I don't want a run-in with her—especially before an event. There's no way she'd let us leave. "I know, I'm not clomping around like a Clydesdale," she replies, rather brusquely. "I'm not going to screw it up this time." I search for my maroon Balenciaga shoulder purse. It has everything we're going to need, and the bag does seem to go with my dress, despite the colour clash. I tiptoe down the circular staircase and head straight for the garage. Millie is close behind, holding onto the fabric of my dress as if she were an infant finding strength to stand up for the first time. I decide not to tackle that issue just now. She hops into the back seat, and I slowly reverse the car out of the driveway. I give her the bag. "Get the tyre iron out now and put it on the floor."

"I've got this, Maris."

It's an eighteen-minute drive into downtown Seattle from Bellevue. I lived with a friend on twelfth for a couple of weeks, so I know the entire area by heart. It's easy to navigate and fairly small. It's a bustling college community, so I expect people to be largely absent, perhaps visiting their families. I don't know very many people who stay around campus during the holidays, but James seems to be the aberration. I park across the street from his shabby share house, where I have an excellent vantage point. He has no drapes or blinds, so there's an uninterrupted view into his living room and bedroom—he has exclusive access to the basement room too. I don't want anyone to say they saw James and me speaking, but I know I'm going to have to muster up a conversation, however brief, in order to lure him into the car. He's moving about the living room in faded blue bellbottoms and a plain white polo shirt. His hair is wet and slicked back, ostensibly from a recent shower. He sits for a while, watching a rather trite episode of Happy Days.

“Do you want some of the gin?” Millie asks from the cramped backseat. She swigs straight from the bottle, still quite jittery. She usually needs to consume a lot of alcohol or at least some cocaine or ketamine to go through with everything. Her nerves have to be steadied, but I need complete mental acuity. I want full control of my body, my emotions, and my target. I can’t do that if my brain is fogged with drugs or alcohol. It’s not often that I enjoy being stone-cold sober, but this is definitely one of the rare occasions.

“No, you can have it. Don’t have too much. You know you get a little sloppy. Get down lower.”

I step onto the road softly, closing the door with as little noise as possible once I’ve scoped out the open windows facing his house. No one appears to be around or, if they are, they’re too busy watching poor quality television to pay attention. I hover outside his front lawn. I don’t want to be seen walking inside toward his house, but I look rather peculiar standing here. I walk to the door and knock twice, rapping my knuckles against the mahogany slates.

“Oh wow, hello,” he says, finally appearing. “What a lovely surprise. You look sensational.” He grins. He’s stoned.

“Hi! I’m so sorry to impose, but my friends bailed on me, and I thought you might’ve been home.”

“You’re not imposing at all, don’t be silly. Would you like to come in? The place is a bit of a mess, but you’re always welcome.” “Well, I would love to, but I was wondering if maybe you wanted to get a drink first? I can’t quite bring myself to go drinking alone, you see.” I smile at him, placing my hand gently on his forearm.

“Yeah, of course, sure. Do you mind waiting for a second? I’ll go get a pullover quickly. It’s cooling down a little!”

"Sure, I'll be out here."

He takes a couple of minutes. I can hear him on the steps and then across the wooden floors. He dashes around and then grabs a set of keys from the drawer of a small table in the hallway. He shoves them into his front pocket and meets me on the stoop. I lead him toward the car, and he goes out of his way to open my door for me. He gets into the front passenger seat, oblivious to Millie's presence in the backseat, as planned.

He sits down and straps his seatbelt across his chest. Millie strikes on command, crashing the tyre iron against the back of his skull with immense force. His body goes limp, and I reach in the bag, searching. Millie grabs my hand, stopping me. She places the handcuffs in my outstretched palm. I handcuff him to the handle of the glove box on the dashboard and speed away from the curb. The wound on his head is bleeding, but he's partially keeled over, so I don't think it'll leave stains. I cannot handle another trip to the carwash, sitting there and waiting for a fucking hour while the Mexicans dither about inefficiently.

I hurry to the I-90 toward Issaquah. There's a site ready. I made sure of it during the day. It's a very secluded spot, bordered on all sides by wild bush and a small stream. One of our nannies used to take us hiking around there when Millie and I were very small, and it's beautifully peaceful. I've spent more time than I care to admit there, mapping it out and exploring the colorful bushland. It's a large place, almost entirely enclosed by the large, overlapping trees. It's perfect for my favorite hunting game. I've loaded the ketamine-filled darts into the gun I bought in Japan last summer. It's always more enjoyable when the male can last over an hour without yielding to the torpor—I like them spirited but not many are. It's a little depressing when they fall over after a hit or two.

He rouses to consciousness during the trip. It's funny

sometimes what people will say in situations like this. I guess not particularly funny, I don't mean I'd laugh in a literal sense, but it's quite strange. He starts incoherently, his speech undecipherable from that of a two-year-old's babble, and then starts talking about a math exam he has for a summer class at college. He's asking if I'm there to help tutor him because he thinks he's failing.

I hit the brakes and allow the car to roll to a mild stop. I grab the tyre iron from the back and clout his skull again—he blacks out. I don't have time for a conversation with him. The last thing I want is to hear him speak. Males talk too loudly, too long. It's repelling. I don't engage Millie in dialogue during the drive. She sits soundlessly in the back, and I spend the time reveling in the overwhelming pleasure and thrill. Adrenaline is pulsating throughout my body, enveloping me whole. My heart thuds in my chest, quick but steady. This is familiar territory.

The site isn't quite designed for automobile access, but I manage to drive through some of the less dense brush. He's still out cold. Millie and I exit the car—I unlock his handcuffs. I leave the door open. I want him to think he has a chance to escape. I would have liked to sleep with him. He's certainly pretty, and there's nothing better than knowing you're going to be his last. The power trip is like an orgasm, morphine, and money combined. It's dubious, now, though, with Millie here.

It's a long wait until he wakes again. He's like a caged animal, disoriented and terrified. His eyes dart around, sussing out the situation. I watch as the panic sets in, slowly at first, then frantic. I'm perched in a low hanging tree cove, my legs dangling and the dart gun in my lap. Millie is across from me, on the other side of the semi-forest, invisible to the untrained eye. She's got a sturdy white rope with her—it's usually used to dock Father's yacht. I'm in the leotard I wore under my dress, which lies folded neatly in the trunk of the car. I see him stumble and fall out of the car, with blood gushing from his head. He crawls around for a little while, endeavoring to gather himself. I think he's crying, but my vision is a little obstructed from the dark, and I can't see all that clearly. When he manages to get to his feet he stumbles and sways, grabbing his head with one hand. He breaks into a clumsy run, limbs moving awkwardly. He manages to gain a little speed. I shoot him in the leg, and he tumbles down, screaming in pain. "I like that you're trying," I call to him, laughing. Millie lets out a little panicked giggle too.

"Wh-why are you doing this?" he asks me, clutching his leg and sobbing.

"We all need to have a little fun sometimes, James." I shoot him in the arm. At this point, ketamine will be flooding his veins. He'll get respite from the pain and if he's lucky, he may slip into a k-hole and start thinking this is all a hallucination. He lies quite still and then shudders repeatedly. He manages to make it back to his feet, and he starts running again, this time toward Millie. He seems to have a fair amount of fight in him and it's wonderfully entertaining. I shoot him in the back. He falls over.

"Keep trying, please," says Millie, laughing harder now. I'm not sure if the thrill has made her giddy or if she's refraining from crying. Millie often laughs when she's suppressing tears. He staggers toward her, uncomprehendingly noticing that she's there. I think it's only now dawning on him that there are two of us. I don't even find it strange. I did, after all, go out of my way to make sure there were no visible differences. I give him a minute to realize he's not getting out of here and then shoot him in the chest. I hop down from the tree and walk to him. He's fallen again, but this time he's unconscious. I can't imagine it's been more than twenty minutes.

"Millie, come help me," I yell, grabbing his limp arms. I

drag him into the brush, with her help once she finally manages to get to us. I left a butcher's knife around here when I dropped by earlier today. I want him to wake up, and I wait. I feel cheated, I've worked so hard and I'm out of breath. The look of sheer, unbridled terror and despair is one that is unparalleled. It quells the restlessness, the boredom, the lack of directed energy. It gives you power. You're in the position to decide whether or not the person beneath you gets another breath. It's like being god, and that's all I've ever wanted to be. If the person is unconscious, you don't feel their fear. You don't hear their desperate sobs and pleas for mercy, about how they want to see their families and their poor darn girlfriends and pets one last time. You don't get to see their reaction once the knife digs in, slicing their skin neatly from ear to ear.

I feel rather empty as I slit his throat. He bleeds profusely and convulses, coughing up phlegm and blood. I push the knife deeper along his jugular, twisting it several times. He's conscious now but not to the point where he can speak or react, especially not with his windpipe carved open. He continues spurting blood from his mouth and nose and chokes on it a couple of times. His eyes don't open. It's so pathetic, I feel so pathetic. It's like killing a toddler. He puts up little effort against me when I stab him again. He keels to the side, and I shine the flashlight on his face. It's stained with blood and sweat, mingled with tears, and his hair is deeply matted. I kick him in the gut, hard. I need him to wake up. He squirms and lets out little yelps of pain, but he's not all there. His cries get weaker with every kick.

"Do you want to do anything to him?" I ask Millie. I offer her the knife.

She takes it from me and jabs him meekly. If I weren't upset, I'd almost feel sorry for the poor boy. I try to awaken him, kicking again and again. When he doesn't, I put him out of his misery. The foul odor of excrement wafts toward me, and I know he's dead. The stillness associated with the freshly dead sets in, and I wash my hands and legs in the stream of water. The body won't be seen for a while. Even Millie had trouble finding the location.

I wait for her to wash up, and she does so painfully slowly. I wash off the knife and leave it in the brush. I take off the leotard and put the dress back on.

We have our father's hotel opening to attend. He's on very good terms with most of the media, and I picked my outfit for the occasion. I make Millie change into a Dior jumpsuit. It's a very generous concession—it cost about double what my outfit did, and it has beautiful flared ends and a low-cut neckline, while mine is positively puritanical. She's earned herself a little treat. I toss her matching blue dress out the window of the car. I let her drive, I'm exhausted. My arms are throbbing, and my cold has worsened.

"Are we driving straight there?" asks Millie. She looks to me as I light a cigarette.

"Well, obviously. It's almost midnight. We were meant to be there about four hours ago. We don't exactly have time for a casual pit stop at home."

"Jeez, alright, I was just making sure." Her hands are trembling on the steering wheel. She always gets a little emotional. I'm hoping soon I can work alone.

When we arrive, we're greeted by an eager valet, a barrage of photographers, and elegantly dressed couples spilling out onto the street. Millie hands over the keys, and we pose for a few photos together. Hunter is standing outside, by one of the columns, smoking. He sees me and rushes over, draping himself around me. I kiss him for the cameras, hold his hand, and lead him inside. I note Father first, dressed crisply in a Valentino tuxedo, his dark hair combed back the way Mother likes.

"Daddy, it's lovely to see you," I tell him, still keeping Hunter's hand in mine as I hug him.

"Maris, you look beautiful. You look fantastic, too, Hunter. Thank your parents for coming for me, will you?"

Hunter laughs out of politeness (mostly, but I can smell alcohol on his breath too) and nods. "Of course, Mr. Caldwell, you know I will."

"It's Henry, you can call me Henry." I suppress a smile. He'd never let me hear the end of it if Hunter were to actually take him up on his bluff offer.

"We're going to get a drink, enjoy your night, Daddy." Mother is on the horizon, her floor-length gown unmissable.

She's heading for Father, and I make a hasty escape.

"Where were you? I've been waiting for well over an hour," Hunter tells me as we walk through the lobby, greeting people along the way.

"I'm preparing early for college, doing my readings. It's only a couple of weeks until we go back."

"You're already studying? Jesus Christ, Maris, you need to chill."

"Why don't you fuck me in the bathroom, that'll probably help me chill," I say, "Oh, and maybe a glass of champagne?" I kiss his neck, briefly. The conservatives are hovering.

"What, here? It's your parents' opening party."

I kiss him on the lips this time, slow, lingering. "Well, when you put it that way, maybe I should stick to the champagne. Fuck you." I start to walk away. I don't have time for his bullshit—there are plenty of other guys around tonight. He tries to pull me back, grabbing my arm, but I shake him off. I'm more delighted than I should be upon seeing Jack.

"Oh my lord, I'm so happy you're here," I say, hugging him tightly. "You know how to party."

"Let's get you some champagne," he tells me, threading his arm through mine. It's strange how he hasn't mentioned

Carol. He cried about her for a full hour on the telephone earlier in the evening.

"That's exactly what I wanted to hear, Jack, you understand me." He looks particularly pretty. He's had his blonde hair trimmed, and his suit emphasizes his swimmers' shoulders and snug little waist. He flags down a waiter and hands me a flute. I take a demure sip, but all I want to do is down the entire glass. He puts his hand on the small of my back, leading me to a seat in a secluded alcove. It's an intimate little spot, away from the din of the party and the loud, outdated jazz music.

"How are you doing, honey?" I ask him, taking another sip and leaning in. I rub his hand.

"I'm alright. I'm trying not to think about it." He takes a swig. "I feel a hell of a lot of guilt, though Maris. I feel like it's my fault. I was dating Carol, and you know I've always had a thing for you and now I feel rubbish."

"Why do you feel rubbish? Carol disappearing is not your fault. I'm sure she'll be found well."

"I was going to end things. I should've been better to her. I shouldn't have spent our time together talking about you—no offense—but she started to feel real insecure about it."

"I had no idea, Carol never let on."

"No, she didn't want to make you upset. She didn't know about us."

"Oh honey, please, this isn't your fault. Obviously, you and Carol were meant to be together, no matter how much I like you. She really loves you."

"I was going to dump her and now she's probably dead. Wouldn't you feel awful?"

"Look, you need to stop blaming yourself. Firstly, she's likely fine, and secondly, I wasn't planning to dump Hunter, and you weren't planning to dump Carol," I tell him. I run a hand through his hair.

"As soon as I got here, things started with her and then I met you, and I made her feel so goddamn lousy."

"Is being this upset going to help anything? We need to be strong right now and stick together until we find her, which we will. Please, she wouldn't want you to be worried." I swig the champagne.

"Maris, sweetheart, what are you doing back here?"

I look up to see Mother, her voice a soothing coo (most likely from the alcohol and a Percocet or two). She stands cross-legged with the bottom of her gown lifted slightly, her tiny frame teetering on six-inch heels. She disregards Jack, not bothering with a hello. She thinks very little of our Californian counterparts, particularly the sun-drenched blondes with a knack for surfing. She's a very indoorsy, reserved person. She eyes him critically with a thinly veiled sneer. She's probably wondering how he found a suit in his wardrobe. "The party is out there, you should be there for interviews with some of the journalists, preferably with Hunter. The Carlyle family is one we should be publicly associating with." She stares pointedly at Jack.

"Hello, dear—Jack, was it? We do need Maris outside."
"Yeah, Mrs. Caldwell—Jack. I've been around for a couple of years now." His laugh is awkward and forced.

"Yes, well, as I said, we need our Maris talking to the very interested journalists. This is our first hotel in our home city, and it's an exciting time for the family."

"I totally understand. I didn't mean to keep her from you guys."

"Mother, don't you think you're being a little rude to Jack?" "Jack, I do apologize if I'm being particularly brusque, it's just an important night," she tells him through gritted teeth. I love to make her grovel. She prides herself on her perfect etiquette, often omitting interactions with those she considers her inferiors. I'm not exactly an advocator for the rights of those on the bottom rungs of society, but Jack's family's net worth is far from poverty. Their money may be new and founded by sheer dumb luck, while ours has traveled down through several generations on both sides, but my treating him as if he were no better than the common vagrant seems out of order.

"Not at all, Mrs. Caldwell, of course I understand."

He stands up and brushes non-existent dirt off his blazer, reaching for my arm. Mother's eyes zero in on his hand and then meet mine. She raises a manicured eyebrow, and her jaw stiffens. She doesn't need to articulate her revulsion. I know the look. I release his hand. "Hunter's been looking for you, dear. Don't you want to spend some time with him? I'm sure Susannah or that Dawn girl can keep your friend here company."

"Jack, come on, I'll introduce you to some of the journos," I say for Mother's benefit. She lets him walk ahead, latching on sharply to my arm with her talons.

"Just what in Christ's name do you think you're doing, Maris?" she hisses, digging into my skin. "First, you come in four hours late, and now you're here doing god knows what with that filthy Californian cast-off. Have you even thought about how important tonight is for our family? You have Millie out there dressed like a common whore, and you're wearing what looks to be a sack from Sears. Are you out of your mind? Are you trying to sabotage us?" "Mother, you're making a scene. Did you not take your Xanax today? I'm not trying to do anything; I'm talking to a friend. What Millie wears is none of my concern, and quite frankly, I adore this dress. You bought it for me if you'll recall."

"I bought it for you when you were fifteen because Millie wanted it, and I didn't want you to feel left out. It wasn't meant to be worn by a girl in college. Jesus, Maris."

"I'm very sorry, I genuinely am," I tell her, looking her in the eye. "Honestly, Mom, you know I wouldn't do this on purpose." She softens. "It's alright, I believe you. I just need you to be more responsible, more accountable. You're not a child anymore, and you know you have obligations as a member of this family." "Of course, I understand. You and Daddy did mention the importance of tonight. I wanted to get prepared for classes as early as possible, and as for the dress, I really like it. It's not from Sears. You know it's an Ossie Clark, and it's special because you bought it for me."

"Oh, Maris, you're very sweet sometimes. You're very sweet. I think you get it from your father."

"I feel awful, I'm really sorry. I'll speak to some of the journalists to make up for my behavior. It's rather uncalled-for, I completely agree with you," I say, waiting for her grip on my arm to loosen. For such a small woman, she sure is strong, and I think she's perforating my flesh. "I would love to spend some time with you, Mother. I don't see you nearly as often as I'd like."

"We ought to get coffee tomorrow and talk. I know you're probably more upset about Carol than you're letting on," she says. "You've always been very...quiet about your issues."

"I would love that, I would. You and Millie are the only people I feel comfortable talking to and I've run myself into a breakdown. I can't seem to cope."

"Alright, honey, we can talk tomorrow. I'm sure you'll be pleased to know that your father will be home for two weeks before he flies to Vienna for that conference." Her hand relaxes, freeing me. "I need you to talk to The Washington Times for me, dear. I daren't trust Millie with that, and besides, she usually requires a little prodding from you anyway."

"Of course, I hope it's Barth? He's my favorite from The Times."

"Yes, he's here with his wife and daughter. We figured if we invited him as a guest and not a member of the gallery, he might give us a little extra something in his review."

CHAPTER FIVE

When I return at nearly 5 AM, the body appears to be in the early stages of decomposition, hastened by the dewy summer weather. Alone, I struggle to strip him of his jeans and shirt. He weighs a lot more than I'd imagined, and I yank on the clothes with all my force to lift his lifeless body into a more comfortable position for me. It's a terrible idea to leave clothes on a body. They trap fibers and hair, soil samples, and bloodstains. If the police had any idea what they were doing, they may be able to trace that information back to you. When the male is naked, I pile his clothes neatly beside him, folding them with the strict corners Rosa accords all our laundered blouses. I take several Polaroid photos of my prey, particularly the savaged bits of his torso and his face, with the eyes still wide open, glassy, and staring. His hair is matted with his blood and possibly some of mine from the struggle—the cut on my hand has yet to heal. I've brought my hacksaw with me as well as a butcher's knife that, once unsheathed, smiles up at me from my bag. I don't know if there's much information around on decapitation, but it is possibly one of the most difficult tasks I've ever taken upon. It's really fucking tough. It takes a hell of a lot longer than the movies and documentaries let on. I'm not exactly a bodybuilder, either, so it takes me forty-five minutes to sever all his fingers at the knuckles alone.

Deaths in movies and detective magazines seem so breezy, almost effortless, but I'm telling you, humans take a very long time to finally give up, and even longer when they know their bodies are about to be cut up. We all have a strong instinct for survival, so we fight until there's no strength left in us. I'm not a sicko; I don't enjoy this part of it. I don't have a morbid fascination with decapitation, nor do I get orgasms thinking about it, but it's pertinent to ensure that investigators take at least a couple of months to identify the remains. This is achieved in a number of ways.

First and foremost: fingerprints. They are the single most-used identifier for found corpses and the people who may have caused the deaths. I sever each of his fingers and his toes for good measure. It's important to not get sloppy. Dealing with knives and hacksaws can cause many injuries too. I seem to have cut myself in many places, but I'm numbed to the pain as I work. My focus is impenetrable with the second object of identification—his skull. It's the most fun, and of course the most strenuous. I work tirelessly with the saw.

The fleshy parts of his neck slice open smoothly, as do his arteries, but the bone is stubborn and unrelenting. I nearly break my arm in the process of beheading him, but a sweet joy floods me when the last of the cervical vertebrae gives way. I sit and study him while I regain my composure. The face on this cadaver gives me more satisfaction than his face in life—fear in his open eyes, defeat, his mouth. His blonde hair is abundant, both on his head and on his body. I feel a wave of nausea at the sight of his bare chest. The hair is thick enough to serve as carpet for the den. His hands appear rugged, a far cry from the actuality of his sheltered, fledgling academic career. His lips are girlish, more so than Hunter's, almost as full as mine. His teeth form perfect white rectangles and whatever's left of his forehead appears clear, lacking pimples and other blemishes. Blood has congealed about his muscular thighs. The stab wounds are still gaping, soon to be infested with maggots. Nature is beautiful; she does most of the cleanup herself.

I'm exhausted and I have yet to go to bed. It takes all my strength to not fall asleep right here. I leave his headless cadaver in a mound of rotting leaves. His head goes into a canvas tote lined with a bin wrapper, along with his clothes and the butcher's knife. I shove more brush onto him, breaking off a weak branch from one of the trees and tossing it onto whatever's visible. The putrefaction will set in soon, and it'll start reeking in no time. Summer is wonderful when it comes to that and trips to tropical islands. In winter, particularly a Washingtonian winter, bodies stay preserved, often freezing over. In summer, the flesh rots, and the insects gorge. There's no good place to hide a hacksaw, so I head back to the car with it in one hand and the overwhelmingly heavy skull in the other.

I dump both in the trunk. My legs feel as if they'll fold underneath me, and my head is pounding from the champagne and the lack of sleep. My dress is conservative enough to not look too peculiar in the daytime should anyone see me. I stash the Polaroids into a small case of mine. I always flip through them when I'm feeling down. My drive home is quiet. The traffic in the city hasn't quite commenced. I listen to the talkback radio instead of the music channels. I love talkback radio. I love to listen to people uninhibited in their conversations. I could listen to it for most of the day if I'm being honest.

I drive into the garage, wearily making my way up the stairs into the house. It's peaceful, without the noise of Mother's voice, Rosa's vacuum, Millie's records, and Father's mind-numbing television. I'm thankful they're all asleep and out of my way.

I head to my room and lock the door. I pull my clothes off, my bra, slip, and underwear, and collapse onto my bed. My aching body doesn't require Valium's holy assistance. I huddle myself in the light summer quilt and pass out almost immediately.

I dream vividly of the Seychelles, sunlight glinting on the calm, impossibly turquoise sea, my legs tanned and flecked with sand whiter than I've ever seen. Anse Lazio beach encircles me and the water laps at my ankles. I look down and see my coral bikini, the matching sarong clinging wetly to my hips. Hunter is beside me, but he doesn't speak. His face soon morphs into Jack's. Carol is on a reclining beach chair behind us, absorbed in a copy of The Second Sex. She's wearing a bright yellow caftan, with what I recognize as my large tortoiseshell sunglasses. I call to her, but she doesn't respond. I try again, but she can't hear me. Stephen lurks nearby, which I find odd as he's never left the United States. I attempt to walk to Carol, to grab her arm, but I can't move. The water feels heavy around me, weighing me down so I'm entirely immobilized. She drifts further from me as I'm drawn into the sea. Jack anchors me and holds my hands as they disintegrate into grains of sand. Carol looks up from her book, glancing in my direction, but I can't tell whether or not she can see me. Her eyes are obstructed by the glasses and her wide-brimmed straw hat. A lone tear slips down her cheek, which is now becoming pallid. Blood begins pooling around her neck, dripping into the cotton fabric of the caftan. She removes her sunglasses, placing them in her trembling lap. The water rises around me. Jack is speaking to me in gibberish, his voice muffled and hoarse as if I had gauze in my ears.

Carol is sobbing now as the blood trickles down her chest. "How could you let him do this to me?" Her gaze travels from me to Stephen.

I don't know what time it is when I wake up—I think I may have knocked my clock down with an errant flip of my arm during my sleep. It's raining outside, the clouds heavy, and the sky lacking any indication of future sunshine. I roll around in my bed, the sheets tangled comfortably between my limbs and bringing me the warmth I wouldn't expect to need in the middle of July. I can hear Rosa outside my door, banging the noisy vacuum cleaner against the banisters of the staircase. I reach for my clock once I find the strength to sit up. It's twenty-five minutes past two, but I don't feel any more refreshed than I did when I went to sleep. I find it difficult to function on less than nine to ten hours of sleep, but I struggle to achieve this. I can only sleep five hours at a time, so I generally wake up for an agonizing ten minutes—popping as many benzos as I can—and then try to fall back to sleep. It's very troubling and inconvenient. I want to go back to sleep, but I know I have a shopping date with a good friend I met in Utah a few years ago. Her family travels back and forth between Tacoma and Provo every couple of weeks or so. They have this nasty little Volkswagen campervan, and I don't really know what any of them do for a living. I stayed with them in their winter house at Crystal Mountain and avoided numerous advances from her acne-ridden little brother. I quite enjoy Heather's company. She's a striking girl, slender and delicate with the lithe, graceful body of a ballet dancer. Her Mormon family isn't at all aware that she's a lesbian. Her closet is so deep that it may as well serve as a black hole.

I run a bath, sitting on the edge of the tub as the water fills. I'm not in the mood for a quick shower. I don't have it in me to rush about now. My hangover is mild, but my lack of sleep takes a great toll. I lower myself into the water, blisteringly hot, and close my eyes. I grab the loofah and squirt a glob of Chanel bodywash onto it, gently running it along my fatigued legs. I savor the quiet, the calm. I pull my hair into a messy bun. My heart slows, and I breathe in the divine honeycomb and vanilla scent of the soap. With a great amount of effort, I peel myself off the marble tub. I put on my terrycloth bathrobe and tie it loosely around my waist. I sift through my clothes, eventually putting on a full-sleeved, ruby red skin-tight blouse and a skirt with horizontal red and white stripes. I drape a white cotton sweater around myself, tying the sleeves in a gentle knot above my collarbone. It doesn't look particularly warm outside, but I hate stockings, so I don't bother to put any on. I sit on the edge of my bed, cradling the telephone in my lap as I slip on some shoes. I dial her grandmother's home phone, the only number I have for her in Washington. It rings for a while before her nasal-sounding mother answers.

"Hello?"

"Oh, hello Mrs. Oldcastle, this is Maris Caldwell. I was wondering if I may speak to Heather?"

"Maris, honey, of course you can. Let me get her for you." She doesn't cover the speaker well as she barks loudly for her daughter. Heather's soothing voice soon takes over. "Hi Maris, I was about to phone you. Would you like to meet in front of Rhodes' in Bellevue Square?"

"That sounds great. I'm going to drive over in, say, twenty minutes or so. You know it's only about five minutes from my place. Have you had lunch yet?"

"I haven't yet. How about we get lunch first and then go shopping?"

"Perfect, I'm looking forward to seeing you; it's been far too long!"

"I'll say. Alright, I'll see you soon, Maris."

I grab a purse from the divan at the foot of my bed, mainly out of laziness. I could look through my collection to find one to match my shoes, but I have neither the inclination nor the energy. I leave the door to my room open, cornering Rosa in the hallway. "I would love it if you could get around to cleaning my room," I tell her tersely. It's a daily struggle to not focus on the rolls of her stomach or her overlapping teeth. "It's getting a little messy." "I'm sorry, Miss Maris, you were sleeping, and I didn't want to disturb you." Her accent is thick, emetic. "I will get to it right away."

"Please, I'd like fresh bedsheets at least once a year," I say. "Or I'll have you deported," I add, under my breath. I watch her fat jiggling from the stairway as she attempts to wrangle the bulky vacuum cleaner into submission. She wears a regulation maid outfit that struggles to contain any part of her. She used to work at our hotel in New York, but Mother developed a bizarre fondness for her and brought her and her horde of illegal immigrant children to Seattle. They essentially sponge off us, and I don't think there's a husband in the picture. I don't even know how anyone found it possible to impregnate her that many times. I think bestiality is a sin, but clearly Luis or Pedro or Julio didn't agree. Rosa is an excellent cook, I must admit, but that doesn't negate the nausea that comes with seeing her. The Hispanics seem to be flooding in, and my parents sure have contributed. California used to contain them, but now it's bursting at the seams and the overflow is rushing into Washington. Thankfully, not many of them have the intellect to gain admission into any university at all, let alone mine. The blacks have been terribly maligned: many are beautiful, talented, and intelligent. The Jews are wealthy and entrepreneurial, but the Hispanics have no redeeming qualities. I could spend most of the day engrossed in the hypnotic jiggling of Rosa's flesh, but I continue down the steps. The house seems empty, and I don't see Millie's or Mother's keys on the table in the foyer. Perhaps I'll get to skip the conversation Mother promised me last night.

Heather is at the front of Rhodes' department store as promised, dressed in a pretty, sleeveless mustard-yellow tunic and Candie's mules. Her chestnut hair is parted to the side, flowing in a glossy cascade to her slim waist. She's not at all butch and masculine like most of the lesbians I've encountered while out clubbing with the fags. They wear their hair short and often don men's clothes and disgusting Birkenstock sandals. Their advances aren't as outrageous and confronting as those from men but are nonetheless distressing. Heather is shy and unassuming. When I first met her, she'd never been with a woman. She's tried dating men, many times, but none of her relationships have passed the one-month stage. I honestly don't blame her at all. Even if she weren't a lesbian, males have little to offer. I give her a long hug, resisting the urge to run my fingers through her hair.

"Maris, you don't know how happy I am to see you! We've been in Utah for the past two months, and I've been absolutely going out of my mind," her arms still wrapped around my shoulders.

"Well, I haven't been in Utah, thankfully, but I've missed you, too, Heather. Come, let's go get lunch. The ethnic food here is a treat if you'll recall." I link my arm through hers and lead her to the food court. Her skin is smooth and soft against mine, no doubt due to the frangipani body lotion she uses religiously. While the male gays are shunned when showing affection to one another in public, nobody thinks twice about two women with entwined arms.

"I'm starved, Honestly, I could even go for McDonald's right now. A cheeseburger with fries and a large strawberry milkshake, oh and maybe an apple pie, I could have it all. I've been eating so much of this goddamn yogurt because of my diet, I want to die, I hate yogurt."

"Heather, please, the last thing you need is a diet. let's go to McDonald's." It's not even a phony compliment. My hands can grip the entirety of her waist, and, even at five eleven, she barely tops 105 pounds.

I don't like to admit it, but I adore fast food. I couldn't go a week without it. Granted, a trip to a fast-food restaurant will usually lead to me being keeled over a toilet bowl with a finger halfway down my throat, but that isn't at all a deterrent. She orders her meal, substituting the strawberry shake with vanilla, and then I order the same. She pays in cash after my half-hearted attempt to reach for my wallet. McDonald's vanilla milkshakes are celestial. The one time I forced Rosa to emulate it at home, it ended up tasting like burned rubber, and I lost the desire for it for at least six months. I smile at the black cashier, a rarity in this area, and collect a tray from her, walking to an intimate table in the corner of the food court. I grab a handful of fries and shovel them into my mouth with the speed and intensity of a fat girl let loose in a chocolate shop. When Heather arrives, however, I return to the dignified manner of only eating one fry at a time. I take tiny bites of the cheeseburger, allowing myself the opportunity to speak without sounding uncouth.

"Maris, what have you been up to these few months? Your life is always so interesting and happening. The most exciting thing that happened to me this week was getting my dress back from the dry cleaners." She sighs and sips her milkshake. Her dainty fingers draw an invisible star on the paper tray cover.

"I haven't been doing that much since I got back from Europe. It's a lot more boring around these parts when you're not here. Are you staying for long?" She grins at me, her entire face animated with glee. "Well, I didn't want to say anything beforehand, in case it wasn't going to work out, but I'll be staying in Seattle for a while. I got accepted into law school! It was either here or Utah, and god knows I can't stand being around that piece of shit area anymore."

"What, you mean you're moving here?"

"I'll be here as long as the University of Washington will have me!" She lets out a little squeal.

"Fuck, that is amazing, honey! It's great you're finally getting out that hellhole. I'm glad you haven't been Mormonized yet."

"Well, don't get me wrong, Maris. I'd still like to have five wives."

"I think an even number might be better, or perhaps seven, a different one for every night of the week."

"Well, it wouldn't be hard for a girl as pretty as you," she tells me. "You could have anyone you wanted."

"Not after this meal," I say, dipping a fry into a pool of ketchup. "I don't want to get on a scale after my holiday. I'm surprised I didn't gain fifty pounds from all the paella in Spain. I don't even like paella, I don't know why I kept having it." Fish disgusts me, extraordinarily so. All types of seafood wreak havoc on my taste buds. The worst is sushi or sashimi. If I wanted to eat raw and unseasoned fish, I'd go swimming in the damn ocean and grab some. "But tell me more, where are you going to stay, what's your schedule like? We need to figure out a day during the week on which we can get lunch."

"I think that's more up to you. Medical school seems far more rigorous than law school, and you're working with your dad, right?" "Oh, well, I was supposed to be working today and yesterday, but here I am."

She gasps as if a thought has just occurred to her, fawn-like eyes wide. "Dear lord, I can't believe I forgot about it. I read about it in the morning papers and saw it on the news when I got here last night. Your poor friend...Carol, yes,

Carol, she was abducted from Lake Sammamish? I feel so insensitive and rude for making you come out to see me. You must be wrought with grief. She's such a sweet girl, although you only introduced us briefly."

"Yes, uh, it was quite traumatic. Maybe the papers mentioned it, I mean, why would they, but I was with her that day." I take a vast bite of the burger. "We were swimming and hanging out at the beach and then it became the worst day ever."

"They actually did mention that you were there, Hunter Carlyle and girlfriend Maris Caldwell if I'm to quote verbatim." "Hmm, girlfriend to Hunter Carlyle, what a winning title." I'm upset and a little surprised. I would imagine that the connection would be spun the opposite way, considering the value and worth of us individually. Hunter floats and drifts, tied down only by his wealthy lineage, while I'm more than a parasite who struck it lucky. His degree will culminate in nothing, and he'll eventually become nothing more than an attractive figurehead for Carlyle Candy.

"It must be terrible for you. I hope she's found safe and well." "I can't bring myself to think about it. I don't want to imagine Carol suffering or being held against her will. I want her to be in Snoqualmie with her other friends. I don't want to think about it, I really don't."

"Of course, I'm sorry, Maris. I didn't mean to be so obtuse about it all."

"It's not your fault. It's a very strange situation to be in. I don't even know how to grasp it myself! Look, why don't we walk around the shops, looking at dresses should get our minds off this. Well, if I can fit into any of them anymore, that is."

"Don't play that game with me. Your figure is unbelievable." "Come, come, come, let's go to Nordstrom down in the Bellevue Collection," I say, taking a final sip of my milkshake. "There are so many things I shouldn't be buying, but I will anyway."

She finishes off her meal quickly, dabbing the remnants of the apple pie away with a serviette. I drag her through the opulent mall, passing one designer shop after another to finally reach Nordstrom. Six stories high and about a mile wide, it has every conceivable item of clothing a woman would ever need. I could get swept away in the silky fabrics and dizzying fragrances.

"Are you looking to buy anything in particular?" she asks me, looking around in awe. I'm not sure if she's been here before. "Maybe some blue jeans and slacks, though I wouldn't mind a few new dresses too. Do you need anything?" I grab a pair of bellbottoms from a Levi's rack and a forest-green mini dress. Father's quite generous with his monthly allowances to Millie and me, and Millie doesn't keep tabs on her credit card, which happens to be sitting quietly in my wallet. I add a pair of gold, shimmery hot pants to the growing pile on my arm.

"I could definitely use some new clothes, maybe things that allow me to show my ankles. It's not done in Utah," she says, giggling. "Maybe some new bras too. I barely have anything stylish."

I stare at her lissome body, rapt by the gentle sway of her hips and her small but well-shaped chest. She blushes, and I look away. "Why don't you try some on?" I suggest. I select a see-through Chantelle demi-cup number, teal with pretty little flowers. I hand it to her and head to the dressing room. I smile politely at the saleslady manning the overflowing racks of clothes. She directs me to a stall. Heather follows me in. She drops the pretense, her fingers tracing along the back of my neck, and I drop the clothes I'm holding. She pins me against the mirror and kisses me, ardent and forceful. I cling to her waist, drawing her in sharply. My breath catches in my chest, and I unzip her tunic. Her soft lips taste of vanilla. They yield to mine without struggle. I lose myself in her, my control evaporating around me. She's warm and inviting, her body a sheltered haven in the middle of a rainstorm. She kisses my neck and unties the sweater from around my shoulders. I gasp as she runs her delicate hand up my thigh.

"I've really missed you," she tells me, playing with the waistband of my underwear. "Hunter gets too much of you. It's not fair."

"I can't argue with you there," I say, unhooking her bra.

CHAPTER SIX

I can remember a time when I was very little, likely no more than four or five-years-old. It was winter, snowing, and blustery outside. Millie and I weren't in school yet, and we'd been staying in our parents' chalet in Sun Valley with our (mostly) sober mother. She was in one of her depressive spirals and had sat us down before the fireplace. She ran her fingers through my hair gently while braiding it. I had on a ruby red turtleneck and a heavy sweater with a teddy bear on the front; it was my favorite. We were meant to go skiing, but Mother was too tired, and Father had left much earlier in the day. It was a paltry excuse of my mother's. She's never been the outdoorsy type. Her form of exercise was primarily stirring martinis and swiping Father's credit card. She wouldn't have been able to ski to save her life.

She was affectionate during her depression. I don't know if it was from a place of honesty or loneliness. If she didn't have Father around, we'd suffice. I was wriggling around because I wanted to wear my hair loose like hers or in one of those beehives she'd make if she planned to go out.

She thought children oughtn't be dressed up like women; it was unbecoming.

It was late afternoon, and the Swiss au pair had made Millie and me hot chocolate before she was done for the day. Mine was in a thermos container and stone-cold as I sipped it. Millie was splayed out on her tummy, beside me, waiting for her turn, engrossed in a coloring book. We'd only gotten trims up till that point, so our hair was about hip length, but hers was blonde and mine had been dark since birth. Mother nestled me in her bony, emaciated embrace to settle me and then returned to the braids. Her cup of coffee sat untouched on the table. Had I the wisdom then as I do now, I would've understood it was laced with Kahlua. She's very fond of exotic alcoholic drinks that masquerade as acceptable daytime beverages.

Her hands were cold, permanently cold, and she wore a cashmere wrap. Her face was puffy as if she'd been crying but when I asked, she was evasive. "Mommy's very tired, Maris," she'd tell me. "Finish your cocoa." Her nails were manicured, curved into arches that were kind to my scalp. She'd make two long, fishtailed braids and secure them as one with a white ribbon. The smell of firewood was intermingled with the smoke from her cigarette she'd denied having, with absolute vehemence. She told us cigarettes were disgusting. They'd rot your teeth, age your skin, and stunt your growth. She'd smoke out on the terrace in the snow when she assumed we were occupied or sleeping. Without the assistance of makeup, she had clear skin, bee-stung lips, and beautiful, heavy-lidded eyes, but she would only allow Millie and me (and occasionally the au pairs and nannies) to see her in her natural state. She primped and primed when she was to see Father or society women or the dark-haired man who'd drop by in the middle of the day while Father was gone. Her moods were unpredictable, but she was usually nicest on her down days. “Mommy loves both of you so much,” she said, tying a small bow with the ribbon. She smiled at me, her eyes swollen with the remnants of a thick, heavy “Sometimes it’s very hard, you know, just very hard to...” Quite frankly, no, I didn’t know.

“Mommy, please don’t cry,” Millie said, swiping at Mother’s face with a Crayola-stained hand.

“I’m not crying, Millicent. I’m tired.” Her tone was sharp, cruel. It was one that was reserved for her and the maids. She’d divide Millie and me when necessary, pitting us against each other, and other times she’d dress us identically. She’d play bizarre games that I still haven’t come to understand. The sleeves of Mother’s woollen sweater were rolled up at the elbows. Her forearms were bruised purple with lingering finger imprints. She always had bruises when Father was around. “Now, come on, sit still honey,” she cooed, giving me a gentle kiss on the temple. “Don’t you want to look pretty?”

“I want to look like you, Mommy. I don’t want to tie up my hair,” I whined, held in place by her unmoving legs. “Please.”

“I don’t want you to argue with me, pussycat, sit still.”

I tried to push against her. I was small, but she was fragile. It had been an even competition at that point, and I’d managed to break free. Her weakness morphed rapidly into rage—her palm crashed against my face with colossal force. I sobbed. Her smacks were unrelenting. She dragged me to her by the hair and rained blows upon me till I was hysterical and had curled in on myself. Millie watched on silently, not attempting to intervene. She knew better than that, and I knew never to count on her to stop a beating. I had to wait until Mother had it out of her system, until she hovered over me, howling almost as heavily as I was. My skin set alight. I burned and ached and cried. Her hands became fists, and her anger found its outlet in my tiny body. I could’ve fought back, but I didn’t. I escaped in my mind.

I'm sitting at the counter of the Oak Bar, a feature of Father's new downtown hotel. I'm drinking a martini with more olive than gin. The bartender is a talker, yappy as all hell. His nose warrants its own goddamn zip code. I don't know how he made it through the rigorous recruitment process. He seems to possess the intelligence of a gnat, but I suppose it could be attributed to affirmative action—the Hispanics need jobs too. I nod and smile politely as he jabbers on about how exciting he's finding Seattle to be. I had plans to meet Hunter for dinner at Canlis, but I'm in no mood to see him nor try their dry-aged duck. I've satiated my hunger with a truffle oil grilled cheese sandwich instead.

The bar is quite busy for a Thursday evening. I see people on awkward first dates and businessmen discussing deals over Manhattans. I'm tired, drained. I went to bed at 6 AM after watching Psycho on television and couldn't get back to sleep when I awoke around ten in the morning. I order another martini and wait for the spic to realize that I won't need a payment method. I hope Father is at home and isn't hovering nearby. I twirl the olives in the alcohol before I take a bite, noticing as a boy slides into a seat on the other end of the counter. He's remarkable to a level that leaves me staring dumbfounded. His eyes are a luminescent light blue, perceptible from this distance, and his hair is dark, as dark as mine. He's built slim and his jaw and cheekbones are deftly carved as if out of porcelain. A blonde girl galumphs on to the stool beside him. She's unfortunate-looking, with the undefined chest of a twelve-year-old boy and thighs the size of Texas. He seems rather disinterested in her, but I recognize the desire in her gaze.

I readjust the straps of my cocktail dress, to maximize the view of my (rather impressive if I do say so myself — yes,

I know it's uncouth, but it's true) cleavage. She seems desperate for his attention, and at this point, I don't really blame her. I have to physically remind myself to look away once I meet his eyes. All I want is to linger. He stares at me until the blonde grabs his arm and forces him to face her.

I turn back to my drink, stealing glances at every available opportunity, noticing how the colour in his cheeks contours his smooth skin. I engage with the bartender to distract myself. His unpleasant face momentarily douses the overwhelming need. I'm almost nervous, but the alcohol is doing its job, steadying me. I don't think I've ever seen someone as attractive as this boy. I'm a lightweight, so the three martinis are making me tipsy. My body tingles from a cocktail of lust, adrenaline, and searing alcohol. Nerves are not normally something I have to deal with. I don't feel much, at most I'd be bored or high, so I don't understand the twinge in the pit of my stomach. The girl's grip on his arm is claw-like and remains steady as if she were grasping on for dear life. I don't know how she's managed to be on a date with him, perhaps his self-esteem is as low as her neckline. He seems unsure of himself, his movements a little clumsy and lacking the arrogance that usually accompanies a terrific-looking male. "Say, bartender, would you mind doing a favor for me? I need to use the telephone, and I don't want to have to go back up to my room."

"Of course, miss, let me bring you the telephone," he tells me, or at least I think so, his accent making his speech almost undecipherable. "Are you calling your boyfriend?"

"How did you know?" I grab the black rotary phone from him and take my time dialing, attempting to keep my focus away from the boy. I can picture Hunter rousing from a Xanax induced slumber to pretty himself for our date. Hunter is very concerned with his appearance, and oftentimes he'll take longer to get dressed than I will. He's the vainest son of a bitch I've ever known. I call him and let him know I'm terribly unwell, wrought with worry about Carol and coming down with the flu. He is a little slow, but he still manages to realize the noise surrounding me is not of that in my bedroom, and I explain that I was forced to visit the hotel with Father. I look up at the boy despite myself, losing my trail of thought. "No, no, Hunter, don't you worry about me. I should be alright, you don't need to come over and keep me company, I plan to go home and right to bed."

"Are you sure?" His voice is insistent like it usually is when he wants to get laid.

"I'm perfectly sure, I'll phone you tomorrow, alright?" I don't wait for a response and hang up. I watch as the needy blonde gets up and walks unsteadily toward the bathroom, entirely out of place in her heels. The boy is left alone for a moment, and he looks at me and sips what appears to be a gin and tonic with lemon. I grin at him, and he smiles back. "Listen, bartender, will you go over and find out what that young man is drinking?" I ask of Luis or Pedro or whatever the fuck his name is. "I want you to give him another one on the house."

"Yes, miss, of course. Uh, I'm not sure if I can put it on the house, though. I don't have that kind of authority."

"Do you not know who I am? I'm Maris Caldwell. My father owns this hotel among, say, one hundred fifty others, so don't worry about your authority," I tell him curtly. "I have enough to cover us both, and likely everyone else in the bar too." I hold back instead of threatening to report him to the immigration department.

"I'm very sorry, I didn't know. I'll go and find out, alright?"

"Yes, thank you, I appreciate it." I sit still, playing with the olive pick to settle myself. I need to get a fucking grip.

"He's having a gin and tonic with a twist. I'll prepare another for him, miss."

"Great, thank you." I run my fingers through my hair, fanning it evenly over my shoulder. Mother always told us it was indecent to touch up makeup outside of the ladies' room, so I restrict myself to a quick check in my compact mirror. I drain the martini and leave the remaining olive in the glass. Only ugly people ought to suffer this kind of nervousness. I stand up, smoothing the silken fabric of my dress down over my hips and walk to him. The blonde is still absent, no doubt powdering her face maniacally in the bathroom to try to gain any possible semblance of attractiveness.

"So, what do you think of the hotel?" I ask, standing beside him. "I don't know if I care for the décor."

He turns to look at me, tracing the rim of his fresh glass with his finger. When he meets my gaze, he blushes. "Oh, um, I think it's nice but, yeah, I don't know, maybe the décor is a bit much." He motions nervously at the five-tiered chandelier.

"Maybe I should've picked a different light fixture then." I smile.

"Wait, what? Did you pick that out?"

"Yes, I picked out most of the stuff in here. I thought the oak for the counter was a good move, though, considering the name of the bar."

"Are you the interior decorator here? I didn't mean to insult you. You look too young to have been the decorator, I'm very sorry."

"I'm kidding, I'm the daughter, I didn't pick any of this. I'm Maris," I say, laughing. I extend my hand to him. While his demeanor is anxious, his grip is firm.

"I'm Charles, or Charlie, depending on who I'm talking to. It's great to meet you. So, your folks designed this place?"

His face is particularly distracting. "No, I'm fairly sure they hired people to do it. Dad wanted his first hotel in his hometown to be just terrific." I remind myself to blink and look away.

"Oh, holy shit, you own this joint? Melissa, uh, the girl I'm here with, said it had a great bar and restaurant."

"Was she right? I think my parents would be thrilled to hear that."

"Yeah, she really was. I appreciate you sending the drink over, too, by the way. Are you staying here?"

"No, I live a couple of miles away. I probably shouldn't be driving since I've had a few drinks, but I like taking risks. Are you here on vacation?"

"God no, I don't know who'd want to go to Seattle on a vacation, not even in July for the three days of summer. I live in Ellensburg."

"You're my type of person. I try to spend as much time outside of Seattle as I can too."

"It sucks, doesn't it? At least it's a little better than Ellensburg. The people here still have teeth." He reaches into the pocket of his t-shirt and pulls out a pack of cigarettes. "Would you like one?" "That would be great, thanks. I've just run out." I place it in between my lips, and he lights it for me before lighting his own. I watch as the blonde returns from the bathroom, attempting to steady her balance in her shoes. I almost feel secondhand embarrassment for her—it's one hideous sight. The dress stretches awkwardly over her ham legs and her pursc looks like the one my grandmother was buried with. She notices me rather quickly, confused, and anxious. I don't know how she's here with him, I really don't. It's making me uncomfortable. There ought to be order in the world. Her inelegance exemplifies that girls like her don't belong with men this attractive, nor in bars as exclusive as mine.

"Charlie, you have a new friend," she says condescendingly, settling into her bar stool. "Hi, I'm Melissa, Charles's girlfriend."

"Maris here owns the joint," says the boy, only briefly looking her way. He's fidgety and nervous—his attempts to disguise this are far from successful. I'm struggling as much if not more. This is a new sensation for me. I don't enjoy it.

She laughs. "Are you kidding?"

"Maris Caldwell. It's a pleasure to meet you," I say, forcing a grin.

"Oh wow, you're not kidding. I brought Charlie here. I heard it was a very classy new place. He's not usually into this kind of stuff. We got a suite—I thought it would be nice to go out for a night."

"I'm sure you'll have a lovely time. There's a fantastic view as long as you're not on a floor lower than five. You can see the Cascades and the whole city from the penthouse."

"I think if you put our incomes for a year together, we still wouldn't have enough to rent the penthouse for a night," she tells me caustically.

Poor people always have a chip on their shoulder, blaming others for their failures and lack of drive. I'm not sure whether her tone is one of derision or envy, but neither concerns me. Judgment from the impoverished is about as valuable as the trash my maid cleans out. I smile at her. "Well, I don't believe it's booked out today. I was planning on going home, but I might stay here. You're more than welcome to come up and check it out. There's a private bar inside too."

"That's so generous, we'd love t—" starts the boy.

"We might stay in our own suite, thanks," she interrupts, hackles raised. "We appreciate the offer."

"I completely understand, I hope you both enjoy your night. If you change your mind, feel free to pop by. The elevator around the corner goes directly to the penthouse—you need to let the operator know who you're visiting, and they'll buzz you up."

"You're wonderful, really. I don't think I've ever seen a penthouse."

"No, of course you haven't, Charles. You dropped out of

college and work at Waldenbooks," says the blonde. "This is like, what, the first hotel you've been to?" Her tone is cruel, scathing. "I love Waldenbooks, working there would be great, it really would. I wouldn't be able to control myself, though, I'd probably buy everything I could," I say, soothing the obvious injury. "Well, he's not academically inclined, general book reading included."

"That's not true, though is it, Melissa?" His voice is sharp. "I'm sorry, she seems to be having an issue with her attitude tonight." While I would usually back away from this situation (I'd rather not spend time licking the wounds of other people), I'm compelled to stay, rooted in my spot. "I feel terrible, I wanted to come over and say hello, I don't mean to interrupt anything here, I may go up to my room," I say with reluctance. "Have a lovely evening."

I walk across the bar toward the lobby. While the bartender failed to recognize me, the bellboys haven't. They smile at me as I make my way to the front desk. Manned by twelve women in matching navy-blue blazers and skirts, the reception is swift and effective.

"Good evening, Miss Caldwell. What a pleasure to see you here! What can we do for you?" The redhead flashes a smile at me dutifully.

"Hi Candice, how are you today?"

"I'm very well thank you, how are you?"

"I'm doing well but, as you can probably tell, a little drunk. I don't think I ought to risk a DUI, so I wanted to check into the penthouse—Daddy did mention it wasn't booked for tonight." I slur my words slightly for effect.

She pauses for a brief moment, flicking through bookings. "You're in luck, Millie! It is free tonight."

"Oh, that's wonderful. I'll check out before noon, so I shouldn't be too much of a bother."

"You're never a bother, Miss Caldwell. Do you have anything you'd like me to send up, any luggage? Would you like anything from room service?"

"I don't have anything with me, but I would absolutely love some French fries. The biggest portion, some stuffed artichokes and a bottle of Coke."

"No problem at all, here's your key."

"Listen, if I get any visitors, please make sure they're sent up right away." I smile at her, sliding her a hundred as I grab the key. She blushes, greedily snatching the bill off the counter and shoving it into the front pocket of her blazer. "I'll be sure to do that."

"Thank you, honey, have yourself a great night."

The elevator for the penthouse is spectacular, with gold panels and only three buttons: one for the roof, one for the lobby, and one for the telephone. It's cordoned off with red velvet rope but is otherwise invisible to those who cannot afford it. A bellboy walks with me, offering to take my purse from me as he ushers me in. I let him carry it. I tell him to set it down on the divan in the foyer. He waits expectantly for his tip, and I shove a twenty into his palm. "That'll be all for tonight, thanks. Go on and get yourself a drink." I offer him a quick smile.

"Oh wow, thanks, Miss Caldwell, please let me know if you need anything else."

I wait for him to leave before I strip down to my slip and pour myself a glass of red wine from the fully stocked bar. I know it's well-aged and too expensive for my father to allow me to drink. I take the small plastic baggie of coke out of my bag and empty it out onto the countertop, dividing it into neat little lines. I do two lines and sway backward on my heels, reeling. It's terrific stuff, it really is. I'd swiped it from Hunter's stash a little while ago and I'd expected it to be subpar, like everything else in his life. I'm glad it's not. I sit on the enormous bed to steady myself. Cocaine and alcohol on an empty stomach can do wonders in the way of head spins. The curtains are drawn, and the panoramic view of the twinkling lights of the Seattle skyline is dazzling. As I lean over and manage an unsophisticated attempt to take off my shoes, there's a knock. My stomach growls in anticipation of the French fries.

"The door is open —just roll the table in, please!" I call.

"What do you mean?" asks a male voice.

"The room service, of course." I sigh, walking to the door.

"Oh, uh, no I'm not from the hotel. It's Charlie, we just met downstairs?"

As much as I could use the food, I feel elated. I pull the door open.

"Oh shit, I didn't mean to catch you at a bad time," he says, glancing at my outfit or lack thereof. "I can leave!"

I laugh. "Don't be silly, come on in. Can I get you a drink?"

"I'll have whatever you're having, and maybe some of that room service you're expecting."

"How do you know I didn't order liverwurst?" I ask, grinning. "Lucky me, I adore liverwurst." He laughs.

"It's a shame I'm only getting French fries, then." I look up at him as I pour his glass of wine, still flustered.

"Look, it's not my first preference. I do prefer raw organs, but sure, I'll have some of those instead."

"I like your ability to compromise." I hoist myself up onto the counter. "So, how do you like the penthouse? I hope it's all that I made it out to be."

"I'm not used to anything this fancy. I thought our room on the second floor was a palace." He looks around in awe at the granite and ivory kitchen, the ten-seater dining table, and the lavish sunken lounge room, eventually setting his gaze on the view. "You can see the Cascades from here."

"I don't think I've ever been to Ellensburg, well, not that I recall, but I hope this is a slight improvement. Where's your girlfriend, uh, Melissa was it?" I take a sip, crossing my legs, and try not to stare. This is the pedigree of boyfriend I need in my life. I can't imagine any of my friends having an accessory so beautiful. It seems unfair that a girl like Melissa, with all the grace and beauty of an old sow, would be with him.

"Well, unless you're interested in the rodeo it's a cesspit, so anything is an improvement. This, however, is incredible. I can't believe you own it."

"My parents are still alive, so, technically, I don't own it yet." "I'd move to Seattle if I could live like this. It's terrific, it really is. Melissa planned this little trip a while ago but wanted to change hotels since this one opened. She freaked when she heard about the kids our age going missing around here."

"Oh yeah, it's a bummer. I can't believe what's happening. Is she down in your suite now?"

"We had a bit of an argument about coming up here. I wanted to. She didn't. She's probably sulking right now, but am I a bit of a bastard if I say I don't care?"

I laugh. "No, she sounded out of line at the bar, honestly. Have you been dating for very long?"

"A couple of months, I think. She lives near me and was persistent, so I thought I'd go for it. I don't know too many girls." He laughs. "Shit, I keep embarrassing myself. I should stop talking."

I can't decide whether he's being dishonest or is genuinely unaware of his attractiveness. My ability to read people usually works far better, but I feel like my brain is wrapped in cling film. Nothing's functioning as it ought to. "I find that difficult to believe," I say slowly, carefully, my brain struggling to formulate a proper sentence.

"That she was persistent?" He looks confused.

"No, that you don't know many girls. I mean, look at you." "I guess it's not that I don't know them, I haven't had too much luck. Melissa asked me a few times if I'd like to take her to dinner so, eventually, I did, and it progressed."

"You shouldn't be embarrassed. It's just me here."

His hands are trembling a little, and there's the slight sheen of sweat on his forehead. He isn't lying.

"I've had trouble myself," I add.

"You're kidding me. You're the prettiest girl I've ever seen.

Melissa would be furious if she heard any of this."

"Well, it's convenient that Melissa isn't here. How's your wine, would you like some more?"

"So I can sound like an even bigger moron when I get drunk?

Probably not, I'll wait for the fries."

"Fuck, I don't know what's taking them so long. I'm starving.

And, in case you haven't noticed, a little high." "You don't look high. You're very composed."

"I'm in my undergarments, drinking wine on the kitchen counter with a boy I've known for all of an hour." I start laughing. "But I'm glad you consider that composed."

"You've got a point there. But I'm kind of drunk, so my judgment may or may not be skewed."

"Room service," calls a female voice from the hallway. I hop off the counter and hurry to the door as fast as my heels can carry me.

"Come in! Roll the table in, please," I say. The portion of fries is about the size of my head and the artichokes look delicious. Charles helps the little orderly push the trolley in.

"Can I get you anything else, Miss Caldwell?" She looks uneasy when she notices my lack of clothing.

"Oh no, not at all, thank you!" I sign the invoice and add a fifty-dollar tip. I feel generous tonight. I close the door behind her as she hurries out.

"Dig in or I'll beat you to it," I say to Charles, popping

several fries into my mouth at once.

"Stuffed artichokes, oh lord, these are my favorite!" He says it with child-like excitement. "I am so, so hungry. Do you know how expensive the food is at your hotel?"

I start laughing. "Yeah, you could say it's a little steep. But these are cooked in truffle oil and that shit is expensive."

"Alright, this tastes like it should for five-dollar French fries.

I don't know what truffle oil is, but I think I like it."

"Well, that's good. I don't think I could ever be friends with a person who dislikes truffle oil." I cut the artichoke delicately with the tip of the knife, separating it into two portions. "So, are you staying here for tonight?"

"That was the plan if Melissa even lets me back into the room. I walked out...not very amicably. She paid for it so, technically, she can keep me out. We were planning on going white water rafting in the Yakima tomorrow morning, but I might drive back to Ellensburg instead."

"Oh, I hear the weather tomorrow will be dreadful—rain all day. But the news stations have lied before. You're more than welcome to stay up here if Melissa is still angry. There are several bedrooms—one down here and one upstairs that opens into the rooftop pool."

"I wouldn't want to put you out like that," he tells me after swallowing a bite of the artichoke. "You're way too nice."

"It's no big deal, there's plenty of room. Plus, I don't want to be presumptuous, but you probably wouldn't like being back on the second floor after having the penthouse suite. Our butler service is pretty nice too."

"There's a butler here? Holy shit."

"Yes, though they're taught to be invisible whenever possible— they'll run a bath for you or help pack your clothes and disappear when you don't need them."

"You're incredibly lucky to have all this. Back home, Mom cooks everything—and by cook, I mean she'll toss a

TV dinner into the oven and let us, my brother Chris, and sister Billie, and me, salvage whatever's edible."

"What's Billie short for? I have a sister named Millie, coincidentally. She's twenty-three minutes younger than I am."

"Her name's Wilhelmina, but she thinks it makes her sound like she's forty-five, so she insists on being called Billie. Is Millie short for Camilla?"

"Millicent, but I think Camilla would be nicer. I suppose we're lucky, but if you met our parents you might reconsider. If we didn't have staff at home, we'd probably be eating TV dinners too. The last thing Mother made us was mac and cheese back in 1960. Or maybe it was 1959. The idea of her cooking is bizarre. All I remember is that I was very little."

"Do you guys usually live in the hotels? If I had hotels, I don't think I'd ever leave." He looks around the place again in admiration.

"No, our father wanted us to grow up like 'regular kids' so, at most we'd spend a night or two in our hotels during their grand openings. Our house is in Bellevue, but we were always in Colorado and New York too."

"What's New York like? I've never left Washington before." He dips a fry into the tiny bowl of ketchup, and I make a mental note to complain to my father about portion sizing.

"It's probably my favorite city in the world, so I could be biased, but it's wonderful. It's always buzzing with people and events, and you don't get bored. I mean, sure, a taxi driver may run you over, but at least you'll get a bit of adrenaline in you."

"I like the way you describe it. It sounds better than drinking enough beer to make you unconscious at Bleachers every Thursday."

"Don't get me wrong, I've been pretty intoxicated plenty of times at Club 82 in New York but definitely not from beer.

The party scene is wild. Alcohol often doesn't even make an appearance."

"I've always wanted to go to New York. Hell, I'd even go to damn Montana if it meant getting out of here, you know?"

His delicate features are overcome with melancholy. I feel the urge to reach out and hold him to me. His long, dark eyelashes shadow the blue, attempting to hide any visible signs of pain as he stares at the floor. When he looks up at me, finally, he grins, and my stomach ties into a little knot. I'm craving him, watching his masculine hands, and wishing they were on me.

"Well, we have a hotel there, and I'm sure I could arrange a booking for a week or two for you and Melissa if you'd like."

"I think if I pushed it hard enough, my ratty car might get me there. I'd park it a block or two away from the hotel, though. I wouldn't want to scare any of your guests away."

"My car is pretty shitty too. I haven't been able to drive much lately at all, what, with all the work it needs," I lie, attempting to give him comfort.

"I'm going to guess you have a Mercedes. Or a BMW."

"You're close but no dice." I smile at him despite myself. "It's a Porsche."

"Please tell me it's red."

"I wanted it to be. It's blue."

"You've disappointed me, Maris," he tells me, shaking his head. "I thought you were better than that." He bursts into glorious, musical trills of laughter. I observe his mouth, the full lips, smooth as mine, and the sparkling teeth. His neck is slender, the ends of his hair meeting tenuously at the nape. "But it sure beats Melissa's Volkswagen."

"She's a pretty girl," I say. I pry slowly. I want intimate details of his relationship and how to dismantle it.

"She's alright, I guess. I mean she's skinny and all, there're plenty of girls uglier than her."

"That sounds like a glowing recommendation," I joke. "I'm sure she'd love to hear that. Any girl would."

"I don't mean to be rude or anything, after all, we're dating, but she's not what I expected. But I care about her, I do."

I want to wrap him around me like one of those elegant silk Hermes scarves Mother has hanging on every hook in her cupboards. "I'm sure you do, but I feel New York is the kind of city that needs to be explored alone. All the little shops and alleys and quaint cafés in SoHo, you don't absorb them as well when you're with someone."

"You seem more like a Park Avenue girl, to be honest," he tells me.

"How would you know that if you've never been to New York?" I retort lightly, knocking back the rest of my drink.

"Well, Billie leaves her Vogue magazines lying around the house sometimes, and you know...I get bored. I always like a little night reading." His smile is sheepish.

"Do you mean you like looking at skinny girls in expensive lingerie?"

"No, of course not...alright, maybe, but doesn't every guy?" "Did you see the January edition of this year?"

"Jesus fucking Christ, you're the one in the blue and red sets, aren't you?"

"I'll have you know I was also in the ankle-length Alberta Ferretti dress—it had a turtleneck too; very conservative."

"You looked...I don't have words."

"I know, even I was ashamed of how the Ferretti dress looked." He moves closer to me, his clothed thigh against my bare one and there's a sudden buzz that I can't blame on alcohol or cocaine. When his skin touches mine, I shiver involuntarily. I feel heat rush to my face, and I hope I'm not blushing as hard as I think I am. My skin has the very annoying tendency to flush deeply, embarrassing me, and ruining my face in one swift hit.

"Maybe you could show me around New York City," he tells me, taking my hand in his own.

I guide myself toward him. I stare into the bottomless ocean. "Yeah, I suppose I probably could,"

He tilts my chin up to him and brushes his lips against mine, soft and sweet. He tastes like honeyed wine and strawberries, and I can smell faint cigarette smoke lingering on his shirt. I hold back, allowing him to take control, partially because I can execute none of my own. My body is frozen in position, from a combination of adrenaline and desire. He kisses me again gently. His lips are indulgently soft, throwing me off guard.

"I'm really sorry, I shouldn't have done that," he says as he retreats, unsure of himself. "You were so lovely taking me in and all when you had no reason to."

"You shouldn't have stopped." I brush his hair back and kiss him on the side of his neck. I breathe him in. He has the right mix of aftershave, cologne, and smoke, with his natural scent slightly overpowering the cocktail. It makes me a little giddy.

"Melissa is downstairs, and I think you're too drunk. I don't want to take advantage."

"I'm not drunk."

"You're one of the prettiest girls I've ever seen," he repeats. My body aches for him. "I'm not drunk."

He kisses me again.

This time I respond eagerly. "I told you. I'm not drunk."

I've rarely felt more conscious. Each sense is pulsing. His hand on my hip, the sound of his voice, the smell of his skin, the beautiful angles of his face, the taste of him. My senses overwhelm me. I want to rip off his shirt with my teeth, but things stay gentle. He's tender, his nimble fingers tracing the edges of my thong, never once stepping outside the confines of decency. "Your skin is so smooth," he tells me quietly, in between kisses. "Are you certain you don't have a boyfriend? Look at you."

"I think I'd remember, Charles." I grin at him. "Boyfriends are parasitic; they're hard to forget."

He's laughing, and I take the moment to unbutton his shirt. I kiss him on the neck.

"We shouldn't do this. We really shouldn't. I want to take you out, you know, to a nice place. One of those fancy joints in Bellevue. They've got some very good French food, I hear."

"I've been to my fair share of fancy restaurants. They bore me. You don't."

"Does your dad own them too?"

"No, I don't think he's acquiring restaurants at the moment. I think he's pretty busy overlooking the management of our hotels." My kisses grow urgent as my body tingles.

"I want to take you out somewhere nice, Maris. Wine and dine, you know? I've always wanted to do that for a girl, but I've never had the opportunity, especially not with someone who looks like you."

"Do you not want to be with me?" I ask sullenly, lying flat on the bed. I fight the urge to cry. I want to feel him in me, the heat of his body on mine. I want to hear his shallow breath and light moans. I want to feel his heart race. "Because I can totally understand if you don't."

"Don't be silly. Look, I'd probably sell my soul to the devil for a girl like you."

"Then what's the problem?" The tears scald my eyes, ready to drip one by one down my face to ensure my humiliation.

"I want to treat you properly. I don't want to take advantage of you. I don't want to be the guy you see cheating on his girlfriend because I wouldn't want you to think of me like that."

I'm not used to rejection. I feel sick to my stomach. "Alright, well, I guess that's your decision to make," I tell him stiffly. I swallow hard to keep my voice level. I draw myself into a sitting position as far away as I can be from him physically, considering the space constraints. When he reaches for my arm, I shift backward, avoiding his hand.

"I hope you're not upset. I want to do this properly, you know.

I've never been able to," he says.

It makes me queasy as if it were a pity thing. He's pitying me. This is mortifying. The pain is visceral like someone's set me on fire from within.

"Oh, I completely understand. Don't worry at all." I force a rigid smile. "Can I get you anything else? The bar is pretty well stocked, or we could get more room service."

"Would you mind if I got myself a scotch?"

"Ooh a scotch man, you're wild," I say, faking my laugh. "I'll make you one. Neat?"

"On the rocks...I'm not that much of a scotch man, but I hear it impresses girls."

"Oh, it sure does. It's irresistible, truly, the height of masculinity," I quip, kicking off my heels as I walk to the bar. I collect ice cubes from the tray and place them into a tumbler, pouring a cascade of blue label over them. I hand him his drink as he sits at the foot of the bed. "My father has some very nice things to say about this scotch."

He takes a sip and then attempts to hide a wince. "Shit, this is strong."

I stifle whatever remains of my rage and pour myself a tall glass of the golden liquor, without ice. "It's not that bad," I say after I gulp down half. I yawn and stretch my arms above my head. "You know, I'm getting super tired. Must be all the food, and I'm sure the alcohol has played its part. I'm going to bed if that's alright. You're more than welcome to stay here if you like. There're several other beds."

"No, I couldn't impose on you like that."

"Don't worry. It's hardly an imposition. I'm tiny, I don't need three California king beds to myself."

"I should really go home. Honestly, I'm in no mood to see Melissa. Could I please get your phone number? I don't think I can even try to hide my interest. We could go out to dinner and watch a movie, whichever movie you like."

"Oh, uh, that's sweet of you. I'm busy these days, you know, with college coming up and all, and a couple of photo shoots with swimwear companies. I shouldn't be lounging around, and I definitely shouldn't be off my diet like I was tonight. It was lovely meeting you." I smile coolly, leading him to the door. I withdraw when he tries to touch me, shirking out of his way.

"Are you saying you don't want to see me? I hope I didn't upset you."

"No, sure, sure, I'd like to see you. Say, leave your number down at concierge, and I'll give you a ring whenever I'm free, okay?"

"Can't I just have your number?"

"I'll get in touch with you, don't worry." I usher him outside. He looks forlorn and confused. He leans in to hug me, and I instinctively step away. My pride is too overwhelming. I close the door on his face.

Once he's gone, I curl up in the bed, wrap the quilt tightly around myself and cry.

CHAPTER SEVEN

When I arrive home from the penthouse suite, dressed sinfully in last night's clothing, I'm accosted by my father. It's five minutes past 10 AM, and I'm certain there's still a little aftermath swelling around my eyes from the crying, so I have on a pair of outdated Chanel sunglasses. I slept at three and woke at seven, groggy and disoriented. I lay still on the bed for a while, maybe an hour or two, fighting the exhaustion and nausea. It's not even helpful exhaustion. It makes you listless—you're unable to do anything productive, but you're not drowsy enough to knock out. I took some Xanax to get back to sleep but got only an extra hour. When I turned on the television, all the channels were playing footage of Carol's mother sobbing and shaky, begging the public to report anything they saw or knew about Carol's disappearance to the police. I showered, threw up a little of the excess alcohol, and brushed my teeth raw. "Maris, where have you been?" asks Daddy, his arms crossed. "Oh, I wanted to check out the developments in the hotel, Daddy. I had a couple of martinis at that wonderful new bar, and I didn't think it'd be a good idea to drive home inebriated, so I spent the night there." I smile at him.

"I'm glad that you liked it. I wanted you to join us for a family breakfast, so I was about to phone Hunter in case you were with him."

"No, I wasn't with Hunter. You wouldn't get a response from him anyway. You know he's never up before noon."

"Well, I think it's important you remain with him. His family is very compatible with ours. Come, Millie and your mother are in the dining room."

"Daddy, I'm not hungry." My stomach lurches at the mention of it.

"Maris, I'm not asking you," he says curtly. "Come along."

I follow him into the dining room. Mother's at one end of the eight-seater table, and Father takes the other. I sit across from Millie who seems only partially conscious, still in her prudish nightgown with her silk sleep mask beside her. She takes a lazy bite out of a croissant and stirs her black coffee. She, like Hunter, doesn't like to be woken before twelve. Mother is perfectly composed in her white linen dress and the opal necklace she received from her sister in Australia. Her honey eyes show no trace of lethargy, but I see purpling bruises along her arms. The maid's brought out the intricately designed Wedgwood china, something she only does for Daddy.

"So, what are we celebrating?" I ask, managing to drink some water. Rosa hovers about, pouring coffee I didn't ask for and handing me a croissant I can't begin to stomach.

"That's all for now, Rosa," says Mother without concern for politeness. "Please go and finish washing the dishes." She sips her orange juice, which I know has been spiked with Krug. "Maris, take off your sunglasses. You're inside, it's obscene."

My jaw clenches, but I know better than to start an argument while Father's around. He has a good impression of me, one I intend to keep up, so I can remain in his will. Mother has no power, so she hasn't earned my respect or servitude. I take my sunglasses off and set them down beside me. I hope the swelling has eased. "Is that better, Mother?"

"People would say you were raised by animals," she tuts.

Animals would've done a better job raising me, but I don't tell her that. "We couldn't have that, now could we, Mother dear?"

"Daddy, what's up? We haven't had a family breakfast in two months," says Millie, her voice strained and drowsy. "Please tell me you woke me up early because you plan to surprise me with another Porsche."

"Don't be ridiculous, Millicent, you've had that car for less than a couple of months and there're already at least a dozen dents in it." He glowers at her when she yawns. "What your mother and I wanted to talk about is the expansion of our business. We want to establish hotels in Aspen, Vail, Denver, and Salt Lake City, and that's going to mean we'll be gone for quite a bit of time. Normally, I wouldn't worry. Maris is very responsible, and I trust her to take charge of the home, but with a lunatic running around and kidnapping or murdering young women in this area, we must reconsider. We don't want either of you to be a target—you're well known and attractive, and due to the media, most people know where we live and where we are if we're traveling."

"Daddy, I don't think it's much of an issue, honestly. I'm twenty-three-years old, I'm a grown woman. I don't need to worry about this lunatic. If I were to be a target, I'd have been one already."

"With all due respect, Maris, your best friend was abducted," says Mother sharply. "And I know you didn't seem to care all that much once it happened, why, you went straight up to take a shower and failed to even mention it to us—we had to find out through the news, and it's been a week without her returning. I think your judgment may be a bit clouded currently. You were at Lake Sam with her—the man who abducted her most likely spotted you too."

I roll my eyes. "Maybe he has a thing for blondes?"

"See, Henry, do you see what I mean? She's so insouciant about it. Carol has been her best friend since she was a month old," screeches my mother. "I told you. She's either in shock or she doesn't know how to deal with this. She's certainly not to be left alone here."

"Mom, why don't you hire a babysitter to keep an eye on us?" Millie interrupts. "That always works, right?"

"Henry, Maris isn't to be trusted in this situation, and Millicent isn't anything more than her mouthpiece, I've been telling you this all morning."

"Fuck you, Mom. Honestly, fuck you." Millie takes a swig from her mug.

"Millie, that language isn't acceptable here. Do you hear Maris using those words?" My dad cuts into his poached egg, and the oozing makes me want to vomit. "I won't tolerate vulgarity."

"How long are you planning on being there?" I ask.

"Well, we expect to do grand openings in early 1975, the earliest being Aspen, so we'd be there for a while. Of course, we'll fly back to check in and make sure everything is okay here. Another option that I was considering was that you both can come along with us. Millie, you're not enrolled at college. You shouldn't have any issue moving to Utah or Colorado for a while." "But you know that I'm in medical school. I can't disappear for a year, can I?" I interject. "I will take care of the hotel and the house here, and you guys can set up what you need to over there." "Dad, you make it sound like I'm a loafer. You know that I've been hosting charitable functions throughout this year."

Millie's animated now, energy delivered to her through displaced indignation.

"Oh Millicent, who are you kidding? You've spent most of your time in Europe and hosted one gala, which, may I remind you, was planned by your mother and Sophie in PR," he bites.

"You know I can hold down the fort, I always have," I say.

"Maris, you're getting too thin, please eat something," says my mother.

"Quinn, now's not the time to discuss her eating habits." He turns to me. "Look, Maris, I've always felt comfortable leaving the reins to you, but with the recent disappearances and murders, I don't know if it's safe."

"We can hire security if you'd like," I insist.

A year without them would be quite the vacation. Otherwise, I'm always a little concerned that they'll walk in on me while I'm with a girl or with a guy that's not Hunter. It's almost as if they're more concerned about my fidelity than he is. "Like I said, I can't just quit medical school—you know how difficult it was getting in, and how much I studied and sacrificed."

"Do you think you could get a transfer?" asks Daddy.

"Of course, but why would I leave UW for a crappy college in Utah or Colorado? You know those schools are for idiots who couldn't be bothered to study. Instead, they go to keggers and protest the Vietnam War. And I don't want to offend the Mormons by showing my ankles."

I can picture myself inviting Jack over for a game of tennis or lazing by the pool with a cigarette and my textbooks, with the entire compound to myself. Granted, there aren't many days over eighty degrees here, but the swimming pool is heated, and the sun is sharp enough to tan me like a trip to the Mediterranean. My mind travels to Charles, and I feel a hollow thud in my stomach. "Alright, well, I think we'll have to compromise. Perhaps your mother can spend more time with you girls, and I can spend more time there."

"The maids are here, they can serve as nannies," says Millie. Her sarcasm is thinly veiled. "Why do you want to go to Utah anyway? There's nothing there."

"Look, Millicent, I'd take your opinions more seriously if you had a degree in business. Hosting one party doesn't qualify you to make decisions about a multinational corporation," says Father. "You should've completed your degree and gone on to do an MBA so you could actually help the family rather than hindering it."

"I'll tell you what, Dad, why don't I just run in front of a fucking bus, so you don't have an extra burden on you, and no more daughters to whinge about."

Daddy rubs his temples. "Girls, you're the sole benefactors to Caldwell Hotels—if you want to have nothing to yourselves once we die, that's up to you. Otherwise, maybe you should be more interested in expansion and development. All I did at your age was work at one menial job after another trying to save up for a better future. You could at least be grateful."

"Dad, you inherited this. You weren't some broke joe slumming it on skid row. You were handed the company. Stop pretending that you weren't born into privilege," spits out Millie scathingly. "Come on now, Millie," I say. I need to keep Daddy on my side if I want to make it out of this alive. "There's no need to be rude to Daddy."

"See, Millicent? Maris has a positive attitude and an aptitude for business, despite her medical goals. She doesn't spend her time tanning by the pool and drinking gin. She has drive, initiative."

"No Dad, she's a brownnosing lesbian who pretends to be ambitious and is waiting for you to die so she never has to work a day in her life."

I turn to her, resisting the urge to throw my plate at her face. "Yeah, I've been in a relationship with a male for over ten years. I'm definitely a homosexual."

She's weak and cracks under pressure, so I don't push too hard. She has too much information on me. There's also a disturbing resemblance—even most identical twins I know have obvious differences, and she and I have none, facially. If I were to injure her, there'd be a decipherable distinction.

"Hunter's obviously a front for all your female involvements." "Well, I can't argue with that solid logic, Mill. You caught me, I'm a raging homo."

"I can't deal with these girls, Henry, I can't. I slave away caring for them and all they want to do is rip us to shreds. We've worked so hard, so hard, and for what?" adds my mother, with as much indignation she can muster this early in the morning.

"Since you clearly don't need me, why don't I go visit some friends in Olympia?" asks Millie, playing with the fruit on her plate. "I'm sure ambitious Maris here can take care of everything." "If I didn't know better, I'd think you were a high school dropout. You can take your resentment elsewhere, Millie. I'm too nauseated to deal with your shit right now," I snap. "Daddy, you can trust me with this. If it becomes too strenuous, I can try and do night classes instead so that I can man the staff at the hotel. I highly doubt this killer is coming for me, and say, if he does, you know how many hunting rifles we have—I know damn well how to shoot one."

"You are such beautiful girls, of course you're going to be targets. Apparently, this deranged individual likes slender women with hair parted in the middle."

"Just leave it with me, Daddy. I'll start parting my hair to the side instead. Let Millie go to Olympia."

"Okay, what I can do is install some more alarms and possibly put in a security guard. I saw a strange boy here earlier, lurking about," says Father. "I've never seen him before. He could be the 'Ted' everyone's looking for. I'll make sure Will, the deputy sheriff, can drop by to see if everything is alright."

"What'd he look like?" I ask inquisitively.

"Well, he looked about twenty with blue eyes and dark hair." "Isn't Ted a dirty blonde?"

"Perhaps he's gone incognito."

"Daddy, I think you're being paranoid. You've trusted me before, and I haven't yet let you down even once." This is a blatant lie, and he gives me a look. A very particular kind of look. He doesn't say anything about it, though.

"Alright, Maris, well, we're still here for a little while longer to watch how things are but, yes, I know you're capable."

Mother watches me, her affect cold. She attempts to cover up her bruises with her Hermes shawl, but I can still see the purple finger indentations. I can't remember an occasion when she remained completely intact during Father's stay. She's a very proud woman. She'll never admit that her beatings are frequent and forceful, that sometimes her slender body succumbs to them. She always has a front and an excuse. She ran into the doorknob. She fell down a flight of stairs. She had an accident in her spinning class. The truth is that Father has her deeply under his control. He apologizes after he beats her, gifting her flowers and Cartier necklaces in the hospital. She always believes that he's genuinely sorry and that he'll never behave the same way again. She hasn't told a single person, not her parents, not her friends, and not even us. He used to beat her, and she used to beat us. Now he smacks her around, and she doesn't quite have the stamina to come after me to take out her rage. One time she'd asked him about one of his female subordinate's lipstick being in his office. He had beat her so severely that she'd had a concussion, two fractured ribs, a broken wrist, bruised thighs and a broken nose. He usually endeavors to avoid her face. She's very beautiful, and there're few ways to cover up a damaged face. He'd momentarily lost control that time. I think I was around fifteen. It wasn't anything new, and I didn't visit her in the hospital. I waited for her to come home and take it out on Millie and me, but she didn't. She pulled on her favorite nightgown and robe, sat at the home bar, and poured a tall glass of brandy to wash down several Xanax pills.

My father has never set a violent finger on me. Millie's taken a couple of beatings, but that's mainly because he has some strange reasoning—she reminds him of our mother. I don't. Whenever he was in town, he'd buy me dolls and books, my only two passions as a toddler. When I grew older, he started with more extravagant gifts: a horse (despite me hating animals), a Porsche, Chanel handbags (picked out by his assistants) and access to my trust fund. He's bought a house in my name—perhaps for the tax break. Millie accuses him of playing favorites, but he constantly denies it. He strongly believes in academics, so Millie never had a chance. She pulled a B+ average through school, and that was far from good enough. His attitude toward Mother has softened of late. Now all he does is shove her around or grab her by her tiny and frail arms. Her fractures have healed, but I doubt much has been achieved in the way of her mental health. Millie fast became her favorite when we hit our teens. My psychiatrist had asked if I felt a certain way about the abuse Mother endures. He knew I'd generally watched it happen, been right there. Honestly, I didn't feel strongly about it either way. I usually went to my room to watch television. If she couldn't take care of herself, it was her fault and had little to do with me. Vulnerable people send out an implicit vibe to those around them, giving them the green signal to use them as doormats, and that's certainly not my problem.

I let the breakfast go on for a while before I excuse myself from the dining room, much to the dismay of my mother who was clearly hoping my father would berate me on her behalf. I need to exercise. It's a strong part of my daily routine, and not just to look fantastic. I have such a clear mind when I run or swim. I can find targets. I can decide what colour to paint my room and what kind of haircut I should be getting soon. I like long-distance running. Sprinters are far too masculine and as a woman, I could spare the extra muscle. I don't want bulging thighs and thick calves. I get dressed in my exercise gear—shorts that could double as hot pants, a red sports bra, and a backless Adidas t-shirt. I still feel a little queasy, but that's never stopped me before. Our house is on the water, so there's a nice view around here. Granted, it's not as beautiful as Colorado or Vermont, but it'll do. I start with a walk as I leave the front door, my new running shoes squeaking on the freshly mopped floor. I stretch a little before I begin to run. My muscles are tense and sore and I'm overdue for a Swedish massage. I like doing a steady six to nine miles when I'm feeling unwell—when I'm well I opt for twelve miles. I feel it's a good regimen for staying slim and feminine. It's also effective should I ever choose to run the half marathon again.

The sun glitters on the water of Lake Sam, now far less crowded than it has been for most of the summer. People are too terrified to go back there, worried that their girlfriends and daughters and wives will disappear into the abyss with no trace of a scream or struggle. The boys and men are emboldened, walking around shirtless with no regard for their safety—only women need leashing, apparently. I get lost in my thoughts once I'm in my comfort zone, the delicious muscle pain traveling through my legs. I look straight through stocky old Mrs. Davenport, only noticing that she'd been waving at me once I've passed her. She likes to do her exercise at this time because, usually, no one's around to see the jiggling fat on her arms and the loose cellulite on her thighs, visible through her Lycra leggings. The divine smell of the river mixed with the scent of the blooming oriental lilies helps calm me. I run uphill and downhill, fast and slow, to give my body the right kind of exhaustion to keep my mind busy. When I'm bored, I feel restless and deeply uncomfortable, I can't give my brain too large a window for thoughts. I like seeing the manses scattered across the vast waterfront. Each house has intricate designs, each tells a story, each holds a family so drastically different from the next. Our house is by far the largest, with a giant gate containing it. The others often take the essence of our house but fall far from recreating it. Ours has a Georgian façade, with a winding driveway and a sandstone finish. The Davenports put in a tennis court after they saw one in our compound when my parents invited them over for dinner. The family is completely geriatric, so I feel it was essentially a waste of time and space, but I like that people want to imitate us. I often bump into Jack while I'm exercising. He spends most of his time on a banana chair in the front yard of his house reading, and I make sure to say hello as I pass. He is still distraught from Carol's disappearance—almost to the level of hysterical Mrs. Greene who has posted missing girl flyers all over Seattle. The day maid let me know how many times he'd phoned me and which messages he left. They were unchanging. He misses Carol. He feels responsible for her disappearance and possible demise. He's terrified about what could've happened to her. She could've been raped or dismembered, her small body diced into neat little squares in some sicko's freezer. She's the absent girl, the vanished girl, the potentially dead girl. He doesn't want that. He also seems to believe it's a fine idea to leave these kinds of messages to the house staff.

I clear my throat as I begin to approach his house, but nobody is there. I can see Mrs. Rutherford next door puttering about, tending to her gardenias. I get a little winded as I turn the corner—the cigarettes always have some sort of a side effect. I take a break, catching my breath.

"Maris?" asks a familiar but strange voice. I turn around, rubbing my eyes to ensure it's not the sun playing tricks on me.

"Charles?" I stand rooted in my position. "What're you doing here?"

"I was in the neighborhood. I thought I might drop by..." He shakes his head and laughs. "I mean I drove an hour and a half and knocked on everybody's doors here."

"Oh my god, you're the guy my dad thinks is Ted. How many houses did you go to?"

"I think twelve, but a lot of them refused to open the door, so I don't know if I should be counting them."

"Jesus, I thought we were a little more important than that. I mean, our house is basically the only one you can see."

"Well, you wouldn't give me your phone number, so I had to do a little snooping. Those bats at your hotel wouldn't give out any of your details, but I remembered that you live in the super upscale part of Bellevue. I figured you couldn't ignore me if I turned up in person."

I give him a smug smile. "You know I have several housekeepers, right? Housekeepers whose names I could give over to the immigration department if they fail to listen to my orders?" I feel a single bead of sweat trickling down my chest. I note as his hawk-eyes follow its descent.

"Look, I thought that might be an issue, but you have to appreciate my effort, right?"

"Are you counting stalking as effort?" I laugh. "Where's Melissa?"

"She's back in Ellensburg. She's at Central Washington State, she's majoring in psychology."

"She's training to become a shrink. Huh. Isn't she a little too hostile for that?"

"I think she was only that hostile because she caught me staring at you for a goddamn hour and all."

"Tell her I'm not competition. I'm not a fan of being a homewrecker."

His sun-dappled skin and beautiful eyes catch me off guard, but my pride kicks in with full force.

"She's not competition because she can't compete. I don't think many girls can. Of course, Susan Anton and Sharon Tate, but I like brunettes more." He starts laughing. "Like Raquel Welch."

"I met her at a benefit for deaf children, she's a lovely woman, and her figure is impossible to believe," I boast. Raquel's photos do her no justice. I'd never been more attracted to a woman.

"Was she nice in person? She sounds so stuck up in all her interviews, a real diva."

"She's the sweetest actress I've ever met."

"Yeah, I don't know why it took me so long to realize who you were."

"Well, now that you're here, what is it you want?" I say it firmly, like my stomach isn't turning in on itself and my chest isn't struggling for air. "If you'd like to take the penthouse suite, I could probably swing it—my father's not too hard to deal with." "No, Maris, I don't want to stay at your hotel. I told you I wanted to take you out properly, a meal at the least, maybe in the Space Needle."

"I appreciate that, but I'd rather not get salmonella again." I dab at my forehead with the sleeve of my t-shirt: the heat is overbearing. "I ought to get back to my exercise." The burn from last night is searing, impossible to ignore. I force myself to respond like a proper human, and not stare like I would otherwise.

"I know this is only the second time I've met you, but I really like you. I wish I could have control over it. Trust me,

I'm not the kind of guy who drives to another city, knocks on random people's houses, and ambushes a pretty girl during her run."

"It didn't seem that way yesterday, Charles. Perhaps it's best you stay with Melissa," I say through gritted teeth, desperate to defy my body's intentions. "I need to get my run in today. I have a photo shoot coming up, and I can't afford to look chubby."

"I don't think it's possible for you to look chubby. You could get blown away with a gust of good old Seattle wind."

"Tell Jantzen Swimwear that."

"Are you not interested in me?" He's pleading now. He tries to make me look directly at him, face him, and say no. He knows I can't do that.

"Okay, Charles. Here's the deal. You'll come and pick me up tomorrow night at seven for dinner. It won't be at the Space Needle because we're not fat, middle-aged tourists from the Midwest. There's a nice French place a bit down from here, Larousse, it's got excellent food and then you'll be more than welcome to enjoy a film at my place. How does that sound to you?"

"It sounds like this entire stalking thing was worth it." He smiles, flashing his perfect teeth.

"I live at 4900. I think you should go back to Ellensburg right now before my dad phones the police about the handsome, dark-haired boy skulking about the neighborhood looking for his next victims."

"Handsome, huh? I'll take that." He beams. "Isn't that Ted guy a blonde?"

"Yes, but I don't think my dad quite seems to understand that."

He kisses me before I can complain about being too sweaty to touch him.

"I'll see you tomorrow, then, Caldwell."

I grin, easing back into a slow jog. "I'm looking forward to it, Charles. I'm sorry, I didn't get a chance to learn your last name."

"It's Elderberry. Shitty, I know." "That's cute. Well, I'll catch you then."

My body is whirring with excitement and energy after he returns to his car. I channel it all into my running, forcing my body to race uphill five more times before continuing along the lake. I push myself to my limits as frequently as I can, making up for the junk I eat from time to time. I need to keep myself in a size four to pull off the bare midriff and hot pants look. My nausea has worsened, but I keep going, taking a loop around Redmond before heading back to my house.

My legs ache and my chest burns by the time I get to my front gate. I head inside, knowing no one will be around to turn on the security gates—usually you have to be buzzed into the compound. I throw my gym clothes into the laundry and pull on a no-frills, one-piece swimsuit. It's exclusively used in my home as I wouldn't be caught dead in it outside. I head to the pool with a towel, tossing it onto one of the chaise longues. The cold water shocks me for a moment once I dive in. I resurface for air and wait for my body to acclimatize. I always do twenty laps in the pool after a run: five backstrokes, five freestyles, five breaststrokes, and five minutes of treading water in the ten-foot end. That's the highest calorie burn of them all. It helps to cool off and tone the muscles comfortably. I've never been much of a fan of weights or other gym stuff. I mean, I'm not a man, and I'm certainly not butch, so this is my main cardio and weight outlet. I like to be thoroughly exhausted once I'm done. I have too much energy, and I can't handle it. I need to get rid of it in any way I can, preferably through a rush, but I do settle for exercise. I splash around in the pool for a little while after I'm done, partially because I've gone temporarily blind from the industrial dose of chlorine the pool boy has put in, and partially because I'm still reeling. I don't use goggles as frequently as I should. I feel utmost serenity when I slip into the shower, tilting my head back to let the water pour down my face and through my hair. My legs struggle to hold me, but I'm calm in the scent of the body wash and the visible cloud of steam. I think about Charles and his wholesome all-American beauty for longer than I should. I towel dry myself and walk naked into my bedroom, thankfully locked. I sort through my lingerie collection and put on a black silk mini-negligee. I wear the matching silk thong and put on a robe for respectability. I moisturize my skin and put on some lip balm before I phone Lilith and ask her to come over.

I meet Lilith in the foyer. My parents are out, and I don't know where Millie is. The night housekeeper is busy vacuuming the family cinema room. Lilith's radiant. She's exactly my height, and her skin is clear, smooth, dark. She's got striking green eyes and a willowy figure, with tousled short hair. I give her a hug, running my hands down her slim, bare back. Her dimples are endearing, but I can't get past the sexual pull of her perfectly shaped lips.

"Aren't you a sight for sore eyes," I say softly into her ear, pulling her closer.

"You always know the right thing to say," she replies, brushing my hair back before she kisses me. "And the right thing to wear." She looks me up and down and grins.

I grab her by the arm and lead her up the staircase to my room. It's not as if she doesn't know the way by heart, but my fear of lack of control is taking over.

"I brought some party favors," she says, pulling out a baggie of ketamine from her purse. I leave the door unlocked when we're upstairs. I always like a little bit of danger, perhaps my mother walking in on me and the girl she takes out to dinner with us because she's one of my "best friends" from childhood.

"Thank fucking god for that." I take it from her and sort lines on my dresser drawer. I ingest a quarter of the bag, an amount that'll make me sick tomorrow. She stands behind me, her arms tightly holding me to her by the waist. I turn my head over my shoulder and kiss her, my hand on her cheek. I feel her against me, the heat of her indulgent body. I turn around to face her, and she pushes me against the wall as she kisses along my neck. With Heather, I feel comfort, security. With Lilith, I feel unfettered carnal bliss. She's very similar to me. She's neither heterosexual nor homosexual but an equal opportunist. I don't care about the sex of the person I'm fucking as long as I climax. I'm motivated by the almost instant gratification sex can provide me, and while I don't want to boast, I know my skills are great too.

She slides her hand up under my nightgown, running her fingers against my skin. I throw her onto the bed and straddle her, using my teeth to pull off her halter top. I pin her arms down and kiss her eagerly, on the mouth and then on her chest with frenzied force. I feel her mouth on my shoulder and her warm breath radiating down.

"You are so gorgeous," I tell her as I unbutton her skirt. I take it off slowly, relishing every second of her lust-filled agony. I kiss her flat stomach and then the insides of her thighs, touching her chest and the small of her back. I take off her underwear and go down on her. She shivers as I start gently, using the tip of my tongue to trace her neat, beautiful vulva.

Now, I'm no feminist. I don't think all pussies are wonderful looking and created equally. Some look horribly messy and hairy, but hers looks like the gate to heaven, perfectly formed and wonderful to touch. She tastes sweet, very sweet, like water when you're parched. I slip my finger into her, and she moans and writhes as I synchronize it with my mouth. I love eating her out; I love her legs around me. I keep going until she climaxes and then go harder, rougher, using two fingers this time. She convulses exquisitely and then goes limp, her breath ragged. When she regains her strength, she holds me close and kisses me as she takes off my nightgown, allowing the luxurious fabric to drag across my chest, leaving me covered in goose bumps. Her lips caress my breasts and my waist, and I feel her lightly bite me on the hip. She looks up to grin at me before she starts. She's usually rather dominant through sheer experience. She knows what to do and when to do it, and it's so sexy to see her so cavalier about it. She goes down on me with the finesse I know Hunter will never learn, no matter how hard he tries. Her fingers feel incredible. I hold her in place with my thighs and sigh in pleasure when she brings me to orgasm. She kisses me, and I taste myself on her mouth. I kiss her harder, savoring every moment of it. She rubs against me in the missionary position, simultaneously fucking me with her fingers until I'm spent.

We spend most of the night laying in each other's arms, naked except for the silk sheets between us. I try to keep myself quiet, defying the urge to scream in pleasure. I hold my hand over her mouth when she starts getting too loud in case someone's nearby. My parents don't tend to spend too much time on my floor but, recently, with Millie claiming I'm a homosexual, I don't doubt they may plan to drop in to catch me when I'm in a compromising position. Lilith and I don't have the energy to speak, but I hold her until daylight hits. Her body blossoms with the sunrise, the beams highlighting her perfectly curved hips and slender legs. It doesn't take long for my eyelids to feel heavy as the ketamine loses control and sleep takes over.

"I love you, Maris," she tells me drowsily as she drifts off.

CHAPTER EIGHT

I'm ravenous by noon. I rub my eyes lazily and throw on a loose t-shirt to get food downstairs. Lilith left before I woke, leaving a note bearing only an imprint of her red lipstick kiss. She must've snuck out while everyone was distracted. Maybe she told Mother that we had a lot of catching up to do. I feel far less groggy than I expected and pour myself a giant bowl of cornflakes and milk.

I sit in the lounge room and eat while watching a replay of the morning news. Another girl has disappeared. She's beautiful, with long, straight hair parted in the middle, looking disturbingly like Carol. Her tearful father talks about how wonderful she is, how vivacious and kind and friendly. Do they ever say that the person was a bitch? That no one liked her, and she was rude to neighbors and cheated on her boyfriends? That she kicked small animals with pleasure as a kid? Surely, they all can't be saints. I know this for a fact. The males I disposed of all have advocates talking about how upstanding they were, how they honored everyone around them when in reality they were little bitches who selfishly wanted to fuck an attractive woman whether they were single or not. If they didn't exude vulnerability, arrogance, and sleaziness, they'd probably still be alive. I only became a master through their idiocy.

"They found human female remains near Lake Sammamish," says Millie as she strolls in. "Two skulls."

"Did either belong to Carol?"

"I don't know, they haven't identified them. They need dental records. Her mother's over there causing a scene, though, because one of the skulls had hair that looked like Carol's attached to it."

"Where's Mother?"

"She's gone down there to support Mrs. Greene. She wanted me to tell you to meet her. The area's been cordoned off."

"Fuck, I'm too tired. Can't you go? She was your friend too," I say mid-yawn. I scoop as many cornflakes into one spoonful as I can. "I wasn't the only friend who knew her, and who knows? It could be someone else. You know how dramatic Mrs. Greene is being."

"They're fairly confident that they belong to the missing girls from Lake Sam a while ago."

"Mill, do you have a cigarette on you?"

"You know we're not supposed to smoke, especially not inside," she tells me coldly.

"What's your fucking problem?" "You don't even care about Carol."

"Of course I care about Carol. She's a dear friend of mine. She's also a good friend of yours, so I'm wondering why you aren't there?"

"You're fucked up. I mean what we do to those boys is different. She's been your friend since we were born. You should care." Her tone is judgmental, accusatory.

"Can you cool it? I just woke up. I don't have enough

energy to be so emotional this early. I think you need to either calm down or go there and help them dig at Taylor Mountain since you seem so invested."

"I never mentioned a location, Maris."

I don't react physically, but I feel a jolt. "You said it was close to Lake Sam. There aren't that many places around there to hide a skull other than Taylor Mountain," I respond, seamlessly covering my tracks.

"Finish your breakfast so we can drive over there. At least pretend to be concerned."

"Fine—go and bring me jeans and shoes from my room. Make sure they don't look like shit with this t-shirt."

"Okay," she acquiesces. "I'll choose something for you." "Make it quick, alright? I have a date later today." "With whom?"

"I don't think that's any of your concern."

She's visibly upset but says nothing, leaving the room as quickly and silently as she appeared. Usually, I tell her most things, but she needs to be put in her place considering her attitude this morning. We're close, very close, but sometimes she's so irritating. She gets on her high horse, pretending she doesn't do the exact same things I do.

The telephone rings, but I don't answer it. I figure it's my father waiting to berate me. Millie brings me a pair of bell-bottoms and camel-colored suede platforms. I put them on, tucking in my t-shirt. Normally, I wouldn't dress like such trash, but I have neither the inclination nor energy to go upstairs myself.

"You're driving," I tell her through my last mouthful of cereal. Mother isn't around to scold me for talking with food in my mouth. I grab a pair of sunglasses from the kitchen counter, Mother's I presume, and follow Millie out the door.

"Can I have a cigarette now, Mom?" I ask her acerbically. She hands me a single cigarette from her pocket and lights it for me with my lighter. I don't know how she has it. She drives joltingly, and I come to understand why there're scratches and bumps all over the car.

"Are you going on a date with the girl you had over last night?

Lilith or whatever her name is, the Negro?"

"You know, Millie, you really fucked me up yesterday by telling everyone I'm a lesbian. I'm not even gay. I don't need Mother and Father on my back, alright?"

"What did you expect me to say? Dad's always on your side. He loves anything you do and thinks I'm useless. I thought, maybe, if he knew what you were like, he wouldn't do that anymore. You fucked a girl last night. How can you deny it? I heard her screaming for dear life."

"I fuck women and I fuck men too. That's unusual for homosexuals. You understand what homo means, right? You just want your name on the inheritance instead of mine. You know how much they hate queers."

"Well, I don't think it's fair that you're the sole heir to the company."

"Maybe you should take that up with them instead of lying about me to make me seem like a pervert. You could earn it instead of whinging like a little bitch."

"Oh, fuck you, Maris."

"You're a parasitic leech, Mill. You should at least go to university instead of being at home all day doing nothing."

"That's rich coming from you."

"I study medicine. I help Father with executive decisions. That's hardly like you."

"You also have an extensive juvenile record that Dad had to pay a lot of money to expunge."

"You realize that records are automatically expunged when you're eighteen, right? It's not like you have a blank slate, either, not even in adulthood. I don't think I've ever had a DUI, which I don't think you could say for yourself."

She rolls her eyes and pauses at a stop sign. I take a long drag of my cigarette, the ash burning up rather quickly. It's gotten chilly out, and I regret not bringing a cardigan—Seattle is probably the worst place to enjoy summer, other than England. We get about a week of heat a year. I've spent time in Tanzania, India, Australia, and New York, so I know what a real summer feels like. I realize we're getting close to the site when I see a stream of people trickling out into the street, gathering. They're held back by armed policemen and crime scene tape, and many of the women are crying, probably wondering if their daughters have been slaughtered and crudely dumped there. It takes me about three seconds to spot Mrs. Greene. She's sobbing maniacally, and she's wrapped her hair up into a towel turban like she's just gotten out of a shower, which I suspect might be the case. Mother is beside her, rubbing her shoulder to comfort her.

"Oh shit, how on earth am I going to get parking here?" asks Millie, thinking aloud.

"Well, I wasn't the one dumb enough to want to come here at this time, Millicent," I say tersely. "I'll get out and let them know we're here. You should find some back street for parking."

"Don't gloat, Maris. Tell Mom I'll be there shortly."

I jump out of the car and rush to my mother and Mrs. Greene. "Oh Mother, Mrs. Greene, I'm so sorry I'm late. Millie slept in and didn't want to come, but I was horrified when I saw on the news that human remains had been found. I couldn't sit idly by if my dear Carol were here. I was beside myself! Please, Mrs. Greene, don't cry."

"Maris, dear, I'm glad you've arrived," says my mother. She clutches her Tahitian pearls, the same black as her dress and shawl. Her hair is perfectly coiffed into a beehive, held in place by a small Jackie Kennedy-esque hat. She hugs me briefly, and I force a hug upon Mrs. Greene. I see her look at me in contempt, wondering why I'm still here and her daughter isn't. It's making me rather uncomfortable, and I wish she'd stop. I can see one of the skulls, even from all the way back here. Investigators are scouring on hands and knees, their shoulders barely an inch apart. The crowd is upset, angry. They confront the police as if they're responsible for the crimes. They want somebody to blame, somebody they can use to ease their pain and loss. They're worried for their children. They think their daughters may be the next to disappear.

"Please tell me that's not my beautiful daughter," sobs Mrs. Greene to a handsome, barely legal cop who stands with his arms crossed over his chest.

"I've told you a dozen times, ma'am, we won't know until we can match dental records to the skulls."

"Well, it can't be my Carol. My Carol could never be reduced to a skull," she insists to herself with tears streaming down her face, slipping past wrinkles and red patches.

"Oh sweetheart, please, we don't know anything yet," says my mother pacifyingly, in her sweetest voice. "Don't stress, Elaine, they're doing everything they can."

"Please, Mrs. Greene, it'll be fine," I say, avoiding her disturbing stare.

"You don't know that. You don't know shit. None of you did anything to help her." There's only rage in her voice.

"We didn't know she was in trouble, Mrs. Greene. She's my best friend, I love her, and I miss her. I wish it'd been me instead of her, I really do."

"Elaine, you know Maris would've gone out of her way to help Carol. They've been thick as thieves since they were a day old," Mother says, almost indignantly.

"If my daughter hadn't gone out with these kids, she would've been fine. She would've pulled up to the house in her Camaro and watched television with me like we did every night. Now I can't sleep, I can't eat, I can't move." Sobs convulse through her body with every word.

"Honey, they're all good kids. We thought they were safe; they always have been. They're not responsible for this atrocity." I can see her holding back anger, smoothing it out with diplomacy. When Millie finally joins us, I'm sure she can tell what Mother is thinking by her posture alone.

"Oh Mrs. Greene, please don't cry," she says automatically. My mother puts up a hand to signal her to stop speaking.

Mrs. Greene lours at Millie too. Another daughter to spare. Another beautiful girl with hair parted in the middle and doe eyes. "I don't know how to cope, Quinn, I don't." She leans into my mother, whose lifelong lack of a maternal drop of blood somehow seems not to matter. "You have your lovely girls, both of them. I don't have mine." She breaks down in my mother's arms.

"There's a good chance that you do have her. She may not be the one whose remains have been found. You can't lose hope, alright? I simply won't let you." Mother cuddles her and soothes her like she never did us. "You'll come home to our place if you feel sad or lonely, we're always here for you, Elaine, always."

"I just want my baby."

"I want my little Carol too. She's so sweet, she lights up our house whenever she's there," says Mother. She's holding Mrs. Greene, rocking her gently like a child. "Can I get you anything, Elaine? I have my car. I can bring you some coffee or tea or a sandwich."

"No, I haven't any appetite. I can't breathe. My baby is gone." "You don't know that," says Millie.

"A mother knows."

It starts to drizzle, the water quickly dampening my white t-shirt. Luckily, I didn't take my bra off last night with

Lilith. It makes Mrs. Greene more anxious, her grip on my arm strong enough to snap my bone in two. She watches the detectives obsessively, noting each of their slight movements and screaming whenever they stumble upon something, whether it be leaves, a rotting rat or a couple of rocks. The detectives become frustrated, shooting her dirty looks. She refuses to move. She flatly declines when they offer to drive her home. She stands in the rain with icy determination. "I'm going to be here as long as you are," she tells the detective resolutely. She has no plans to back down.

"I don't think that's a good idea, ma'am, you're hindering our investigation. We won't be getting any results for at least a week." "How would you feel if that was potentially YOUR daughter's skull?" she screams.

"I don't think that's necessary, ma'am," he says hesitantly. I see him looking at her, particularly weary. I can only imagine how annoying she's been up until this point. She's frustrating at the best of times.

"Oh girls, you'll catch a cold, didn't you think to bring a sweater?" asks Mother as she wraps her shawl tighter around herself.

"It's summer, Mother," I tell her, trying not to shiver.

"My sweater is in the car," says Millie. She watches Mrs.

Greene. I don't know if she feels the hostility and envy I do. "Elaine, do you think it may be better to come to our home and wait for news inside? You'll get drenched out here, and you need your rest. It's been an extremely tough couple of weeks."

"Yes, Mrs. Greene, you can come and stay with us," I offer. I don't want her in our house. I need serenity when I decide what to wear to see Charles. I also don't want to be stopped from leaving, which Mother sometimes does if we have family friends over. In this emergency situation, there would be no chance of me leaving.

"I'm staying here as long as the police do, Quinn."
"Alright, well, I'm staying right here with you."

"As will I, Mrs. Greene," I add unctuously. Maybe it'll lessen her creepy vibes.

The police work tirelessly, but I know how inefficient they are. Even if you leave goddamn clues right in front of their offices to taunt them, they'll still fail to figure anything out. They could've probably found the girls if they hung around this area during the week after the disappearances. Killers generally come back to the crime scene. Once you do a good job you want to savor it before disposing of evidence.

I'm surprised at the rate of decomposition, though. It's not hot enough for the girls' flesh to disintegrate this fast, not even with the presence of rodents and insects. I suspect the skull belongs to someone else, but Carol's can't be too far away. I spotted her body when I was here dismembering one of the males. It was mostly intact, and it seems medically impossible for it to be in this state already. She was nude and maggots were feasting on her abdomen. There was both putrefaction and decomposition, but there was more flesh on than off. I'm sure he planned to decapitate her as he did the others, but when I saw her last, her head was fixed on her body. I thought about leaving once I saw her body, but I knew that important work had to be done so that the male couldn't be identified once he was eventually found. Even if her killer did walk in on me at his special crime scene, I had enough weapons on me to protect myself. I had more to lose by leaving. Plus, I kind of enjoyed the thrill and danger of it all. "I'm sure Carol will be alright," I add. I smile at her gaunt mother, placing my hand on her arm. "There's no need to stress at the moment."

"I wish I could be as delusional as you," she snaps.

"I'm being optimistic, Mrs. Greene. Carol is my best friend." She ignores me, only to stare at the cop, imploring him to help her with her pain. He doesn't. He stands there in silence, watching as the diggers sift through what's become mud. The rain grows heavy, the dark clouds threatening a storm. The crowd thins, leaving only us and parents of a few missing girls. Mrs. Greene is still choking on her sobs and hiccupping loudly. Mother looks around in distress, deeply uncomfortable, and clearly wanting to leave. How would she do so without looking selfish, though? She knows she has to stay, but there may be water stains on her Hermes pocketbook and that's not a risk she's ever willing to take. "Oh dear, I'm feeling a little dizzy. My blood sugar must've dropped," she says, attempting to be clever. "Go home, Quinn. I'll be alright."

"No, I couldn't leave you here alone. Don't be silly." "Look, Maris, take your mother home. She's not well."

"Mother, let's get you home and something to eat. I don't want you fainting again like you did last week."

My mother does not have diabetes, but I want to get out of the rain. I want to go home and decide on an outfit. I'm tired and need my rest a lot more than I need Mrs. Greene's obsessive stare. For a boy as beautiful as Charles, some effort has to be put in, not just the lip balm and eyeshadow I wear for Hunter. I have a dozen dresses that would make him forget Melissa's existence.

I had court-mandated sessions with my psychiatrist until I was eighteen. My parents forced me to continue them into my adulthood, thinking that they could cure whatever was wrong with me. They could never pinpoint what it was, but they tried their best, attempting to stifle any urges I may have had. It didn't help, I just learned to lie better. My mother was the worst; she would fill my father with lies about me, ensuring I couldn't miss a single appointment if I wanted to keep my inheritance. She wanted an explanation. She couldn't understand how she could produce such an internally defective product in a beautiful body. She has always been proud of how attractive Millie and I are.

She actively encouraged everyone to comment on our beauty from the age of three. I guess she thought it reflected badly upon her. If her daughters were beautiful, she would have to be as well. We were her trophies. It's what made her harsher on me. She didn't want my behavior to reflect poorly on her. I started pretty early. It would have to be blamed on her and Father's genetics and the environment they raised me in. I was always bored and restless as a child, and I had to find an outlet.

There was a puppy that used to sneak into our chalet whenever we were in Colorado—I don't know which breed, but it was little and garrulous. I think I was perhaps six or seven, and I'd always despised animals. I found them curious, these little creatures that we slaved over. My mother loved dogs, especially the fluffy, little thing that always found its way inside. I fucking hated that dog; it would wake me up at five with its incessant barks. I let it into my room and closed the door as I went to the kitchen. My mother had a set of collectors' butcher knives because she told my father she had a passion for cooking. I took two of the larger ones back into my room. Everyone was still asleep—I could hear the nanny's deep, rumbling snores. The dog started barking again. I kept looking at it, wondering what to do. I wasn't hesitant when I picked up one of the knives. I wanted to see how it would react. I held the dog tightly between my thighs and severed one of its ears with all the force in my body. Blood started rushing down my white bunny-patterned pajamas. It started screaming like a human child. I went for the second ear. It frantically tried to free itself from my grip but failed. It trembled and cried, and I didn't know if it was having a seizure. The noise was enough to wake the family.

Mother rushed to my room, and I was temporarily distracted. The dog jumped from my lap and started running in panicky circles. It took Mother a couple of seconds to realize what was happening. Her eyes were wide and horrified. The ears were next to me, dropping blood onto my quilt.

"Are you insane?" she asked me with a strained quietness, gathering herself. "ARE YOU FUCKING INSANE?"

"No."

"What on earth are you doing, you sick little monster?" She made an effort to soothe the puppy. "HENRY, PLEASE COME HERE," she screamed in her shrillest voice, the sound reverberating off the walls.

"I wanted to see what it would do," I explained to my father who had hurriedly put on his smoking robe, rubbing the sleep out of his eyes.

"Oh my lord," he whispered in disbelief.

The dog was still screaming and crying. The knife was still in my hand. I felt a strange sort of rush through my body. Father took the knife from me, and Mother slapped me so hard I can still feel it. I lost my allowance for a month, and my mother was hysterical around me for the same amount of time, calling me deranged and depraved at every opportunity. Of course, no one outside the four of us knew. They couldn't have the media find out about their deviant daughter, despite the amount of rage they had for me. The next dog I experimented on was in complete seclusion, and that time I put it out of its misery, slitting it open from the jaw to the bottom end of its stomach. It wasn't a criminal offense but, even if it were, my parents would never have reported me, despite how much my mother loved dogs. She found the carcass a few days after, rotting and covered in maggots.

"She's very beautiful, but there's something wrong with her," was all she could say for years about me. "There's something missing. She doesn't have any humanity in her," she would tell my father. "Look at her eyes. They're so lovely, but they're so empty. She looks right through you."

I didn't take heed of any of it. I knew there was nothing wrong with me. I knew I had an intellect she couldn't understand. She was never on my level, and she never will be, as is the case with most other people. I eventually lost my fascination with animals. I knew what they were going to do, how they were going to react. It wasn't interesting anymore, and my mind wandered. I tried to control it, I did. I wanted to get into medicine, and I wouldn't be able to do that if I were a deviant. I did all I could to stop myself.

I was a late bloomer, but Hunter and I got together when I was about thirteen. I was flat-chested and flat-hipped like a boy. My parents encouraged the relationship, even though I was barely an adolescent. He came over one night, and we watched The Moon is Blue—some wild movie made the year after I was born. He pressed his body to mine, cuddling me well into the film. He grew hard against my thigh, and he pulled my skirt up, prying my legs apart painfully. He climbed on top of me and forced himself inside me as I tried to fight him off. He was larger and stronger. I had no chance. The loss of control hurt more than my aching body. It was more offensive than the blood trickling down my thighs. Of course, he thought it was what I wanted, and he was incredibly proud of himself. He bragged to the boys at his school. After all, he was the only almost thirteen-year-old who'd nailed a girl—and not just any girl.

I was filled with rage, and I had no real outlet. I saw a little boy walking past our house alone during the summer of 1964. He looked about ten or eleven and stood at the front edge of our property, gazing down at the sparkling view of the sun beating down on the lake. I was on our front lawn, tanning myself on one of the five days of summer. My mother was away, visiting her parents in London, and Millie was with a couple of her friends. I called the boy over to me, asked him what he was doing. He was a little apprehensive at first, but I managed to talk him into coming to the house. He was very interested in the view and the pretty sailboats. I told him the view was better upstairs, that he could see almost all of Seattle. It was rare for me to be in Washington at that time. Usually, we'd summer in East Hampton. He followed me inside on my command. I led him into the spacious attic-come-gym. It was, and still is, a stunning room. The ceiling is mostly made of glass, as are the walls. My methods were messy and uncontrolled back then. After all, I was just entering my teenage years. I couldn't be as sophisticated or trained. I was a child. He was a child, younger but the same size. It was a fair fight. While he was looking out at the water, I rendered him unconscious with a crowbar. I tied his arms together with a skipping rope while he was out cold, and when he eventually came to, I walloped him, focusing all my anger and boredom on his slender body. He wasn't great to look at, but I didn't care all that much back then. I didn't have standards for attractiveness.

I couldn't control myself as I beat him with anything I could grab. I smacked him again and again with the crowbar on the head, on the torso, on the legs. I could hear parts of him cracking and blood seeped into the flooring. He was still very much alive, and when he tried to scream, I shoved my sock into his mouth. I left bruises on every inch of his skin and beat him relentlessly about the face until he was unrecognizable. I knew I'd broken every facial bone. I wanted to see how much a human could take. I wondered how different it would be from the dogs. I didn't expect it to be as exciting as it was. I sodomized him with a glass bottle of Coke, and he screamed through the sock as he thrashed about in agony. The smell was truly awful. I'm telling you, it was pure hell. He'd defecated himself. I didn't know that happened as a person died.

I was going to set him free by slitting his throat from ear to ear but, instead, I sat silently with him as his body gave way. I think it was an hour until he finally died. I'd never felt as powerful. I never knew something could feel so phenomenal. I left his body there and went down to shower. I ate a packet of chips and drank some lemonade. Only then did the panic set in. I had no idea what to do with his body. With animals it was easy, I could dump them into shrubbery and ignore any missing child posters. With a boy, I imagined people would start looking for him eventually or that he'd end up on a billboard on the freeway. Kids from our area appeared in the media quickly. It was the one negative of being wealthy.

I left the body upstairs for a couple of days, hoping that no one would find it. Mother hadn't used the gym even once after the initial week of its purchase. I didn't think there would be any risk. I was a smart kid. I knew it would start stinking, but I'd planned to remove body by then. It was very messy, far messier than I'd expected—his head was barely connected to his body, and he weighed a ton. There were splatters of congealed blood on the windows, and there were shit and urine on the floor. I thought I'd done a pretty good job. I scrubbed at the bloodstains until they were gone and used latex gloves while I mopped around the body. His face was bloated and battered, the eyes swollen shut. It only got uglier as time progressed. I hadn't planned it. I never meant to actually kill him, but when it happened, I realized how relaxed I felt for once, not restless, not bored, not in pain.

I prefaced a conversation with Millie with a pithy excuse, telling her he tried to steal from me. The smell had begun to radiate from the top floor. I warned her it was a messy scene. But I needed her up there. It was impossible for me to throw out the body alone. I wanted to wrap his body in one of the rugs, but most of ours were Oriental and as expensive as the house. I remember how upset Millie was when she saw his ravaged corpse. She inevitably started sobbing, and I think she was a little traumatized. She kept telling me I had no right to kill him for stealing from me. She was much slower than I was back at that age, so I claimed that the wounds I had from the stabbing struggle were from him attacking me first. "He hurt me, Millie. He had a weapon on him. He said he wanted to come up and look at the sailboats. Look, just look, I have so many injuries from him," I insisted, showing her the gaping wounds on my hands. I started crying for effect. She ran to the bathroom to vomit. I watched as she heaved over the toilet bowl and held her hair back with one hand.

"You're going to have to help me get rid of him. You love me, don't you? You know I can't do this alone. He assaulted me, Millie, I didn't instigate. I did whatever I could to protect myself," I said with primed tears.

"I can't—I can't help you with this. You killed someone," she said with the stutter she wouldn't lose until she turned fourteen. "Would you've rather had him kill me? He was going to. I had to fight to save myself," I urged.

"Maybe we should ask Mom or Dad what to do. I don't want to touch it," she cried. "I can't touch that thing, I'll vomit again. It stinks so bad in here. What are you going to do when his parents come looking for him?"

"Millie, haven't I always helped you? I gave you my hundred dollars last month so you could finally have that trainset you wanted. Who else would do that for you? How can you abandon your sister like this?"

"Just tell Dad. He loves you, I'm sure he can help you."

"No, you know I can't do that."

"Well, if he attacked you first, it was...okay to do this... wasn't it?" She struggled to catch her breath. "I'm going to get Dad. He can fix it. He can always fix it."

She was right, I knew that. He could help me, but I didn't

want him to think any less of me. I didn't want him to think I was this aberrant excuse for a child. He always knew what to do to get us out of a situation, but I didn't know if it would be worth the cost. "Okay, bring Daddy," I said quietly as I braced myself. "Make sure Mother doesn't come up too." "Just wait here, alright?" "Yeah, just go."

I paced back and forth as she tried to find our father downstairs. He could only be in his home office, the den, or his bedroom. I had no idea what was taking her so long. Every excruciating minute felt like an hour. When I heard them on the steps, I felt my body freeze. Father surveyed the damage silently, stationary. Those two voiceless minutes seemed like an hour.

"Did anyone see him coming into our home?" he asked me, showing no sign of emotion.

"No, I don't think so. There wasn't anybody around." "Have you told anyone other than Millie?"

"No, Daddy," I told him solemnly.

He wasn't frenetic like my mother. He acted based on rationality, not emotions. He was level-headed, like me. He used to tell me stories of his boyhood when he would do the same things I was doing.

"Millie, why don't you go help your mother set the table?" He was calm, collected. He put his arm around her shoulders as she sobbed. She agreed eventually and left after promising not to say a thing until he told her it was okay.

"Okay, Maris, I don't know why you're behaving like this," he told me. "But I will try and fix things. You need to tell me what happened."

"Do you want the sugar-coated version?" I asked him boldly. "No. I want you to tell me why and how you did this." "Daddy, I'm really sorry."

"I don't care about all that, what fucking happened?"

I'd never heard him swear before. He always claimed to

be above that kind of vulgarity. It shocked me a little, despite the context. "This kid was outside looking out at the sailboats at Lake Sam. I was, I don't know, upset. I told him to come inside because we had a better view. I don't know why it happened. I knocked him out cold and then kept beating him, over and over, and the next thing I knew, he wasn't breathing. I don't know, I didn't expect that to happen. I didn't think I could be strong enough to hurt anyone, let alone, you know, kill someone."

"Why did you tell Millicent?" "I needed help."

"She's hysterical like your mother. Did you think that would be wise?"

"I couldn't drag this body out by myself. I can barely even carry shopping bags."

"What were you planning on doing with it?"

"I don't know, I was thinking maybe I'd dump it out in the wooded area."

"And then what? You'd get caught, Maris. You'd get caught in thirty minutes flat. You wouldn't have a future."

"I don't know what to do." I began crying.

"Stop that nonsense. We need to figure this out," he barked irritably. He rubbed his temples as he strode about. My father hates crying or any form of weakness. "You've really done a number on this one."

"I was angry."

"Couldn't you have taken it out on another neighborhood poodle?"

"I told you, I'm sorry, what can I do?"

"You're doing nothing at all—I have to handle this."

He stood quietly, thinking. I could almost see the mental calculations as if he'd done this before. It was a long while before he spoke again, and I sat on the floor, my back against the bloodstained window. I stopped the tears now that they were no longer necessary. The body was disgusting to look at, but I couldn't look away.

"Alright, Maris, I'm going to make a few phone calls and see what can be done considering the mess we're in—both literally and figuratively. You know the maids clean up here, right? Did you think about that?"

"I've kept them away so far, haven't I?"

"If you talk to me like that, I'll have you thrown in jail myself," he says coldly. "Go downstairs and eat your dinner while I fix your mistakes."

He wasn't someone whose buttons I'd push, so I shut up pretty quickly and went downstairs. He made his phone calls and struck a deal with some political and judicial heavyweights, ensuring I would never see the inside of a juvenile correction facility or deal with a criminal record as long as I attended court-mandated therapy sessions with a criminal psychiatrist on a weekly basis. I don't know what he did with the body, but I learned two things: firstly, the boy was from a lower-class ethnic ghetto—not our neighborhood as I assumed, and secondly, that I very much enjoyed killing.

CHAPTER NINE

I rake through my extensive wardrobe multiple times. I go through Millie's clothes too. I've shortlisted four dresses that are worthy of tonight's affair. Charles isn't from an affluent town, but he deserves more consideration than Hunter and the other men I've dated, purely because of his beauty—I feel overall that's worth more than money. My monetary sources are plentiful. I eventually decide on a beautiful navy-blue, bell-sleeved dress. It has a deep neckline that shows the right amount of cleavage, and, paired with the heels I've chosen, it elongates my legs. I shower and then moisturize my entire body, leaving myself smooth and soft. I spend a fair amount of time applying makeup. I use shimmer shadow, mascara, and this bronzing powder that's always confused the hell out of me. My lip gloss is shiny and clear, tinged with wintergreen and ginger to emphasize the fullness of my lips. I leave my hair down and take a classic brown Yves Saint Laurent pocketbook with me.

Charles greets me at the door with a smile, and I feel that twinge in my stomach again. I don't let on my excitement.

"You look wonderful, Maris." He kisses me on the cheek.

I glance around quickly to make sure my family isn't in the vicinity before grinning back at him. He's incredible in his suit and tie, conveniently also navy blue.

"Okay, my old rambler isn't quite as fancy as your Porsche, but I hope it'll do."

"We all have to make compromises sometimes," I tease him. "I'm glad this time you didn't knock on all our neighbors' doors. My father was getting seriously concerned."

"This time I was aware you lived in the fanciest house within the fanciest neighborhood."

"Well, you'll be inside later. You can tell me if it really is the fanciest."

"I can't believe you guys don't just live in your hotels," he says to me incredulously.

"When you're in as many hotels as I'm in, you want to be in a house, to be honest. I sometimes want to hurl when I see a lobby." "You should see my apartment in Ellensburg, you'll be hurling for a while." He laughs.

"I'd love to go see your place over there. Get me out of here." He gallantly opens my door for me. It's cute watching him fumble for the right moves as he aims to understand how dating works. I don't think Hunter has opened a door for me in about five years. His charm now only appears when he's in the company of those who've known him for less than twenty-four hours.

The drive to Larousse is approximately ten minutes. It's handy having excellent French food so close by. My taste is a little eclectic. I usually love trashy junk food, but Larousse's fine dining offers some serious competition.

"I've never had French food. Is it really snails and stuff?" He turns to face me, ignoring the road in front.

"All snails, nothing but snails—they're slimy and delicious." "Maybe I'll stick to a side salad," he says wearily.

"Just in case you aren't joking..."

"Oh, well, that's no good, there're snails in that too."

"Maris, I'm going to kill you. I'm the one driving," he says, amused. "I'm not going to be able to pronounce anything, and I'll be eating snails."

"Okay, why don't you let me do the ordering for you?" I glance up. "Oh, turn left here, the valet can handle parking the car."

"Do you want the valet to see you in this piece of shit?"

"Well, he's seen me in my sister's battered Porsche, so how much worse can it be? Luckily, my company doesn't look as bad as the car," I tell him. "And Lorenzo isn't that much of a dick because he isn't actually French."

"You're on a first-name basis with the valet guy? Aren't you a woman of the people."

"If you keep talking to me like that, I'm not going to put this on my parents' account."

With the way he's driving, I'm not sure how we even made it to the restaurant. "You drive like a fucking grandmother, by the way. Not my grandmother, because she drives over ten an hour, but definitely a geriatric," I add.

"Well, maybe I want to delay the slimy side salad." He manoeuvres the car into the little spot in view of the valet stall. I smile at him, running my hand up his thigh as we roll to a stop. colour flushes his cheeks, and he freezes, eventually scrambling for the keys to give over to the waiting and joyful Lorenzo.

"How are you? You're looking wonderful!" I say, still working my fingers along Charles's leg as I speak to Lorenzo, who is wildly out of place working at a French restaurant. "Come on, Charles." "Oh, Miss Caldwell, I'm so glad to see you. Where is your lovely mother?" He leans down into the driver's side window. "She's at a rave with a lot of MDMA, Lorenzo." I start laughing.

"No, she's at home, but I'm sure she'll drop in sometime soon."

Mother won't ever be dropping in, considering her perpetual diet and her feverish fear of butter and carbohydrates. We only have a tab here because my father brought her in once during a family meal and then continued to frequent the restaurant with all the blonde twenty-something girls he hired as our staff. He's always been the stereotypical attractive businessman and has had more affairs than he or anyone can remember. He takes the hidden, most intimate booth, thinking that might spare him if Mother were to casually waltz into her dietary nightmare.

The maître d' is a frazzled Frenchman I've never seen before. He's taking reservations on the phone while arranging a table for us. He eyes me up and down.

"Do you always have this effect on men?" Charles whispers into my ear.

"Without fail," I tell him, before asking the man to sit us in a beautiful little nook near the grand piano.

"I recommend the boeuf bourguignon, not a snail in sight. You do eat beef, right? You're not one of those hippies, are you?"

"Thankfully, I'm as far from vegetarianism as possible. Melissa has tried to make me stop eating meat because she thinks it's cruel and unfair but, look, that's never going to happen."

"You're my kind of man, Charles Elderberry." I try hard to stop myself from staring at him. All I want to do right now is sit in his lap.

"I'm happy to hear that. I thought I may be too low brow for your taste."

"If low brow looks like you, I'm pretty happy about it."

The waiter stops at the table with the menu and wine list. Charles pales a little when he sees the prices. This place is relatively cheap compared to the other restaurants around here, but I can imagine that most people from Ellensburg can only afford the likes of McDonald's. I normally wouldn't pay, but since it's on my parents' account, I see no problem accosting the waiter with the bill before Charles can.

"Okay," I tell him excitedly, "I think you'd like the gruyere soufflé and the coq au vin if you're not up for beef. All of it is wonderful, to be honest. They cook their fries in duck fat."

"How can you eat all that junk and still have a body like that?" "I burn the fat off by murdering and dismembering boys," I jest, giggling when his eyes widen. I look up to the mustachioed waiter. "What're your specials tonight?"

"We have crêpe au four, the chef recommends it," he says after overcoming a little bout of concern at my comment.

"Okay, I think I'll stick to the soufflé and the chicken, but he'll have that first." As soon as I say it, my stomach rumbles in anticipation. They flavor it right here.

"Um, can I please have the b-be-beauh, ugh, I mean the beef?" "The boeuf bourguignon?" asks the waiter helpfully.

"Yeah, yeah, I think I'll have that."

"Jean-Claude, could we get a bottle of Dom with that? Whichever one you recommend," I say. I know for a fact that he's an ugly Ukrainian who has traded his unpronounceable name for one that sounds at least mildly French if a tad cliché.

"Of course, Miss Caldwell, is there anything else you would like?" He has on his most eager smile, expecting a large tip like the one I gave a couple of weeks ago when I got absolutely tanked from a combination of red wine and dolls.

"That's all for now, dear." I want to slap myself when I realize how much I sound like my mother.

"I knew I wouldn't be able to pronounce anything here," Charles tells me in embarrassment.

"You can stop worrying now and thank me later. If we

were at the restaurant you suggested, I assure you we'd be throwing our guts up tomorrow. We had guests come in from Australia and took them there because they insisted upon it, and I was sick for the whole week after."

"Maris, I know so little about you. Tell me everything, so I can focus on something other than how good you look in that dress. I told my mother about this date, and she said you're a major socialite. I don't know how I've never seen you on TV."

"Oh, that's not true. I'm not a socialite. I just go to my parents' functions whenever they force me to and model if it's a company I like. I'm a student. I'm in med school at UW."

"You're in med school, how do you do it?"

"I don't know, I love it. I'm not even enjoying these holidays. I want to be back in class as embarrassing as that sounds."

"I want to go back to school eventually," he says. "I'm hoping I can get a good score on the LSAT and do law at UW or at Puget Sound. I know it's a little far-fetched at the moment, but I think if I buckle down and save, I could probably do it."

"Have you considered modeling?" I ask.

The waiter appears with the champagne, the bottle dripping condensation into the ice bucket. He pours a glass for me and then Charles. I smile up at him.

"Modeling, what? Me? You've got to be kidding me."

"Why is that so preposterous to you? You're what, six foot one? You have excellent bone structure and beautiful eyes. You could model until you earn enough for college. They throw boys out pretty quickly anyway, so you wouldn't have to stick around for too long."

He scrunches his nose in disbelief. "No, I doubt it. I could never be a model. I'm not good-looking enough."

"Are you fishing for compliments?" I ask with a grin. I rub

his leg underneath the table with my foot. "I'm happy to give them out if necessary."

"I feel like I'm being set up here. Women usually aren't that forthcoming with compliments." He blushes again.

"Somehow, I don't believe that'd be the case when it comes to you."

"This is why you make a good socialite, all that charisma. Does it come to you naturally?"

"No, I have a false personality that I've carefully cultivated that, when altered slightly, is suited to different individuals," I tell him sarcastically.

"Have you considered stand-up comedy?"

"I think comedy is about the only thing I don't have an aptitude for." I pause. "Oh, I'm only kidding. I'm not that conceited, I know I suck at most things."

"Not from what I hear."

"Really, what else have you heard?" I lean forward.

"My mother thinks you're a celebrity. I don't think she's ever been more excited about a date of mine. She doesn't think much of Melissa. She tells me constantly I could do better, and now, finally, she seems to be happy."

"Wow, your mother sounds terrific. I'm glad she thinks I'm a celebrity, but I hope she doesn't get too disappointed when she finds out I'm only a moderately intelligent medical student. My sister Millie generally does more of the publicity stuff. Everyone confuses the two of us, even our parents."

"Don't tell me it was your sister in that Vogue piece."

"No, that was actually me, thankfully. I wouldn't want you to be thinking of Millicent right now."

"Does she look exactly like you?"

I consider it for a moment, whether I should tell him things most people wouldn't know. "I'll tell you a little secret. She's an inch taller than me and unless you look closely at her, you wouldn't notice a teeny tiny crescent-shaped birthmark on her left shoulder. That's the only way to tell us apart."

"My brother Chris looks almost nothing like me. He's a blonde, and he has green eyes. I think maybe my mother cheated on my dad. The rest of us all have dark hair and blue eyes."

"Maybe she did, that would've been scandalous in the fifties.

How old is he?"

"He's twenty-one, three years younger than me, fucking pain in the ass."

"Why's that?"

"He's a loose cannon. Though, I guess you could say the same about me right now, dropping out of school and all."

While for the past half hour I've been fixated on Charles's face, I look beyond him to the circular booth right at the rear of the restaurant. I see "Ted" with a diminutive brunette, whose long, thick hair overpowers her mouse-like features. He looks sharp in a tweed coat with a bow tie, and his dark gaze scans the room.

"Oh, you're not incompetent in the least, Charles." I'm a little distracted when I see Ted standing up. "Will you excuse me for a moment? I need to drop into the powder room. Hopefully, my food doesn't get here in the meantime."

"That's alright, I'll stave off from mine till you get back." He beams.

I hurry across the restaurant, toward the bathrooms where Ted is heading. I don't know what I'm doing or what I even want to say to him. I catch him before he's about to enter the men's room. "Did you end up finding a pretty girl to help with your sailboat?"

He's a little shaken but recovers quickly. "I didn't end up going sailing at all, actually."

"Can I still take you up on that offer? I'd love to see your boat." "Yeah, yeah, of course, that would be great. You said you had a boyfriend, though, right?" "Not anymore."

I know this nice-looking, sweet-talking boy was the last person to see Carol alive. I like the feeling of being around someone so much like me, despite the carnage that he most probably caused my best friend of the past two and a half or so decades. His thoroughly chewed fingernails starkly contrast his stylish, smooth outfit and expensive patent leather shoes. I don't think he has upper-class breeding, but he is pretending he does.

"That's good to know," he tells me, finally cracking a smile. "Say, how about you call me sometime? I can have the maître d' send over my number to you when your girlfriend goes to the powder room if you like?"

"That would be wonderful. Don't worry, she's not my girlfriend."

"Okay, well, I'll hopefully see you soon," I tell him, doing half a wave as I head back to Charles.

He waves in return for a while, apparently forgetting he'd gotten up to go to the restroom or perhaps considering the possibility that he may have found new prey.

"You're one lucky girl, or this is one slow restaurant," Charles tells me with the same beautiful beam when I slide back into my seat.

"Oh, it's not me, this is definitely a slow restaurant." I find myself staring at his lips. "But it's worth it, I promise."

"I'm going to hold you to that," he says spiritedly.

"Alright, we should at least get drunk in the meantime," I say, pouring the bubbly amber liquid into two flutes.

"This is embarrassing, but you have no idea how badly my chest burned when I had that scotch. I can't do the manly man thing with liquor."

"I'm hopeful this champagne will go down a little easier, then." I giggle against my better judgment. "I could've made you a full French meal at home, but I figured this setting would be more like a first date, as opposed to having my family around."

"You know how to cook a full French meal?"

"I went to cooking school for a couple of months when I was in Paris in the summer of 1970. I was never as good as those Frenchies, but the food came out pretty damn good." I'm not being entirely honest, as I went to only one cooking class and decided to quit and smoke Gauloises outside with the French boys. I flew home soon after because I couldn't stand the accents or Mother's constant bitching anymore. She was so whiny there without my father. She was the one who'd taken up the cooking classes so that she could woo him with a homemade meal like a true housewife who didn't depend on her maids. She quit shortly after I did, but neither of us confronted the other about it. She never learned how to cook as a young girl. Her father was a steel magnate who lavished her with gifts and trips and whatever else she wanted. She was the only daughter in a family of four children and was spoiled rotten. Cooking wasn't on the cards. That's what cooks and maids were for.

"What don't you know how to do?"

"Well, I truly suck at singing. Honestly, I could make your ears bleed quite a bit. It's one of my favorite torture techniques." "Okay, I'm going to need to hear you sing when we go back to your house."

"I don't know if I want to torture you, though. I had better things planned."

"Maybe we'll stick to your plans, then. Also, I, uh, heard that you do have a boyfriend. He's another stupidly rich boy, heir to a candy fortune. Hunter, I think?"

"You shouldn't believe those tabloids. Everything is sensationalized. Hunter and I are just good friends—we have been since we were tiny." I lean in closer to him, gently touching his arm. "Don't let it slip to anyone, but I'm kind of his beard. He's an avowed bachelor."

"He does not look homosexual at all! What a shock."

"You can let your mother know if she's the one who told you. I imagine you don't read the tabloids."

"No, I can't say I do. But they certainly sound interesting." "They never let the truth interrupt a good story."

The waiter arrives with our appetizers, and Charles is hesitant as he pokes at his with the wrong fork. Being raised with perfect etiquette, it's difficult to watch. I feel the burning iron prod urging me to tell him, but I feel another not to be like my mother. She's so pathetic that that's one of the only things she does in life, and I can't do it. I cut my soufflé delicately. The rupture in the center is marvelous to look at, and it tastes even better. It's everything I like in a food item—carbs, butter and cheese. Everything my mother hates.

"Okay, I didn't want to prove you right, but this is not at all slimy."

"That's a shame, I asked for extra slime on my way to the powder room."

"I might need to start trusting your judgment. This is phenomenal."

"I'm glad you like it. It's the only non-junk food I can stomach." "Are you a caviar kind of girl?"

"God no, it's foul. Even the good stuff like Beluga tastes like shit. Don't tell my parents I said that, though."

He starts drinking his champagne slowly, reminding me that he can't get too drunk since he needs to drive us back and doesn't want to get caught for driving under the influence. I finish the appetizer faster than my manners would usually allow, but I have an excuse since I haven't eaten properly all day. The only thing I've eaten was that bowl of cereal and besides, I know I'll work off the calories shortly. I feel strange. I've never been this tongue-tied, at least not in the past decade or so. Words generally come to me smoothly, without a second thought.

"I still can't believe what's been going on in Washington, with all the recent disappearances and murders," he tells me in between bites.

"Yes, unfortunately, it's such a shock. I don't remember anything this bad happening around here. This kind of stuff always happens in New York and Los Angeles and Detroit, not in Seattle."

"There was one in Ellensburg. I didn't really know the girl, but she was in one of my classes before I dropped out. It was some heavy shit. Her parents have been on the news constantly. It's the wildest thing to happen over there. Nothing happens over there."

"It's been a bit more personal for me. My best friend Carol went missing from Lake Sam a little while ago. They think they found her remains at Taylor Mountain."

He looks at me for a while, assessing whether I'm making another macabre joke or not. He's flustered. "Are you serious?"

"Yeah, I was there today with my mother and hers." I simulate mourning. He, of course, needs to see my devastation.

"And you still came out to see me?"

"Well, my parents taught me to always honor my commitments, and I don't mean to make you conceited, but I was very much looking forward to this."

"I really appreciate that. You have no idea how excited I was. Hmm, actually, I'm pretty sure the majority of what I was feeling was nervousness."

"Why would you be nervous?"

"Look at you, Maris. I'm so glad that you were able to see me tonight despite what's going on."

"I wouldn't have missed it." I smile.

"Did they find out what happened to Carol?"

"They didn't have much to go on, but I think they found skull fractures from a blunt object."

"Do you think it's the same guy who's abducting those boys? I've never seen guys this worried for their safety. I've had people warning me too. Apparently, they were all tortured and killed with different methods. Some were held captive and all were decapitated, like the girls."

"Yeah, I would assume it's the same guy. Maybe he's bisexual.

He sounds like such a sicko," I say.

"None of them still had their heads or fingers intact. It's so disturbing. I wonder what he does to them."

"Well, I hope to do forensic psychiatry, so maybe I'll have answers for you within about a decade. It's so depressing. I don't know who would do these kinds of things."

Our mains arrive, and the waiter tops up both of our drinks before Charles can refuse. "Are you enjoying your meal, Miss Caldwell?"

"Oh yes, it's lovely. Please pay our respects to Francois if he's cooking tonight."

"Yes, I absolutely will."

"Are you on a first-name basis with all the staff here?" asks Charles light-heartedly.

"I'm here a lot if that explains any of it away," I say. "Okay, the more I say that, the more I wonder why I'm not obese."

"Well, I'm guessing your exercise has something to do with that."

"You mean the exercise that you interrupted the other day? If I've gained weight, it's on you."

"Now I've got that and your dad thinking I'm a serial killer lurking around your neighborhood." He smirks.

"Well, my parents are going out of town for a while pretty soon, so you won't have to deal with him too often."

"Where are they going?"

"They're opening new hotels in Colorado and Utah. I don't know why anyone would want to open a luxury hotel in Mormonville where only the churches have money, but my parents have a habit of making bizarre decisions, so it doesn't surprise me."

"So, it's just going to be you and your sister at your place?" "Well, actually, Millie might be going to stay with some friends in Olympia, so it'll be me and the house staff."

"I can't in good conscience leave you all alone with the house staff," he tells me with his eyes lit up.

"That's so kind of you," I tease. "I know I need company." "I'm sure guys are lining up for that."

"Girls are lining up too." I strategically place my hand on his.

This is something I do without fail.

I've always had a system when it comes to behavior. I find it difficult to comprehend why people do the things they do, and I've never understood what makes one attractive to another for friendship or dating when it comes to qualities other than physical appearance. I'm a fast learner, and I've been watching people and strategizing since I was a young child. I never had the same reactions as them, nor the deep, unwavering emotions that altered their behavior. I rarely feel things strongly, but I now understand how to make it seem like I do, after years of intensive personal programming. I don't know what went awry as I was growing up. I thought eventually I would be like everyone else, but I knew there was something different about them. They would cry about silly things like their pets dying or hurting another person and their rage would be hot and irrational. I'm not a robot; I mean, I do have emotions. I get angry, I get very angry. I feel sad when I don't receive the appreciation I deserve, and I feel adrenaline when I take party favors or have sex or finish a killing. The rage I feel, however, is cold and clear, allowing me to respond in a calculated manner—for the most part.

I came up with a system that I would use in my personal interactions with everyone around me, altering it based on circumstances or the individual in question. With boys, I always dress in a certain way and take on a flirtatious affectation because it gets me what I want. I'll put on a nice dress that accentuates my body, often a dipped neckline or a short hemline will come into play. I wear high heels that make me look long-legged and feminine, and jewelry that is tasteful and eye-catching—nothing gauche. I don't want anything taking the focus away from my face or figure. I keep my hair shiny and wear it down, so I can be coy while I speak to them. I have a mental play-by-play handbook telling me what to do in any possible situation with them, and I perform these tasks mechanically. I find myself at a loss at the moment, however. I don't know whether to follow protocol or not with Charles and Ted. I don't know what I want from them. I don't have a set goal, and it's making me uncomfortable.

"Well, if you have any room leftover with all of Seattle's most eligible bachelors there, I'd love to stop by," he says, knocking me out of reverie. I wonder how long I've been staring.

"You're coming over tonight, aren't you? You can pick a room, and I'll be sure to save it for you." I run my fingers gently down his arm, stopping at his wrist. I see goose bumps rise on his skin. "If you'll have me, of course I will. Do you think your father will be home? I'd really like to let him know I wasn't skulking around the neighborhood looking for girls to kill," he says, laughing.

"God, I hope not," I say accidentally under my breath. "There's a chance. I think he's trying to make up for his upcoming absence by being around all the time before he leaves."

"That's sweet of him. My father did a runner on us before I turned five. I don't remember him well, only that he used to curse a lot."

"My father isn't as much of an upstanding family man as he pretends to be. I think he was there for a total of three of our birthdays. He spends most of the time away from us. It was always the nannies and occasionally our grandparents."

"To shitty parents," he says, raising his glass in a toast. I clink mine against his. "To shitty parents."

The coq au vin is delicious, and I'm certain he's enjoying his beef. It would be impossible not to. This time he uses the right cutlery and takes liberal sips of his drink. He's loosened up substantially, not as awkward or hesitant in his moves. The shy confidence penetrated the surface.

"Okay, we're having dessert, right? Please tell me you have a sweet tooth too," he says.

"I'm very much of a savory kind of gal, but I can't pass up an opportunity to have the crème brûlée here."

Once we're finished with our food we head outside, clambering half-drunk into his car as the valet drives it around. He's excited on the drive back to my place, perhaps from the champagne or the sugar in the dessert. I didn't wave to Ted as I left but smiled at him when I realized he'd been watching me. I didn't want to seem too conspicuous to the girlfriend he was claiming to not be dating. Charles drives at a normal speed this time, the grandmother in him left behind at the restaurant. When he pulls into the winding driveway, I notice Mother and Father's matching Bentleys, but Millie's Porsche is not in sight. He looks around in awe while I think of a way to elude my parents and their upcoming onslaught of questions.

"Jesus Christ, this is the fanciest house in the fanciest suburb," he tells me, taking in the Georgian architecture and the vast, perfectly manicured lawns. I tried when I was little to get them to put in a moat at the entrance, but they shut me down fast, telling me how silly the idea was. They weren't big on caring about our feelings. My parents aren't the type to humor small children— perhaps the children of others but not their own.

"Does the entire population of a small nation live here?"

"I guess you could say that half of our staff members are Hispanic."

"Will your parents mind me coming over?"

I lie through my teeth. "No, they won't mind at all, don't worry."

I lead him up the driveway, struggling a little from the tipsiness and my heels and try to slide the key in as quietly as possible. I know they're both likely to be awake. No one in my family sleeps early unless there's a media appearance the next day, and they don't want to look tired and ugly on television. The doorknob turns before I get to it.

"Maris, honey, I'm glad you're finally home." It's Father and he's caught off guard by the sight of Charles. "Oh, hello there, you look familiar. Have I met you before?"

"Hi sir, I'm Charles Elderberry. I don't think we've officially met, but I think you saw me yesterday around that sandstone house down the road," he's cheerful but very, very jittery. He extends his hand to my father.

"Yes, that's right, I saw you near the Weston estate. I didn't know you knew my daughter. Maris, is he in your classes?" He shakes Charles's hand and then remembers his manners, stepping back into the foyer to allow us in. "I'm sorry, come inside."

"We met at the hotel, Daddy. Charles thought it was terrific, just terrific. He loved the décor."

"It's a beautiful hotel, sir. I was very much in awe the entire time."

I keep from sighing when my mother enters the room, her heels clicking against the marble floor to announce her arrival. "Well, hello," she says, taken aback when she sees him. She's flustered when she notices how attractive he is, patting her coiffed hair into place.

"Quinn, this is Charles. He's been saying wonderful things about the new hotel."

"I'm so glad to hear that," she says, unprecedentedly lost for words. Her charm is usually effortless and smooth, but her speech has halted, and her cheeks are flushed. "Are you a friend of the girls?"

"Just Maris, I'm yet to meet Millie, but I've heard a lot about her," he says nervously.

"Can I get you something to eat or drink, Charles?" she asks, still staring.

"No, I'm alright, thank you, Mrs. Caldwell, I appreciate that." "Oh, dear, you can call me Quinn. Come on inside, it's getting chilly out," she says, regaining her composure. "Maris, honey, I have some terrible news. I didn't think you'd have company but—"

"What's wrong, Mother?"

"I'm sorry that you have to hear this on your first visit here, Charles. Maris, they identified one of the bones. It was matched to Carol. There's a small memorial service tomorrow at Sacred Heart before the police take the remains back into custody."

"This is awful, oh my poor Carol. I'm glad we finally have some answers, though," I lament.

"I'm so sorry to hear that, Mrs. Caldwell, uh, Quinn, I heard about the search this morning on the news," says Charles.

"Yes, poor Carol was Maris's best friend."

"It must be a very difficult time for all of you. Maris, would you like me to leave? I know you might want to be alone right now." "No, no, absolutely not," I say quickly, panicking at the thought of him leaving.

"You are more than welcome to stay. I'm sure Maris would appreciate the company right now, dear," says Mother in her softest voice.

"My mother's right, I could use the company."

"Okay, sure, well, I'm happy to stay if that's alright with you guys."

"Daddy, Mother, may I be excused?" My jaw is set as I meet my mother's eyes. It's a statement, not a question.

"Yes, of course, sweetheart," she allows, knowing she has no choice. Her manners are impeccable. Not once would she cause a scene in front of someone outside our immediate family.

"Come along, Charles, my room is up this way," I say, leading him toward the stairs. I don't have any physical contact with him in Mother and Father's presence because I don't want to have to answer questions about my supposed infidelity tomorrow morning. Mother seems to be rather charmed by Charles. She's like a high school girl swooning over the quarterback. I'd perhaps consider it creepy if I didn't need her to be lax about him staying here. He sits on the divan instead of the bed once he's inside. I lock the door behind us.

"Are you doing okay?" he asks me.

"I'm alright, I don't really want to think about it right now. It might be better to deal with it in the morning. Would you like a drink or are you buzzed enough for the movies?"

"I'm pretty buzzed right now. Your room is far out. It's even better than the hotel room."

"Now this is something I actually did design. Well, I mean, I chose the furniture, the layout wasn't up to me like it should've been. Look at how swell my canopy bed is, though."

"I think my room is about a tenth of the size. Shit, how many of these rooms do you have?"

"I don't know, I think all up there're nine bedrooms if we're not including the pool house which has two rooms and a bar." I smile. "But none of that is particularly interesting. What do you feel like watching?" I kick off my heels and my feet are finally in peace. I walk to the television and my large collection of VCR tapes. I have almost every horror film made in the last decade and a smattering of comedies and dramas.

Before I get a chance to look through the tapes, I feel his hands on my shoulders. I turn around to face him and his hands travel to my waist, where he holds me tight. He doesn't wait for me to speak. He pulls me to him and kisses me with the intensity and craving I felt the other night in the hotel room. I kiss him back and let the heat flood my body. He's considerably taller than I am now that I've no longer got my heels on, so he picks me up, and I wrap my legs around him. His kisses grow almost aggressive, and he sets me down hard on the bed, my back flush against the newly changed quilt.

"You have no idea how much I wanted to do this in the hotel," he tells me, almost breathless. He runs one hand underneath my dress and the other unzips it, forcefully pulling it off.

"It didn't seem like it at all," I play, yanking him to me by the collar of his shirt. I meet his eyes and I still feel jittery. I've slept with my fair share of attractive men, but I'm in a new league.

"Well, I hope this'll change your mind." He kisses me down the neck, biting a few times along the way. He delicately slides the straps of my bra over my shoulders, reaching behind me to unhook it. I feel a wave of pleasure wash over me when he looks up to grin at me, tiny crinkles about the nose, and I moan as he travels across my body with his lips. I try to take off his shirt but fall back in defeat, immobilized by pure euphoria as he goes down on me. For someone who claims to have not been with many women, he certainly knows what he's doing. I try to keep it down, knowing that my room is far from soundproof and my parents are around, but I struggle. He brings me to climax, and I expect him to be like his straight male brethren and stop right away so the focus can be shifted to him, but I'm wrong. I keep my legs around his neck and run my fingers through his tousled hair. "Are you sure you haven't slept with every woman in Seattle?"

I ask as I gasp for breath. "I don't know many guys who can do that after only being with one woman."

"I guess she taught me well." He goes back with excitement. "Aren't you going to let me do anything for you?" I ask. I want him to take me in missionary so we can be face-to-face.

"You're having me over as a guest, that's more than enough." I grab him, trying to pull him up to me. "Can you kiss me? Up here."

The sex with Hunter is, quite frankly, lackluster. The sex with Jack is moderately better, but neither of them can make me climax regularly. They never have me in this shape, but I need sex at least once a day, and sometimes it's a hassle trying to bring in a new person. I'm finally able to take off his shirt, and I lap up the sight of his slender, toned body. He has a tan that flouts Washington's sullen weather, and his muscles are well-defined. His boyishness is endearing.

"Do people tell you that you have an amazing body all the time?" he asks me in between kisses.

"All the time," I say in jest. "Do people tell you the same?"

"Yes, all the time." He starts laughing and slides in a second finger to make me draw in my breath.

I climb on top and kiss him while I unbutton his pants and wrestle with the zipper. I straddle him, wincing in agony as it first goes in. He grows concerned and puts his hand on my cheek before gently tucking my hair behind my ear.

"Are you alright?" he asks. "If it hurts, please tell me, we can stop."

"I don't want to stop," I tell him, maintaining eye contact. I gradually ease myself down. The stabbing pain soon turns into tingles of pleasure.

He goes slow, trying not to hurt me. He's rosy-cheeked, and his skin is lightly slick with sweat.

"Don't worry, I'm not that fragile," I say.

"I'm glad to hear that." He overpowers me, pinning my arms down as he gets on top.

He's spent when he falls asleep beside me, and I watch his long, dark eyelashes flutter as he dips in and out of dreams. I wish it were that easy for me. I've had insomnia for longer than I can remember. But it's not all bad. I get a lot of work done at night, and if I need to sleep, even those four or five disjointed hours, I have access to all the benzodiazepines and barbiturates in the world. I use barbiturates sparingly. I don't particularly want to die yet. When school is in session, I spend the nights studying anatomy and molecular structures, but when I'm on holidays I like to focus on my passions. I dexterously unwrap him from around me and pull on my lingerie, a long-sleeved shirt, and my 32-inch flare Lee jeans.

I skulk out of the house as quietly as possible, collecting my car keys from the bowl in the foyer. It's past 12 AM, and I'm comforted by the dark and silence. I climb into my car, still a little intoxicated, and drive around. I love driving around, I really do. It gives me time to think, time to explore, time to plan. I normally drive for miles and miles, but I know I'll have to be reasonably lucid by early tomorrow morning, so I go to the UW campus. It's still quiet, with all the students having flocked back home or to various tropical climates.

I stop at Dante's Tavern, which is still lit up and filled with the less fortunate students. I don't discriminate. I don't care. I park further down the road, away from the crowds. I comb my hair with my fingers and rub a little cherry ChapStick onto my lips before heading inside. I sit at the bar and order a gin and tonic while I survey the crowd. They pass by, with various drunk males stopping to flirt with me.

Into my second drink, I make a discovery. In the back booth by the jukebox is a group of four boys, three with shaggy hair and two with unsightly beards. With them is a clean-cut, blonde all-American type. I'm not entirely sure from here, but his eyes look green, and he's arguably quite attractive. I have a keen eye when it comes to prey. I watch him unobtrusively for an hour until he gets up to leave. I don't want to be seen near him or with him, so I wait as his friends disperse and trickle out the door. I pay for my drinks and follow several minutes later. He walks slowly. It's clear he's a bit tipsy. He walks half a mile down the street. I trail slowly behind, and he's too drunk to realize. There's no one else around once we're far enough from the din of the tavern. I quicken my pace to catch up with him, careful to not make too much noise with my Salvatore Ferragamo flats.

"Excuse me, I'm so sorry to bother you," I call out. "I'm really lost."

He turns around, at first not sure if I'm speaking to him. "It's cool, what do you need?"

"I can't find my friend's house. She said she was a couple of streets down from Dante's, but I don't know where it is. Do you think you could help me find it? It won't take too long. My car is right over there." I point at the Porsche and smile. "I'll drop you back here."

"Okay, yeah, sure, I can help you. I know this area well." "Oh, thank you so much. I've been struggling for half an hour."

"Totally, no problem. Have I seen you somewhere? You look really familiar."

"I doubt it," I say with a forced giggle. "I just transferred here from New York."

"I think I'd recognize a pretty girl like you," he says as he walks drunkenly beside me.

I fumble around, pretending to struggle with the keys,

giving myself enough time to unlock the door and reach under the seat for the tyre iron. I drop the keys to the floor of the inside. "Oh shit, I'm so clumsy today. Do you think you could get those for me? I'm short-sighted, and I don't have my contacts in." He stretches over to grab the keys, and I smash the tyre iron against the base of his skull. He falls face-first onto the seat, and I hurriedly push the rest of his limp body inside. Luckily, Charles slept over—my alibi is airtight if the police ever catch on. I handcuff the boy's hand to the side of the seat and drive as fast as I can, the lights turned off.

CHAPTER TEN

I return home at 4 AM and fall asleep beside a very benumbed Charles. I'd expected him to be asleep, but I didn't expect him to be completely unresponsive. I'd ingested a nice mix of Ativan, Valium, and Xanax in the car so getting to sleep wouldn't be a problem, but I awaken at 6:30. I lay still in bed for half an hour as I think about what to say in Carol's eulogy. Of course I have to mention her physical beauty because that's what's most important to mention about a woman these days, and I need to talk about how we were friends since our infancy and how untimely her death was, yada yada yada. I wake Charles up at seven and ask him to get dressed. Mother will barge in soon or, at least, she'll send Millie to do her bidding, and I can't have them thinking he and I slept together. There are too many guest bedrooms to justify him staying in my room.

"Maris, are you throwing me out?" he asks, rather peppy. He smiles.

"No, of course not, I just need you to go to the bedroom next door, and I'll come in within twenty minutes after I've showered." "I'm joshing you. I wouldn't want your parents thinking I'm that kind of guy. I'll be next door." He kisses me gently on the mouth. "I know this is a really difficult time."

"Thanks, honey, I appreciate it. I'll come and get you soon, alright?"

Once I've showered, I put on a somber navy-blue blouse with starched wing collars, a black sleeveless vest, a black pleated suede miniskirt, and a purple belt—Carol's favorite color. I comb my hair and put on mascara, but I still feel listless and imagine I look it too. I put on black stockings and a conservative pair of three-inch heels. I still have one of Mother's Jackie Kennedy style veiled hats, and I know she would dare not confront me about stealing it at such a tumultuous time. She comes in, as expected, to collect me, wearing a neat black Givenchy suit. It's bland but still very flattering. I'm glad I inherited her figure.

"Maris, where is that lovely boy?" She looks me up and down. "You've managed to dress appropriately. Isn't that very thoughtful of you?"

"He's in the guest room, Mother, right next door." I haven't had enough sleep to tolerate her politely. "It's my best friend's funeral, alright? I don't need the third degree. I couldn't sleep all night."

"Put on some concealer. You look like you're the one who belongs in the casket," she tells me coldly.

"Oh, that's so nice of you, Mother. What a wonderful way to begin mourning. Maybe you ought to spend more time watching your weight instead of criticizing me. Your hips look like tripled in size. Please leave my room. I need to work on the eulogy."

"Yes, well, we need to leave in thirty minutes, so don't dawdle." "I hope Daddy beats the shit out of you tonight," I whisper in her ear. "You've earned it."

She's furious but knows she can't make a scene. The

walls are thin. "You're a nasty little bitch, you know that?" she hisses back.

"Get the fuck out of my room."

I tower over her in my heels and use the intimidation to back her against the door. She leaves without speaking. I wouldn't get into a physical altercation with her because I need to stay in the will, and I like picking on people my own size, unlike her. I don't channel my anger out onto small, weak beings. It's primarily she who's insisted on my weekly therapy even after I turned twenty-one. Father had relaxed considerably and thought that the shrinks were doing more harm than good. The bitch has taken accumulative weeks from me. I stand before my mirrored wall and survey myself. I do have the dark circles Mother so crudely mentioned, but I feel the look is fitting for a funeral. I'll have to shed a few fake tears, and the veil of my hat covers most of the damage. I'm tired and achy. I have bruises and cuts all over my arms, but thankfully my shirt has long sleeves. I know the police will be at the funeral in the hopes that the killer's dumb enough to show up, and I don't want their attention on me. I carry a small purple clutch and leave my room. I knock on the guest bedroom door twice, very loudly so my parents can hear before Charles opens it. He greets me with a bemused smile, perhaps in response to the obnoxious knocking. "You look very nice for someone who's going to a funeral,"

he tells me candidly before placing his hand on his mouth. "Oh, shit, I'm sorry."

"That's alright, my mother told me I look like I belong in the coffin, so that's a nice upgrade," I say.

"Jesus Christ."

"I know, that woman sure is special!" I hope the sarcasm hasn't been lost on him. "I know funerals are a bit of a buzz-kill, so I'm sure you don't want to go, but I really want to see you later if you're around."

"I should be heading back to Ellensburg. My brother's coming over for dinner, and I haven't seen him in a while. He goes to your college, actually. I could come and take you to a movie tomorrow if that works for you?"

"Give me a call tonight, and I'll let you know what my schedule looks like tomorrow. Come on, let me walk you out at least."

Father drives us all to the funeral in complete silence. No one's spoken since we left the house. Millie is wearing one of Mother's black dresses, and her hair is pulled into a small, semi-deflated beehive. She has on a purple Hermes scarf, something she decided on only after I told her that Carol would appreciate the colour scheme. Mother sits stoically in the front passenger seat. The church Carol's mother has chosen is what she calls "small and modest," or in other words, a dismal hovel with a choirboy-raping priest ready to tell us all about the ill-conceived heaven that's waiting for us when we pass. Mrs. Greene is even sloppier than before, without any semblance of a working mind. Her eyes are boring holes through me, and she heads over my way. Thankfully, Hunter gets to me first.

"Oh Hunter, I'm so glad you're here. I couldn't cope without you, I really couldn't." I hug him tightly, forcing my way into his arms.

"I've been trying to call you," he says, his eyes either red from crying or smoking one too many doobies. "You didn't get back to me."

"I did, I tried to call so many times. Consuela kept telling me you were out."

He realizes his discourtesy and says hello to Millie and my parents, his Colgate smile front and center. They give him a polite, measured greeting, and my mother finds her way over to Carol's mother, ready with our family's deepest condolences.

I find funerals in this type of weather totally puerile and needless. It's too hot to wear gloves and a nice coat, and it's too cold to wear a linen summer dress. If I died in this weather, I'd want them to drop me into a grave as soon as possible and wait until winter for a proper commemoration, accentuated with Burberry coats, Hermes leather gloves, and glamorous high heels. I note Hunter's purple tie and wonder if someone sent out a memo of all my ideas to this band of morons.

He holds my hand firmly, leading me to the front pew, beside the others who've been chosen to present eulogies in front of the skull and three skeletal fragments they're now counting as Carol. Her mother is usually as vain as she is hysterical—in other circumstances, there's no doubt she'd be holding an open casket funeral. She was always very proud of how beautiful and alluring her daughter had been. I mean, considering how terrible both she and her husband look, it was a sheer miracle for Carol to come out as a solid seven. Dawn and Susannah are both seated in the front pew, along with Jack, Carol's two brothers, Stephen, and a cross-eyed cousin from Mississippi who I'd venture was a product of incest.

We're assembled based on our order of speeches. I'm to go third, following Mrs. Greene and her son, with Hunter and Jack right after me. I avoided Carol's brothers for years after they approached puberty and started making advances on me, but I notice David still has a tremor in his left hand and an abominable bowl-cut hairstyle. I lean into Hunter, using the warmth of his body to lull me into a comfortable position between consciousness and slumber. I regret not bringing the dark sunglasses that would allow me to sleep right through Mrs. Greene's dramatics and her son's morose thirty-minute speech about accidentally pushing Carol down a flight of stairs when they were toddlers.

I wait my turn patiently and when the weepy eyesore

is finally done, I climb the stairs to the podium. I didn't get much of the speech done, but I'm an impromptu kind of girl anyway. I make the speech as I think about the delicious thrill of going out with her killer. I figure we both like the colour cyanotic blue.

"Twenty-three years ago, I met the girl who would go on to become my best friend, my sister, and my closest confidante. We were barely a couple of weeks old, but the bond grew as quickly as we did. Carol Marie Greene was a wonderful, gorgeous, vivacious girl who made life just that little bit better. We laughed together. She was always there when I needed to cry about a boy or about how I didn't like the handbag my parents brought back for me from Milan." I pause for expected bittersweet laughter. "She was there with me when no one else was, and I cherished her dearly. Carol was my world and will permanently have a place in my heart. I was envious of her beautiful brown eyes and a smile that always lit up the room." I pause and force out a sob. I see flashes of her corpse putrefying in the wilderness, how one eye had been foraged and the other open and still in death. "I know Carol wouldn't want us to cry or mourn her. She would want us to commemorate her brilliant life, her talents, and her charisma. She was bigger than this, she was more than a funeral could ever show. My heart aches for my loss and for that of her family. Carol, I know you're watching over us, and I want you to know I'll fight to get justice for you. I adore you and I hope you're at peace."

Applause breaks out in the packed church, with the women openly crying, and the men's eyes reddening with strain. I wriggle back into my seat in the pew while Hunter clears his throat and jiggles his foot. It's his turn, but public speaking has always frightened the living daylights out of him. It's another reason why he's a terrible heir to a multimillion-dollar conglomerate corporation.

He takes the stage anxiously, flipping through a notebook in which he's written the eulogy. I sit straight, keeping my posture in line and incredibly uncomfortable to keep from falling asleep. I glance over my shoulder at the undercover cops who look the furthest from undercover. I lean toward Jack, gesturing for his flask. He hands it to me underneath the pew, and I take a quick swig. His eyes are almost as swollen and puffy as Mrs. Greene's. Carol's brother is now beside me and his breath smells like raw sewage. I control the urge to retch and place my hand appropriately to cover my nose without looking uncouth. The mourners take the stage one by one until I feel like severing my carotid artery just to leave the room. They're all saying the same things I said, but their copies are cheap and have none of my poetic flair. Jack finally bursts while up there, crying like a little bitch, slurring his words. The guilt of fucking me while dating her still seems to be there. My thoughts keep drifting back to Ted—it's kind of impressive how he pulled off a double heist in one day, especially when there were dozens of pigs around for their annual picnic. I'm lucky to get one in a month, almost always needing Millie's help too.

When I turned twenty, I'd decided I wanted a little distance from my parents. I didn't want a job or anything, I mean, I didn't want to pay for this independence, so I pleaded and cajoled and manipulated my father into funding it. My mother was happy, very happy, to get me out of her hair and fully supported my father's decision to buy me a small one-bedroom cottage a couple miles from Bellevue. I'd been at the top of my class for years. In my father's eyes, I'd earned it. I was never there for more than two or three days at a time, and I'd have help from the maids at the family house for meals, but I really enjoyed that little sliver of freedom. I had a great television set up and this cute little sofa set, very similar to Mary Tyler Moore's apartment on the show. As long as I turned up at school, achieved high grades, and saw the shrink, I was allowed to stay there for any amount of time I decided. It came to great use when I turned twenty-one, and the urges grew stronger, though I'd tried so hard to contain them after the previous incident. After the funeral, I stop off at home to eat a sandwich and finish off the bit of cocaine I have leftover, and then head to the little cottage. The boy from last night is still tied with rope and gagged. I've been extra safe, using the handcuffs to keep him in place. He's conscious and frenzied, screaming continually once he sees me.

"I'll take the gag out if you'll behave," I offer charitably, hopping up on the counter opposite him. "There's no need to be scared, honey, we all have to go sometime."

He starts crying, weakened from the lack of food and water. He wriggles to free himself to no avail. He thrashes and kicks. Eventually, he starts nodding, agreeing to behave. Surrounded by the beautiful bushland and a lake, there's no one around for miles to hear him. I rip the tape off and pull his underwear out of his mouth.

"Why are you doing this to me? I'll do anything you want me to. I won't tell the police. I won't tell anyone. Please, I'm begging you, please let me go," he cries.

I always enjoy watching men beg for their lives. The bravado and masculinity disappear so quickly, it's funny how weak it is. "I won't hurt you, I promise." I grin, the adrenaline knocking me out of my earlier stupor. There's no better feeling than complete domination and possession. He's mine now. "Would you like a drink or something? I'm sure you're thirsty."

"Why are you doing this?" he asks another four times.

"Are you saying you don't want any water? I'm not sure if I'll want to offer it again. I'm feeling pretty generous at the moment."

"Please, let me go. I'll give you money."

I pretend to be interested. "Oh, really, you'll give me money?

How much money are we talking, sweetheart?"

"I have, uh, I have $10,000 in my account right now. I'll give you all of it if you let me go," he begs.

"It's a shame for you that my family earns that in well under an hour, so it doesn't mean too much to me, but I appreciate the offer."

"I just want to see my family, please."

"Oh, your family will see you, I promise it's all the same," I say, laughing. I walk to the kitchen and retrieve my gleaming chef's knife. I brandish it, letting it dangle before his eyes. "They'll see every little bit of you."

"No, please, I'm begging you, please don't hurt me."

"Can you make some more interesting conversation, please? You're boring the fuck out of me and the more bored I get, the more mutilated you get."

"Are you going to kill me?" Tears begin to run down his cheeks.

"That depends entirely on you." I feel terrific and put on 'Dream a little Dream of Me' by the Mamas & Papas on the record player. "Do you like this music?"

"It's fine, I like it," he says, weary.

"It's nice, isn't it?" I home in on him, meeting his terrified green eyes. He starts thrashing as I put the knife to his throat. It gives me a real kick to watch him squirm. "Oh relax, you little bitch, I'm not killing you yet. I want to have some fun."

"Please don't kill me. My father has cancer, and my brother and sister can't support the family."

"Don't lie to me. You don't have a father. He left your mother a long time ago." I use as much force as possible to gouge his thigh with the knife. He starts screaming and screaming, so loud that my ears hurt. I pull the knife out.

"See, lying to me probably isn't going to help."

"How the fuck did you know that?" His face is colored, wrenched with agony. "Who the fuck are you?"

"Listen, little boy, you're not the one allowed to ask questions here." I plunge the knife into his other thigh. He starts bleeding down the legs of the mahogany chair. "You're not in charge."

He screams in anguish. "WHAT DO YOU WANT?"

"Do you think screaming at me is going to help you?" I take off the purple funeral belt. "Do you want to see what happened to the last guy who spoke to me like that?"

"What do you mean?"

"Well, when you work this hard, you generally want to keep souvenirs—it's a lot of effort, I'm telling you."

I walk into the bedroom. It's sparsely decorated. There's one king-sized bed and two bedside tables with beautiful crystal Baccarat lamps. There are three lines of shelves on two of the walls. Each shelf contains five well-spaced human male skulls. The room is my trophy case, displaying my total thirty kills over the two-and-a-half. I like spending time here; it brings me closer to my victims, giving me a sense of permanence. While the kills only last for so long, mementos last forever. I grab the latest one, the college boy I hunted with Millie. I'd left it to decompose in the greenhouse in the garden, and thankfully the heat sped up the process, leaving only the bones. It's in perfect condition, pardoning the giant skull fracture on one side. I show it to the blonde.

"He was at UW too." I set it down in front of him. "I had a lot of fun with him. My sister and I took him to the woods and shot him with ketamine darts until he couldn't walk anymore. He was almost as pathetic as you, maybe a little better."

"Why are you doing this?" he cries. I see him wince as I position the knife to his neck again. "Do you kill people for fun?" "It's a shame you'll never get a chance to kill. It's so much fun, it really is. I love watching people beg for their lives. All that control, it gives me a rush, you know? I like switching it up too. I play all kinds of games with different victims. I am God." I stick the knife into his arm and twist it. "How many do you think you could take before you die? I'm guessing, by the look of you, twenty. None of mine, so far, have been critical shots. I purposely missed your femoral and brachial arteries. These are all surface wounds."

"I don't know, please, just please let me go. I need a doctor. I need to see my family. I'll do anything you want me to."

"You're lucky I'm in med school, then." I pick the belt up from the floor and whip it against his bare chest. He screeches. I whip it at least a dozen times until my arm gets sore. Red indents form all over his abdomen. I carve an M into his chest for fun. "If you don't stop blubbering, I'm going to gag you again."

"What do you want, I'll give you anything," he yelps as I whip him again. His body is a bloody mess.

"I want your skull for my collection." I fill a glass of water for him and force him to drink half of it. "But I don't want you dead yet. Do you want the knife, the belt, or my lighter?"

"None, please, none. I'm begging you. Please have some mercy," he beseeches. Tears begin to flood.

I pull my lighter out of my blouse pocket. I yank his underwear down. "Your friend here is going to have a bit of fun," I say.

"NO, PLEASE, NO, NOT THERE."

"Do you think your girlfriend will still want you without this?" I gesture at his small, limp dick. I set it alight. His body convulses in pain for several moments. I finally put it out with the rest of the water once the smell of burning flesh starts stinging my nose. I whip his pretty face with the belt, using both of my arms this time. "Would she still date you if your face were to be permanently scarred?"

"PLEASE DON'T HURT SUSAN."

"I don't hurt women. I don't gain any pleasure from watching a woman in pain. Men, on the other hand…" I whip his stomach and then use the knife to run long shallow lines down his arms.

"I could let you bleed out and die from hypovolemic shock, or I could put you out of your misery. What would you prefer?"

He's sobbing hysterically. "Please let me go."

"How would that work? You'd probably walk fifty feet, and then you'd fall over and die of sepsis. What're you trying to achieve?"

"Just let me out of here, I'm begging you, please let me go."

I wait for the heat to die down a little, so I don't burn my hand. I place the knife against his dick, giving him a second to realize before I slice whatever charred remains of it off. The floor is submerged in blood. Luckily, the floor's made of polished marble and is super easy to clean. Plus, I never have visitors here. "Do you want to wait to bleed out or do you want me to end your suffering?"

"Please let me go." His voice is considerably weaker, faint and fading.

"All of this cardio is making me pretty hungry. Do you mind if I eat some chips?"

He lets out a feeble moan I can't comprehend. I open a bag of Hostess salt and vinegar chips and eat while I watch him slowly slip away, leaving behind a limp, battered carcass. I finish my food before I spend an hour severing his head, fingers, and toes and then another two hours cleaning up. By the time I'm done, it's already dark out, the sunlight waning. I take a shower and smoke a cherry-flavored cigarette. I haven't felt this satisfied in a long time.

CHAPTER ELEVEN

I have finally managed to get some sleep, unhindered by the presence of someone else in my bed. I haven't been alone in bed for a while. Hunter or Jack or Heather or Lilith or someone new, recently Charles, there was always someone. I need to be fresh for class, sleeping alone offers that privilege; I'm as clear-headed as the virginal boys who vie with me for first place. I have a solid 4.0 GPA and that's not something I'm willing to let slip. I graduated from my bachelor's a year early; Hunter is still in his third year of his BA, and Jack, Susannah, Stephen, and Dawn are in their fourth. I always used to pick up Carol on the way because she was too nervous to drive her new car without bumping it while parking. Instead, today I'm only stopping at Hunter's and Dawn's. Jack has been far too emotional for me to handle. Charles phoned soon after I woke up, asking to meet me for lunch, since he has the day off, and I'm glad I have an excuse to be away from this morose, whiny group. I don't understand why they haven't stopped talking about it.

"Did you guys hear another boy disappeared from UW?" asks Dawn. She's tied up her long hair, afraid that she'll be the next to be abducted. "He was only thirty feet from his frat house."

"Yeah, I saw it on the news," I say, "it's just awful. I don't know why the task force is sitting around doing nothing at all." I speed through a yellow traffic light.

"No one even saw anything. I hear he wasn't reported missing for five days," adds Hunter. "He was in my psychology class."

"Hunter, do you even do psychology?" I ask. He's notorious for dropping any subject that has a midterm and final.

"Well, I dropped it, but when I was there for two weeks, I sat right behind him. I wonder if it's that Ted guy."

"Who else would it be? It seems like a rather large coincidence that there's one dumping ground," says Dawn, with the intelligence I had no idea she possessed.

"The police are looking into the idea that there're two killers because the modus operandi is different," Hunter adds. "The girls were raped and strangled, and the boys have either been shot with tranquilizers or stabbed or burned or shot with a gun. I think two had their throats slit, too, and one was drowned. What's similar is that they've all been beheaded, but the boys are missing their fingers and toes too."

"Jesus, Hunter, you seem to know a little too much about this," I say. I'm somewhat alarmed.

"Our friend died because of one of these lunatics, you should know just as much," he says haughtily.

"Wow, you must care so much more about her because you've managed to read some newspapers and lifted your head to see a TV, bravo!" I stop myself from smacking him.

"I'm being safe. One of them has struck the group. Who's to say the other killer won't?"

"Sweetie, I assure you, you're fine," I say condescendingly. “That’s what you fucking said about Carol, and now look where she is. They can’t even find her full body, for Christ’s sake,” he snaps. “They had to bury a spine and three bones.”

“Can you calm down? You’re giving me anxiety,” says Dawn from the backseat. “I tried to meditate this morning to balance my chi and bring myself to terms with my grief, but now I feel like you guys are undoing it.”

“Were you meditating with Rain and Chakra?” I ask snidely. Only Hunter picks up on my derision. For once in a long time, he grins.

“I was, but what good is it now?”

I do rounds through the university roads, eventually finding parking about a mile away from my side of campus. I have approximately ten minutes to make it to the anatomy labs, put on gloves, a coat and borrow safety goggles because I forgot to bring my own.

“I’ll walk you to class,” says Hunter as I collect my textbooks from the trunk. “Dawn, where are your classes today?”

“In the Schaefer building. I’ll catch up with you guys at Dante’s later if you’re going.”

“Yeah, I’ll see you then,” I say, with no intention of meeting them if I get a better option. “Hunter, you’re going have to run me to class, I’m so fucking late. Can you carry these for me?” I dump the books into his arms before he can respond.

“Jesus, what the fuck is going on here? I haven’t seen this many pigs together in a while,” he says, gazing across campus. I only notice them when he brings it up.

“Oh my lord,” I say. I’m genuinely surprised and slightly on edge. Considering the number of them, I wonder if there’re any left to police the rest of Seattle. They’re swarming like bees on honey, but I don’t know what honey.

“Do you think someone else has gone missing?” asks Dawn in a panic.

“Based on how many there are of them, I’m pretty sure,” I

say. I can't see any cordoned off areas, and I don't know if it's a crime scene or not. They're mainly crowded along frat row. "Why don't we go and check it out?" As much as I don't want to look suspicious, I figure it wouldn't hurt too much to have a look. The last I recall, they don't assume college coeds kill frat boys.

"Oh god, what if someone else is dead?" This time Dawn looks like she's on the verge of tears. "I can't handle this anymore. I can't even go to class without seeing a fucking massacre."

"Can we have a look before you start having a nervous breakdown?" I ask, speeding up my pace. There's no evidence left as far as I remember. I know he only bled once he was in the car, but I can still feel my chest tightening. I have to remind myself that the police are inept and will find no trace of him on campus. I made sure of that. I approach the scene cautiously, and Dawn and Hunter fall into step. While there is a bit of anxiety, I feel pretty good that all this is because of me. I have the entire King County Sherriff's Department at my beck and call: all I need is a dead, decapitated male. I've always enjoyed being the center of attention. Once we're closer, we can see the police spread out in sections finely combing the street for any speck of forensic evidence. I imagine they're hoping for a drop of blood or an errant item of clothing with a hair conveniently tucked into it. The other cops are either drinking coffee out of Styrofoam cups or walking around the perimeter, talking loudly on their intercoms. I see John crouched down behind a car, looking underneath it.

"Excuse me, officer, could I ask what's going on here?" asks Hunter, causing John to almost bump his head on the trunk.

"Oh, Hunter," he says, surprised. "I'm sure you've been watching the news." He crouches lower, grasping the asphalt of the road.

"Is it that guy—the one on the news?"

"Yeah, I'm afraid it's him. You wouldn't have seen him around, would you've? It seems he and Stephen were good friends," says John.

"You've got to be kidding me, right?" I ask, feigning disbelief. "I can't believe Stephen never mentioned that!"

"Miss Caldwell, you're here too?" He squints up at me. "Well, yes...I mean, I do study medicine here."

"But you didn't know the boy?"

"I don't even know his name. He's a pretty average looking dude," I say. I used to have trouble talking with the police when I was younger. I'd get agitated and sometimes scared, enunciating to overcompensate. My father's advice was always to say no more than ten words unless you were to include "I want to speak to my 'lawyer.'" People think that being truthful will help you with the police, but it's the easiest way to put yourself in the slammer. "I think...I think I've seen him, around Stephen," says Dawn.

For once, I appreciate hearing her voice. John brings himself to a standing position, brushing dirt off the knees of his green uniform slacks. "Do you know anything about him?"

"No, I've never spoken to him. I've only seen him with Stephen, I think twice," she mumbles, staring absently at the cop.

"Do any of you know where Stephen is?" asks John.

"He'd have class about now. You can catch him outside the law library most days. It's the place with the least sun exposure," I say. "He's a redhead, he burns pretty quickly." I try not to laugh at my own lame joke.

"Have you got any leads, or are more of our friends going to turn up dead?" Hunter is cold, hostile.

"Now look, we're doing all that we can. If you can help our investigation, please do so, if not, go to class and let us do our jobs," replies John in contempt.

"You're not fucking doing anything. You still haven't found out who killed Carol, which maniac is trawling through Seattle picking up college kids to mutilate and murder. Oh, and that's assuming there's only one, which I doubt is the case," says Hunter through clenched teeth.

"Go on to class, boy," says John with a southern drawl he so clearly has been suppressing. "Get out of here."

I wonder when they'll finally end up linking all the male victims to Stephen. He knew all of them, bar none, and most people would be able to verify that. Stephen is generally a popular dude despite his awkwardness. I selected people who would be easily tied back to him. I mean, I have standards, so I picked the attractive ones. But they all have strong connections to Stephen— it's a lucky coincidence that Carol has one too. The police might think only one predator is using this area as a hunting ground, one killer who attacks both males and women. I know the M.O. varies significantly from the males to the girls, but the links to Stephen will add up to a strong case against him, as will all the circumstantial evidence that I've deftly been working on. Stephen doesn't have an alibi for the bulk of the killings. He is an acquaintance or friend of most of them, and we all know how likely it is for a person to be murdered or raped by those closest to them. Stranger killings are very rare.

Stephen fits the profile almost entirely, minus the terrible sketch of Ted. I hunted carefully, stalking the victims, and finding out Stephen's schedule. I had terrible sex with him twice, which consisted of three minutes of missionary and two of cowgirl, and I made sure to rip some hair out to leave on the headless bodies. I pretended I was into that gross, kinky shit, and I never knew how much he enjoyed submitting. I kept him under surveillance for months, watching every one of his moves and everyone he interacted with.

It's nothing personal, of course, but if I wanted to satiate my thirst to kill, there had to be a scapegoat. Hunter was a poor choice—I'm far too close to him, and I need him around to be the boyfriend, and the girls were too easy to be targets. It was between him and Jack. I knew them both quite well, so I could get away with spending a lot of time with them. It wouldn't look suspicious to hang out with my friends. I slept with both and decided Stephen was the lesser—he'd be the one to take the brunt. He's also very timid and is awfully afraid of authority figures, which would make him easy to intimidate into a false confession. Jack does have a mind of his own, and is reasonably intelligent, so I'm pretty sure he'd immediately know to lawyer up or stop talking. Stephen has a deep inferiority complex that anyone with an elementary education would recognize. That explains why he's murdering these young, wealthy, conventionally attractive men with such brute force. They would always represent what he lacked—charisma, confidence, and character. Sure, he has money, but he's never had much luck with women, at least, not before Susannah.

"Hunter, sweetie, save the anger for the killer," I say gently, placing my hand on his arm. "I'm sure you'll find Stephen around today, detective."

"I'm sure we will. Take him to class." He gestures toward Hunter.

"I will. He's a little upset, understandably," I say. I can't help but stare at the pig's sideburns. I wish he'd do the world a favor and get rid of them. "Come on, Hunter, I'm late for class."

"Guys, my class is on the other side of campus. I'll see you at Dante's later," says Dawn, scurrying away.

Hunter walks me to class, holding my books in one hand and my arm in the other. He holds me firmly, pulling me to him as we make our way across the giant pool of cops. "Maris, are you sure you're okay? I don't think suppressing all your feelings about Carol is going to help. I know you feel something. I love you and I know you."

"What do you want me to do, Hunter? Do you want me to sit down in the middle of the street and start crying? Do you want tapes of me crying at my psychiatrist's office? She was my best friend, trust me when I say I miss her. Of course I feel for her." I stop in front of the labs. "Now, look, I need to get inside. You know how O'Brien likes to make an example of his tardy students."

"I love you, Maris. You'll be coming to Dante's after class, right?" He puts his hands on my waist and tucks my hair behind my ear. He kisses me, his lips soft from the balm he pretends not to use.

"Yeah, sure I will. I love you, too, honey."

I rush into class and put on all I need to avert a demerit—the coat, the gloves, the eyewear. O'Brien notices I'm late but doesn't do anything about it, for which I'm glad. Today we're working on human hearts. Diseased hearts beside healthy ones. Without the cadavers they'd usually be contained in. I've read ahead. I know what congestive heart failure looks like, and I know my way around the aortic and mitral valves. I love being in the lab. I love learning about the body in such a clinical, impersonal way. It's a way I understand. There's a heart very likely from an obese person. It's grossly enlarged and covered in overwhelming, sickly yellow fat. Another heart is also enlarged but not ensconced. "Can anyone tell me why this heart is enlarged?" O'Brien asks of the entire class of forty. I put my hand up first. "I would suggest severe aortic valve regurgitation that led to an overall loss of efficiency, causing the heart to overcompensate."

"That's perfect, Miss Caldwell—perhaps if you turned up to class on time, you'd be the best student here." He glances over at Jennifer Nguyen, my main contender, a butch-looking refugee from Vietnam. Her English is poor, but her study method is meticulous. She always looks awful with her flat face and frizzy black hair, but I can't say much today: I barely even looked at the mirror when I pulled on my brown Beatles t-shirt and olive green, wide-flared slacks.

"Where would you make the incision to find out?" he asks.

I take the carefully presented specimen from him, placing it on the workbench. I make a small incision with a scalpel above the aorta. "Is that it?"

"It is. Good work. You just missed a demerit."

Jennifer eyes me contemptuously. She's assigned the iron-loaded heart with stenosis. I've been studying all through summer, even while I was overseas. I know the entire syllabus for the year, and I took a particular liking to the heart, brain and pancreas. I have a deep fascination when it comes to the human body. I enjoy the clinical rounds most, though. I like visiting patients and figuring out their innards; it's like a puzzle. I've always liked puzzles. For the upcoming three weeks after cardiology, I'm doing neurology and I've been reading up on different types of cancers and their effects on various parts of the brain. I like to know which are operable and which are inoperable and which symptoms are caused.

Jennifer may be almost at my level academically, but she couldn't possibly have my excellent people skills. She'll be demolished when she has to start speaking to patients. I have a nickname for most people and hers is Agent Orange. The rest of the class often calls her a chink, but I have no reason to use racial slurs against Asians. They try to engage with me, speaking with me and asking me to hang out after class, but in the academic sphere, nothing is more important than doing my work and getting the highest GPA. I don't need friends here, nor do I want them. I prefer working alone, but when we partner up, I always choose Agent Orange. She's all work, no chat and it's great. Thankfully, today is not one of those days, but I watch her struggle with the diagnosis for the condition she's studying.

"I'm not very sure," she tells him and the class timidly. "It could be a number of different things."

"Sir, do you mind if I venture a guess?" I don't wait for his permission. "I think it's stenosis from an overloading of iron—I think perhaps the patient resisted chelating treatment or wasn't aware of the problem before it got out of hand."

"Maris, you've earned enough brownie points for the day. Let your fellow students venture guesses. We know yours are anything but," he tells me.

I want to smack him, but I smile politely and keep my mouth shut. At least he's aware that I know as much as he does. He's not exactly a fan of his female students. He's from the old traditional school that doesn't allow women a position outside of the kitchen. The faculty obviously wouldn't support that view, considering how liberal it is, so his disdain is often well disguised. Agent Orange and I are two of five women in our class. I focus on the heart assigned to me—peripheral artery disease—to stop myself from critiquing everyone else's faulty diagnoses. I take careful cuts of the muscle to neatly fix them onto slides for the microscope. I never did any units in molecular biology, but I do think it'd come in handy. I could spend all day in the lab, taking specimens of different tissues of the body. The academic sphere is one I've always excelled in. You don't need to put on a façade. It's you and the textbooks or you and the cadavers. I feel disappointed when the four-hour lab wraps up for lunch. There'll be clinical rotations for several hours in the evening but after my rendezvous with Charles. I get the feeling he's about to tell me some juicy news.

"Charles, I'm over here," I call out across the lush courtyard outside the medical labs. I smile and run toward him, trying to pull off my lab coat in the process. My handbag is hanging off my shoulder. He's wearing a turtleneck argyle sweater and chinos—not entirely unreasonable despite it being summer and all. He's radiant, beautiful, but his eyes are bloodshot. "Oh no, what's wrong?" I hug him tightly, holding him to me for several moments. His arms are limp around me.

"My brother, my brother is missing," he says, pausing to hold back tears. "We only found out today."

"What are you talking about?"

"Do you see all the police on campus? They're trying to find him. He just...I don't know, vanished. We haven't heard from him in a week. That was one of the reasons I needed to come to Seattle."

"The blonde boy was your brother?" I pretend to be surprised. It was very convenient that his brother Chris was also attractive and had ties with Stephen. It fit right into my plan and fed my appetite. I've never felt as satisfied as I did then. Most kills don't live up to your expectations, let me tell you. They're not worth the several-hour cleanups. Chris, on the other hand, was perfect. He was handsome, tall and had very pretty eyes from which tears constantly trickled. He lasted for a long time. I'd kept him in the house for roughly fourteen hours, and he stayed very much conscious for most of it. I don't like to admit it, but I tend to be quite sadistic with my kills. I enjoy the suffering and the fear the most. It gives me a thrill to watch them writhe in pain. This was definitely a case of two birds with one stone. He wasn't my first choice, but Robert had decided to visit his folks in Spokane, and I wasn't given much notice. I stalked and hunted and by luck came across Chris, knowing very well about his connection to both Stephen and Charles. I don't know, maybe I'm fucked up, but I love watching Charles's reaction. "Come on, sweetheart, let's sit down for a minute."

"He didn't come home, Maris. He's done this before, but he always comes home. He always comes home." A tear slips down his cheek.

"There's nothing to suggest he won't come home. Does he usually go hitchhiking?"

"Yeah, he does, he turned up in Portland a little while ago, but he phoned us to let us know he was okay. He has his freedom being here instead of back in Ellensburg, but he calls us weekly, and he didn't call."

I sit down on a bench and pull him down, too, holding his hand in mine on my lap. "We have to have faith, Charles. He could be with friends."

"No, he wouldn't do this to us. He knows how hysterical our mother can be. What if he's dead like your friend? That's what the police think."

"What did they tell you?" I ask, stroking the back of his hand with my thumb sympathetically. "Do they know who could've done this if it does end up being ruled foul play?"

"They think a male, probably gay. They don't know if it's that Ted dude because, apparently, it's not his M.O. I don't even know what M.O. means."

"Modus operandi but never mind, that's not important here. We need to make sure your brother is okay. What was his name, again?"

"His name's Christopher."

"Yes, I think I remember you mentioning him to me. He's the only blonde green-eyed one in the family, right?"

"You remembered, yeah, that's him. He's a kid. He doesn't deserve this."

"He looks like such a cutie, he really does. I hope he's found alive and well. With all this going on, I'm scared to even go to my clinical rotations at night. All I've wanted to do lately is stay home and watch The Brady Bunch to get away from this nightmare," I tell him. "I'll be staying nearby, just in case—I think one of the motels downtown, so if you need company, I could do with a little of The Brady Bunch too," he says. He grips my hand tighter.

"Don't be ridiculous—stay at our place for a little while. I have plenty of space in my room, but if you feel more comfortable in one of the guestrooms, there are quite a few spares."

"I couldn't impose like that. You've been so wonderful."

I would love for him to stay at my place, not just because of the pretty face and the great sex but for watching his reactions every time his brother's face pops up on the television. It's such a sweet thrill knowing I'm the reason for it. It's hard to explain. I suppose it's a little narcissistic, but they have a whole task force trying to pin me down. As long as they stay on the Stephen trail, and I have Charles or Hunter as an alibi, I'm free to do as I please. Hunter's possessive and jealous a lot of the time, but even he couldn't argue against giving refuge to a boy who's just lost his kid brother. He'd look like a monster if anyone were to find that out, and Hunter couldn't have that. His reputation is very important to him, more important than anything else. Of course, he'll play the benevolent boyfriend, and he already dresses a little fruity, so Charles will probably continue to buy the whole gay thing. They can sleep during the night, and I often can't, which gives me a fantastic window of time to stalk more prey.

"You are more than welcome. My parents really like you, and none of us would mind at all. In fact, I'd be really happy, and I know you'd feel more comfortable being nearby just in case the police want to speak to you," I say. "We can watch The Brady Bunch and my favorite Mary episodes and cope with missing Carol and Chris. I'm hoping he's alright, though. I couldn't save my dear Carol, and I don't wish that fate on anyone."

"Maris, you are the sweetest girl. You don't know how much this means to me."

There isn't too much of a resemblance between him and Chris. He was probably right. I imagine his mother was having an affair. Charles is taller, with better bone structure and vividly blue eyes. I don't think I could've ever chosen Charles as a target because that kind of beauty doesn't deserve to be violated. I wonder how Charles would react if he knew his brother sat tied to a chair, slowly succumbing to death while he was going down on me in my bedroom. I mean, if they ever did look into a woman being a suspect instead of some sick faggot, I could have Charles support my alibi against his brother. It's such surreal perfection that I'm still surprised I've accomplished it.

After I met Charles, I started doing some digging. I have some friends who are pretty good with finding out information if there's enough money in it for them. I found out plenty about his alcoholic mother and absent father. I learned about Wilhelmina and her troubles with eating disorders. Billie is beautiful and dainty. She looks very much like Charles and obviously she wasn't going to be on my list. When I found out about Christopher, it turned out to be quite a happy coincidence. I know most people on Greek row. I'm close with many girls in Delta Omega, so I find out gossip about the most eligible frat boys. Stephen surprisingly hangs out with them on the regular, despite being mercilessly bullied by them throughout high school. Christopher was only a distant acquaintance who Stephen saw sporadically, but the odds were stacked in my favor—he had dated Susannah. The police will at least try out the theory that he was jealous of Chris. Why wouldn't he be? He's a skinny little ginger mess. His maternal grandparents are oil tycoons, and that was Stephen's ticket into our lives. Otherwise, he'd be stuck outside the golden gates envying like everyone else.

"The cop told me that perhaps my friend Stephen was a friend of his, I'm surprised that I never met Chris," I say.

"Wait, Stephen Winthrop? Is he the scrawny redheaded kid?" "Yeah, do you know him?"

"My brother brought him back to Ellensburg, occasionally.

They're both on the fencing team."

"Oh god, trust that loser to fence." I catch myself quickly. "Stephen, I mean. He's very eccentric. He's never been one of those normal guys on the football or baseball team. When we were like ten or something, he did ballet with me, Carol and my sister."

"Do you think he could've harmed Chris? I don't know if I need to ask that considering he did ballet, but even so?"

"Well, like I said, he's a little odd, so I don't hang out with him too often. I think he could do something, but I wouldn't be certain one way or another. Maybe you should talk to the detective about it?"

"Yeah, I have to go in for an interview tomorrow morning. Can you believe they told me I could bring counsel? What the fuck would I have to hide? He's my brother," he says indignantly. "They usually ask the people closest to the missing person first, to eliminate them from the suspect list. I wouldn't be too worried about it. I doubt they think you're involved," I soothe.

"If you want, I can ask Daddy for a lawyer."

"Nah, I don't think I'll bring one. I just want to know what happened to my brother."

He'll find out soon enough. The scrub that I dumped his headless, mutilated body into is often frequented by overzealous hikers on Saturday mornings. I'd give it about three days to hit the newspapers and televisions. I wonder if they'll go into gory detail or spare the public. Sensationalism sells, but disembowelment may be a little much for the weekend news.

"Wait a couple of days before you panic." I stroke his back. "We don't know anything yet. It's not right to make assumptions that hurt us." I'm hoping he'll stay long enough to watch the breaking story with us over breakfast. It was one thing watching Mother react to Carol's death, but it's quite another when it's your own flesh and blood. The theodicy would've been spectacular in Carol's conservative Catholic family, but I missed it. Considering I'm one of the very few people he knows in Seattle, and that my house probably looks like the Taj Mahal to someone from Ellensburg, I think it's likely he'll stick around.

"I don't understand why this happened. He never had any enemies. Who'd want to harm him?"

I think this line of reasoning is worn and pathetic. How is it that every person who goes missing or dies is suddenly a wonderful, flawless person who was well-liked by all the people they encountered while alive? Surely, while they were in good health, they would've been criticized for their actions, but they gain martyr status the minute their heart stops beating. I would love to see someone on TV or a newspaper saying that the person who died or disappeared was a fuckwit whom everybody hated. I could respect that kind of statement. Most of the males I've targeted were especially vile in several ways. They were arrogant, pretentious, misogynistic, and entitled, but all I hear about them is praise. The great things they did for the community (nothing), their positive attitude toward life (non-existent), and their devotion to their families (also absent). The glorification of murder victims in the media is truly pitiful. Posthumously they're angels of the highest order, apparently. I suppose it has its upsides. When I'm dead, perhaps people will forget the things I've done, like the police when my father pulled a few strings. I'd love to die in an exciting situation. I've done all these boys a favor. They weren't just old people who'd fall into death during slumber. They were part of a game, part of a mission. That's how I'd want to go.

"I imagine if he was anything like you, he would've been a truly delightful guy," I say. I hold him against my chest, running my fingers through his freshly washed hair. "They'll find him."

"They probably will, but dead or alive?"

"All we can do now is keep you in good company and pray." It's a giant struggle not to laugh. I love imitating religious zealots. If there really was a god, he'd have swooped in and stopped me before I slit the throat of a rather religious Christian boy that I found a couple of months ago. I gave him an hour to pray to his Saviour. His father is a reverend, and his mother does what she can around the church because she firmly believes that women only exist to serve men and can't or shouldn't try to lead or have initiative and drive. I wonder where Yahweh was on that day because he sure wasn't in my cottage. "I have a good feeling that he's alive."

"Do you think I should talk to Stephen myself?" he asks helplessly.

It would be quite beneficial to have a public confrontation between the two of them. Stephen is generally a coward, but when he's cornered, he acts quickly, violently. If he strikes Charles, the chances of him having assaulted or killed Chris increase exponentially. There's already a strong shadow of doubt over our good pal Stephen. I just hope he doesn't cause any marks on Charles's face.

"If that might make you feel better, you definitely should go and talk to him. He's a little unreliable and lies frequently. If you intimidate him, however, physically I mean, he probably will break down and tell you. I'd recommend getting to him as soon as you can and preferably not when Hunter is around."

"He's not violent, is he? Well, even if he is, I should probably confront him."

"Oh no, he's very timid, not violent at all," I reassure. "If you have trouble telephone the police in King County."

"Is he around today?"

"Yeah, he's always around here. I'll show you where he'll be, and then I have to head over to the hospital for clinical rounds. I would invite you, but I doubt you want to sit in a hospital for four hours when someone you know isn't even sick," I say. "Look, I can't deal with Stephen now, especially not after the whole Carol situation, but I'll point him out. It's a little unsettling that he knows all the people who've gone missing. I don't want to think that way. He is one of my dearest friends, but I can't help it."

"It must be such a difficult situation for you and your friends." He's sympathetic.

"It is. I don't know what to do anymore." I slide my hand into the pocket of my slacks, using the engraved silver band I ripped off Chris's limp finger as a thumb stone.

CHAPTER TWELVE

My favorite keepsakes are the skulls. I display them proudly in the little cottage, the only decorations I need.

However, I'm not always able to go there, sometimes it's just out of the question, so I keep smaller souvenirs at home. They sit in the walk-in closet, in a locked drawer I'd otherwise designate as my jewelry storage. I have rings from several of the boys, settling for a bangle from the one Sikh boy I killed last year. I have other small items, too, often strips of clothing, locks of hair, and personal affectations such as glasses. It's my prized treasure chest. I keep Polaroids of each victim in varying states of decomposition, and some that were taken moments before the murders, catching the sheer, animalistic fear in their eyes. In between kills, I enjoy nothing more than to reminisce while looking at the pictures.

When I return home from clinical rounds, my mother tells me Charles left earlier but will return for dinner. I go upstairs and see my father in my room.

"Daddy, what're you doing?" I ask, tired and confused. "I didn't know you were still in Seattle."

"Are you on something at the moment?" he asks emotionlessly. "Are you high?"

"No, of course not, I was in the hospital for god's sake. They do surprise urine checks. You can go find that out for yourself," I respond, more defensive than I ought to be. "I'd get kicked out of the medical program."

"Then what's wrong with you?" he asks.

"Excuse me?"

"You've gotten Millie involved in your business. You have goddamn Polaroids in your drawer. Have you lost your mind?"

"Why are you going through my things?"

"This is my house, Maris."

"What do you want me to say, Daddy? I don't have an explanation for you," I say matter-of-factly.

"Let's go step by step, then," he says. His voice is calm, but the expression on his face frightens me. "When did you start again?"

"I don't know, maybe a year ago?" "Be honest with me, Maris."

"I started when you bought me the cottage. I wanted the cottage to be able to do this without involving you guys."

"Are you telling me the sessions with the psychiatrist aren't helping at all?" He sits on the sofa opposite the four-post bed.

"They've never done anything. I don't have control over it. I tell the shrink what he wants to hear. I don't know what else to do. I told you that it was a waste of money, but you decided to listen to the delusional, hysterical harpy downstairs," I say coldly. "You could've saved that solid 10K."

"She thought it would help you, and from what we'd been hearing, it seemed to have good results."

"Of course it would, Daddy. That's generally what happens when you tell people exactly what they want to hear. I wasn't going to go to that social climbing loser and tell him about how much I enjoy killing. He wants to see me as a victim, and I let him. I'm the girl who was raped by her boyfriend and abused physically by her mother. You know that he has a moral and legal duty to report to the police if a person intends to harm themselves or someone else, right? I'd be locked up right now."

"What are you talking about? When were you raped?"

"Hunter raped me when I was thirteen. It's fine, honestly, I don't give a shit about that, but I can be the raped girl the shrink wants to see. I can be the one who's persecuted by her abusive mother. I don't need to be the one who talks about homicidal tendencies—why would I give myself up?"

"Why the hell wouldn't you tell me what happened?" He's furious.

"I told mother. She told me to not mention it to anyone else because it's embarrassing and because no one would believe it. Hunter comes from a great family. How can he be a rapist? I would just be considered a liar." I don't bother with fake tears. He's never believed them, and he won't now.

"Well, it wouldn't be the first time Quinn had a lapse in judgment. I think we both know I didn't marry her for her intelligence." His face pales despite himself. He always tries to keep up the façade, and he's much better than me at it. He's had two decades more experience than me, but I can see he's on the verge of tears. I don't think anyone likes to realize their little girl has been raped, especially not by the boy you've devoted so much energy and resources to.

"Do you need a moment?" I ask formally. "Or can I continue?"

He covers his face with his hands for a few moments. When his hands drop, his eyes are strained and red. "Go on."

"I tried to control it. I killed animals, like you suggested, to alleviate tension. It stopped working, and too many neighborhood pets had disappeared. I asked you for the cottage so that no evidence could be traced back here, and so that I would have a little freedom with it all. You were the one who told me morality was nothing but a man-made cage, Daddy." My legs ache, and I take a seat on the bed. "I involved Millie because I'm not strong enough to always do everything by myself. She needed something to do anyway. She's a lazy good-for-nothing."

"You understand that she's as hysterical as her mother, right?" This is something he's repeated endlessly for the last twenty years.

"Unfortunately, I am aware."

"Did you kill Carol? I'm reminding you to be honest here because I can't fix things if I don't know what's happened."

"I don't kill women. I know who probably killed her, though. He did approach me, about an hour before she disappeared. He asked me to help him unload his sailboat, but when we got to the car park, he told me it was back in Issaquah. I knew something was off about him, so I didn't go."

"Well, I'm glad you used your brain properly for once. Quinn is getting too sloppy with you girls. Why didn't you tell us about him?"

"What would you have been able to do?" I snap. "What do you guys ever do? Are you planning to send me to another crappy shrink?"

"All I have ever done is to try to protect you, Maris, but you're making it very difficult for me. There're only so many strings I can pull, and you're digging yourself a grave."

"Dad, firstly, you weren't in the country—I would've had to speak to your wife who would've immediately phoned the police. Secondly, why would I want to get this guy caught? It's his presence that's casting doubt on mine, I wouldn't want to fuck that up, and that's all mother would've done. Thirdly, I'd rather spare Carol's life than mine, I'm sure you'd understand."

"I thought you'd solved this problem when you were younger. You told me you were doing fine and that you didn't have the urges anymore."

"Well, I guess they came back," I say caustically.

"Don't fucking take that tone with me, or I'll phone the police myself."

"No, you won't. You care too much about your own reputation." "How many have you killed, Maris?"

"I don't know, maybe thirty or thirty-five? After a while it gets hard to keep count."

"And, apparently, after a while you forget how to clean your own mess. Really, Maris, you keep Polaroids? Do you have some strange desire to go to jail? I just don't understand." He shakes his head. "Look how easy it was for me to find them. How long do you think the police would take?"

"The police haven't been even remotely on my trail, Daddy. They think it's a queer trying to fulfill a fantasy. They would never suspect a woman, much less a woman like me," I say, calmly this time. He's not someone I can afford to piss off. "But tell me, please, why were you going through my things?"

"Your sister let me know about your little stash. I suspected that you may have been involved in the killings, but she confirmed it and led me to this treasure trove. She told me you were forcing her to help you. That, if anything, was your biggest mistake— apart from this collection, of course."

"She's a fucking little bitch. I do so much for her, and she can't keep her mouth shut? She's lucky I don't crack her skull open," I scream. I'm losing control and the room spins.

"I've told you since you were tiny that your mother and your sister are not cut out for this type of lifestyle. You and I are a different breed, a higher one, and we can only be pulled down if they're involved. I know about your problem, and I want to help you, Maris, but you've got to help me. We're a very public family. We can't handle any more scandals. You know that."

I fight against myself. I want to go into her room and shatter all her crystal lamps and cut holes into her designer dresses. "Well, I know now that she's a snake."

"I told you many times to talk to me when you're having trouble, not to involve your sister. She came to me in a panic, crying like a child. She's terrified of you, of what you'd do to her if she didn't listen to you. And on a side note, I don't want you using uncouth, unladylike language."

"What does she think I'll do to her? She's my sister."

He rubs his temples. "Maris, you're missing the point. I need you to tell me everything, and I need you to tell your sister nothing."

"I don't feel anything, Daddy. I'm nothing, I feel nothing. This is the only thing that lets me experience something human. I keep the Polaroids to remind myself that I've been able to achieve something," I say, trying not to cry. At this point, I'm not sure if he can tell if I'm being honest or not. For the most part, it's true.

"You've achieved a lot, Maris. You've been in magazines. You were Miss Washington. You have a 4.0 grade average in medical school. You've done surprisingly well in the half marathons you've been in. You were the homecoming queen and valedictorian. Why do you need this?"

"I told you, I feel nothing. I was playing different characters. When I hurt these males—now let me assure you, they are not the wonderful boys the media makes them out to be—I feel a rush. I feel better."

"While I find this utterly abhorrent, I understand it's always been in your psyche. I did accept it when I started to assume what was happening. I need you to be careful. I know you have no regard for anyone other than yourself, and I think that can be a good trait overall—it'll get you further in life, but I know that if you act poorly, it'll reflect on our family name, and we can't have that. What do I need to clean up?"

"I started two years ago, in 1972, early in the year when it was still snowing. I found this boy at college. My double majors were in Chinese and Psychology back then, remember? He was in my Chinese lectures, and he was always sitting next to me, no matter how many other seats were available. It was a rookie move, I mean lots of people had seen us sitting together, talking, and I knew Stephen occasionally went jogging in a group with him. I lured him into the cottage, I drugged him after sex and then strangled him to death while he was out cold. He didn't fight back, and I wasn't at all satisfied, so I thought I needed to keep doing it until I was. I mean, I panicked a little after it was done, but since I'd done it before, it wasn't that much of a shock. I knew what to expect, but I guess it still fell short."

"What did you do with the body?" The tension is increasing. "I kept it there for a while, I guess. Millie came to help with the cleanup and when she went home, I dismembered it and severed the head. You know Millie is no good with blood, so I spared her that," I say. "I gave it a gap after the first one—I wanted to avoid it as best I could, to quell that part of me. I don't want to be some sicko. I couldn't, though, and I caved a month later. That's when I started bringing Millie along because it was easier. She vomited and cried a lot, but you know that Millie will do pretty much anything I tell her to."

"There's the issue, Maris. Well, one of the issues. Telling Millie or involving her in the crimes is not a good idea—she doesn't have the stomach for it, and she will buckle under pressure. I hear you've been blackmailing her too. She told me that you'd said you would let the police know about her involvement should she turn you in. She's very weak and untrustworthy when it comes to these things. Plus, she knows about your little stash. You might as well go announce your crimes on the fucking news for Christ's sake."

I'm silent for a little while, taken aback by his language and the rage in his voice. It's not often that I feel fear, but it's now coursing through me. I try to placate him. "Daddy, look, I'm really sorry. I didn't want to get you involved in this addiction."

"I need you to stop, Maris. I need you to get rid of all this evidence, neatly and permanently. I'm not asking you: I'm telling you. Even if I were a multibillionaire, I wouldn't be able to get you out of this. Is there any other stash that I don't know about?" "No, Daddy, honestly, there is nothing else." I evade divulging the information about the collection of skulls. "I would tell you." "You're going to tell Millie that you've stopped, and you have no intention of repeating your behavior. You're going to get rid of this evidence and let her know of that too."

"I have a plan, and if none of this evidence gets out, I promise you that you'll have no reason to worry. Everything I've done will get traced back to Stephen. He knew every victim, and he'll have an alibi for none of the murders. I made sure to attack when I knew he'd be alone, and for other times he hung out with me, so I can sell him out easily. I'm not an idiot. I'm your daughter, remember? I'm just like you. All I've ever wanted is to be like you."

A woeful smile appears. "You have."

I confront Millie when Father leaves for his flight to Aspen. She's in the home library, hidden on a chesterfield among the sea of mahogany wood and first edition novels. She's curled up with an anthology of short stories by J.D. Salinger, who she only came to appreciate after I led her to his work. She's wearing one of my plaid miniskirts and a sleeveless mustard-yellow turtleneck that belongs in a trash-can somewhere in Idaho. I perch on the edge of the seat, and she looks up at me, her face hiding the guilt.

"Can I ask why you've told Father everything?"

"I'm really sorry, Maris. I didn't know what else to do. The police were asking questions and the only person I could think of was Dad."

"What are you talking about?"

"The police were asking me if I knew anything. They wanted to talk to you, but you weren't here."

I feel my pulse quicken. "What was it regarding?"

"Him, the stupid college guy we picked up a couple of weeks ago. Apparently, he was friends with Stephen, and the cops were sniffing around."

I can't tell if she's being honest or making a cruel joke to scare me. Millie is not quite as innocent as she lets on. She makes me out to be the manipulative bitch in the family, and while I'll accept that she is less so than me, it doesn't negate her own behavior. She often has a penchant for emotional carnage. Her academic record may not be fantastic, but she's got a quick wit and is disturbingly cunning. She always plays second fiddle to me, but I think that's due to her lack of assertiveness—she is very much of the passive-aggressive persuasion. "You're kidding, right?"

"Why would I be kidding?" She turns to look at me. "They wanted to search the house. I told them they couldn't, and they should contact Dad, and I filled him in. They thought I was you." I keep a grip on the emotions that threaten to rupture. "Did they say why they wanted to search our house and not Stephen's?"

She starts laughing when she speaks. "Got you, bitch. Don't worry, we're good for now."

"I'm going to break your fucking neck if you try that again," I tell her, my body trembling with rage.

"I was upset when you took my car out for a joyride," she says, shrugging.

"You decide to tell Dad this because of your dented-up shit mobile? God, you are miserable. You should've done a better job when you tried to slit your wrists in January. Anyone with half a brain would've known to cut along the radial artery, not across it. Do you want me to show you? Maybe this time you'll do more than waste a tub full of hot water."

Tears begin to pool in her eyes. "You're sick, you know that? I wish the police had come around. If anyone deserves to be in jail, it's you."

I can't breathe, I can't see. I lose control of myself and smack her forcefully across the face. I knock her to the floor and put her in a chokehold while she grabs my hair. I knee her repeatedly in the stomach and hit her head against the burgundy floor several times. "I'll kill you. I'll break every fucking bone in your body, you worthless pile of trash!" I shove my elbow into her neck to bar her clawing at me with her long fingernails.

"I'm sorry, I'm sorry, Maris," she cries. Blood starts trickling from the head wound.

I take a deep breath and stand up, showing her mercy she doesn't deserve. "If you try that again, I will kill you."

"I think I need to go to a hospital," she says, wailing. "You're out of your mind if you think I'm going to be doing anything to help you. You can lie here and figure out why you're such a cunt. Oh, and if you go to Mommy or Daddy or the police, just remember how much of you they'll find at the crime scenes." "I'm not going to tell anyone, I swear, Maris. Please don't be angry," she begs. She strains to sit up, dragging herself up by grabbing the arm of the sofa. Her lip is bruised and bleeding. "What did you tell Dad? Tell me, or I'll render those thousand-dollar braces useless."

"He already knew everything—he said I shouldn't bother acting like I know you more than he does. I told him where you keep those little mementos."

"Which you wouldn't know about if you didn't try to swipe my coke stash, right?" I stare coldly at her. "I didn't tell you a damn thing; you're just a dirty sneak. You knew when I'd be away and acted then, yet you pretend I'm the only manipulative person around here."

She starts getting fidgety like she always does under emotional pressure. While my psychiatric sessions aim to control my urges, hers are due to major depressive disorder and panic attacks, with a little bit of PTSD thrown in. She has a different psychiatrist, and my mother tends to argue that her conditions are solely due to my influence on her. She's attempted suicide about four times. It's terribly embarrassing.

"I don't know how many times I can say sorry, Maris. You can keep hitting me if that makes you feel any better."

"No, I don't want to bruise my hands. I have company tonight," I say.

"Yeah, Hunter told me he was coming over for dinner."
"Who invited Hunter over? I was talking about Charles." I don't recall offering him a meal at the house, and I certainly don't think it'll be beneficial to have him around Charles, though I suppose he's loo-loo enough to pass for gay.

"Mother invited him. She wanted to have a family dinner. I don't know. I don't know what the fuck that woman wants anymore. Dad isn't even going to be around."

"Isn't she still worried about Daddy fucking some broad in Colorado?"

"I don't know why she would be. She knows he will," she says. "Floozies have always been his hobby."

"Do you want to get blottoed before dinner?" I can't stop picturing Father's perfectly stocked liquor cabinet. All of his alcohol is of such a high quality that when I was drinking at parties, I was repulsed by the vile taste of their cheap drinks and nearly stopped. He has the finest wines, aged scotch, and several hundred-dollar bottles of cognac and brandy. "We'll clean you up a bit, too, so you can look presentable."

"Brandy please."

"Jesus, Millie, this isn't 1940. Have some merlot like a normal person."

"Ooh yes, Maris, I'd much rather be some housewife with a stick up her ass drinking wine until she forgets how many women her husband is cheating on her with."

I start laughing, I can't help it. I've helped her develop a solid sense of humor. "I'll drink to that," I say, pouring our drinks liberally. "I wonder if Daddy's whores have spread venereal diseases to Mother. It would explain her anger issues."

"Doesn't he go to those high-class ones?"

"Even the highest-class whores get chlamydia at least a couple of times." I roll my eyes. "And he tells me that I'm reckless."

Millie and I are both lightweights as, I imagine, is expected for two slender females. I need two glasses of wine to get drunk or a shot or two of spirits. Martinis generally work a little slower because the gin-soaked olives put a little food in my stomach, slowing down the intoxication process. I'm blitzed by the time the first doorbell rings. I've raided Millie's closet, so I don't have to wear the abominable outfit I turned up to class in. I smooth my hair down, parting it in the middle, and put on what my mother calls "whore crimson"—a bright red lipstick that contrasts the aquamarine of my irises. Millie is dressed more casually at my request. I don't particularly like being upstaged. She's wearing a Marcia Brady inspired gradient turtleneck and faded jeans, while I'm in a very flattering evening playsuit with the right amount of casual to justify wearing it in my home.

"Oh no, Mill, you can't wear red lipstick. That's my look

tonight," I say when she reaches for it, slapping her hand away. I dab concealer onto her bruises as best I can and send her down to greet Hunter or Charles—whoever's managed to show up first. They'll see Millie, and she's quite a vision, and then they'll see me, like her but prettier and taller (I forced her to wear flats), and slimmer. She's the entrée, and I'm the main course, as always. I put on a pair of six-inch platforms and take my time to get downstairs, stumbling a little despite my best efforts.

I'm disappointed when I see it's just Hunter. "Hello, sweetheart," I say, giving him a brief peck on the lips. He lingers, his hand on the small of my back. I can feel Mother's gaze boring holes through my spine. I untangle myself. "It's so good to have you here right now."

"You look lovely tonight, Maris," he tells me. He leans in a little closer, whispering directly in my ear. "Where's Millie?"

"Well, you know how clumsy she can be. Remember in homeroom when she'd fall off the stool without fail every morning?"

He bursts into laughter. "Oh my god, that was far out. Every fucking morning."

"Hunter, would you like a drink? Renata's been quite rude not offering you anything," says Mother, appearing beside me.

"That would be great, Mrs. C, whatever you're having. Thank you for having me over."

"It's always our pleasure, dear. Maris, take his coat."

"Give me your coat, sir," I say sarcastically, reaching for his thin cotton jacket.

"I could get used to you calling me that." He grins.

"I wouldn't do that if I were you." I hang up the coat in the closet, watching the door in anticipation.

"Why didn't you turn up at Dante's? I half-believed you'd disappeared too."

"Trust me, I'm not about to disappear. I'd totally forgotten I had clinical rounds. I only got home, like, twenty minutes ago. I didn't even know you were going to be here."

He glances at the dinner table. "Why is the table set for five? Isn't your dad in Aspen?"

"My friend Charles is dropping by. His brother was the one who went missing. I didn't want him to have to suffer alone, you know. We can relate. We lost Carol."

"What friend? I've never met a Charles, Maris," he tells me. "Is it mandatory for you to know all my friends in order to validate their existence?"

"Well, there's no need to be so catty about it. Isn't a guy allowed to get angry when his girl is inviting a random dude to her house for dinner?"

"Hunter, give it a rest and sit down," I say evenly, trying not to screw an ice pick into the side of his head. "Stop calling me your girl."

He doesn't answer, instead, finding his seat at the table beside Millie. If anyone's going to put up with his shit, it's her. I stand by the door and shoo the maid away, feeling a jolt when the bell finally rings. Charles's lower middle-class lineage is far from visible in his crisp Ralph Lauren shirt and chinos. It's the unofficial uniform of the wealthier boys around here. Eyes still bloodshot from the tears, he falls into my waiting arms, holding me close to him. Everyone in the room stares at him before their manners and breeding kick in. Mother is far from prudish, but I can't recall a similar reaction on her part for any other man—excluding, of course, Clint Eastwood. Charles becomes discernibly uncomfortable when even Hunter stares.

"Come on, let's get you something to eat, you must be starving," I say as I lead him into the formal dining room.

"Yeah, I haven't had a thing to eat all day. Thank you so much for having me over."

"Oh honey, don't be silly. You're always welcome." I smile. "Charles, meet Millie, my sister, and Hunter. I think you've met my mother."

"Have a seat, dear," says Mother. "I'm so sorry to hear about your brother."

"Thank you, Mrs. Caldwell, I appreciate it." He sits beside me, and I put my hand on his knee under the table, drunkenly caressing. "This food looks wonderful."

"I'm glad you appreciate it. I slave away all day, and my girls barely bother to even pick at it," she lies. The only time she steps foot in the kitchen is in the morning to drink her ridiculous African tea. She makes his plate, doling out generous amounts of truffle oil-infused mashed potatoes and grilled Moroccan lamb chops that she most certainly did not prepare.

"So, do you go to UW?" asks Hunter, barely concealing his hostility toward Charles. Maybe he finally realizes he has some competition, however poor and insignificant as he had first imagined.

"Central Washington State in Ellensburg," says Charles. "How do you even know Maris, then?"

"We met at the hotel, Hunter. Why don't you have some more wine?" I pour more merlot for him before he responds. "There are more pressing issues currently."

"Did you watch the evening news?" asks Charles. His eyes begin to well with tears.

"No, I was doing clinical rounds. What happened?"

"Oh my lord, I did see the news," says Millie, pale. "You don't think it's possible, do you?"

"What are you guys talking about?" asks Mother.

"They found a body, and they think it's him. They don't know right now, and the sick bastard decapitated him, so they can't use dental records."

I'd hoped to be with him when the news came out, but

his reaction currently is more than sufficient. "What about fingerprints?"

"He cut off his fingers and toes."

"That is disgusting. How foul can this animal be?" says Hunter, dropping his fork. "No, 'animal' is too nice a word."

"I remember when Stephen was talking about amputating fingers to delay identification, he learned about it in his forensic psych subject. This guy has clearly been listening in," says Millie without prompting.

"Does Chris have any distinguishing features like scars or anything?" I ask.

"He has a scar on his leg from a bike injury, but they won't let me see the body yet. They're still processing everything." He looks up at Millie. "Stephen Winthrop?"

"Yeah, the redheaded guy, do you know him?"

"I'm wishing none of us knew him. The police mentioned him a couple of times," I say.

"Hey, Stephen is a good guy. I've known him for years. I don't know why everyone keeps talking about him," says Hunter indignantly.

"Because he's the only one that can be linked back to all the victims, Hunter," I say.

"That's conjecture," he tells me.

"I'm surprised you even know a word that big," I say. "Now's not the time to be defending your good old pal. People are dead."

"He's your friend too, Maris. You know he has nothing at all to do with this."

"I don't know that and neither do you, Hunter. You went to scout meetings together. You didn't share every thought," I snap.

"Maris, honey," says Mother tersely, giving me a look that only Millie and I understand as a threat.

"Of course, it was very insensitive of me. I apologize. It's best to not speculate, innocent until proven guilty, am I right, Hunter?" I speak calmly, making him appear uncouth.

"Yes, absolutely. I don't think it should even be brought up when we know this Ted lunatic is running around killing people. Who's to say he isn't the one behind all this?"

"You can bury your head in the sand all you want, Hunter." says Millie, "His process is completely different, but I'm sure you'd know that, doing forensic psychology and all...Oh, wait, you don't actually do any of that do you?" She pushes a portion of lamb around her plate.

"I think, perhaps, you've had a little too much to drink, Millicent," says Mother, face flushed with anger.

"No, Mom, I don't think I've had enough to drink. I need to be tanked to deal with your bullshit. Charles's brother and Carol are dead, but let's focus on Hunter's feelings."

"You know that's not it, Millie. He's our friend," says Hunter, this time more emotional.

"What I know is that Stephen's middle name is Theodore," she replies. "But I'll let you deal with your cognitive dissonance on your own."

I safely show Charles to the better guestroom, only three doors down from me along the hallway. Since we don't often have guests staying in our house, the floor is pretty much mine, affording me privacy on the occasions my mother doesn't decide to stick her head in and interfere in my business. Hunter's still throwing a snit, moody from the direct attack. Millie, however, was the aggressor, and this makes me look angelic in comparison. I'm too tired to deal with his tantrums, but I need my satiation for tonight. If I don't have sex, I'm left with too much pent-up energy and boredom, and that does no good for anybody, particularly those around me. I don't want to seem too crabby in front of Charles. I've almost perfected the sympathetic façade. It's a shame Charles wouldn't be able to perform as I'd much rather be with him. I don't really understand it. I mean, if Millie had died, I'd be upset. But it would have no effect on my activities. It's taken me some time to realize others aren't quite the same. Millie is very much like them. When our first cat (uniquely named Fluffy) "disappeared," Millie was depressed for weeks, crying at least several times a day until Father became fed up and bought her another one. I didn't tell her that I'd been the one who drowned the ragdoll at Lake Sam.

I do the usual stuff that gets Hunter hot. He resists initially out of his indignant solidarity, but his body caves when his mind does not. He undresses me without passion, and the fucking is no more personable than the term. I don't suppose I've ever "made love" or any of that gooey, disgusting stuff, but I've definitely experienced some more ardent (even with Hunter) or at least wanton liaisons. Hate sex does a lot for me on some occasions. I make sure I get mine and then push him off—not too aggressively, of course. I can't listen to his voice any longer; it's making my ears bleed. The last thing I need is to start an argument. When he pulls me close to him, the quilt tucked around our tangled limbs, I turn away from him.

"What, you don't even want to cuddle anymore, Maris? I remember when you never wanted to stop." He says it like he's been mortally wounded.

"I need some sleep, Hunter. It's going to be a big day tomorrow, you know that. I can't be looking awful in the newspaper."

"How am I preventing you from sleeping?"

"I don't need an interrogation. Just go home," I snap. "I've always hated having you sleep over here. I can't get to sleep with you laying on me or snoring. Do you know how much

Xanax I've had to take over the years because of you? Just fucking go home."

His face is flushed, and it'd be funny if I weren't trying to get to bed. "What's wrong with you today? Are you on the rag or something?"

"Look, sweetheart, from our relationship, I do understand that you're not at all familiar or confident with female anatomy, but menstruation is generally difficult to miss. Don't read into something that doesn't have meaning. I want to get some damn sleep."

"Why are you so angry with me? What did I do?"

"Are you fucking deaf? I just told you what's wrong. Several times. I need to get some sleep, and you know I can't sleep with someone in the bed. If you cared enough to listen, like a good boyfriend, you would've left by now," I tell him coldly, turning to face him. "Do you want me to explain it to you the way they taught us the alphabet in pre-K?"

"You're insane lately. First, you go ahead and blame Stephen for Carol and however many others' deaths in front of some fucking stranger from the middle of nowhere, and then you come up here and convince me to have sex and throw a hissy fit. He's our friend. I'm your boyfriend. I don't understand why you're behaving like this. It's embarrassing, to be frank, the way you're acting with that dude around. He's basically homeless."

"Hunter, if you don't get up right now and leave, I'm going to phone the police," I say. I'm very matter-of-fact about it, but I feel the rage bubbling in my chest. A wave of disgust and nausea washes over me as I meet his eyes, and I want nothing more than to claw at his face with a screwdriver.

He laughs. "You'd never call the police."

"Why don't you test that theory, and I'll count to five. They're on the lookout for a young, white male approximately six feet, attacking young women with long, dark hair parted in the center. I'm sure they'd appreciate the tip." I smile. "One..."

"Fuck, alright, I'm going. Call me when you're done being a nasty bitch, okay? I can't deal with this." He scrambles to his feet, searching unseeingly for his clothes.

"You're going to be my date, obviously. Don't look like shit, alright?" I ball up his shirt and hurl it at him. "I'll be wearing purple. Wear that little purple bow tie number you have. It's hideous, but we need to match."

"Yeah, yeah, alright, stop being a bitch," he says, hopping around as he pulls his pants up his legs.

"Just go and close the door behind you, I'm not getting up." "Don't screw the homeless dude." He laughs.

"He's from Ellensburg. That doesn't make him homeless," I tell him. "You're an uncultured swine."

"Coming from the chick who thinks anyone from south of Seattle is Mexican and can be deported."

"Get out of here, Hunter," I say.

He grins at me, buttoning his shirt. "Even if you do screw him, I still had you first. You'll never get that cherry back."

"I can't believe you still call it that. What are you, a twelve-year-old girl? No, wait. You're the guy that rapes them. Silly me."

"Who are you kidding? You know you wanted it," he tells me huffily. "Prancing around in those little skirts."

I think he can see my distress, the rage building. He knows the manner in which it can result. I stare at him, trying to control myself—mental images of a hot iron in my hand, ready to scald him should he linger.

I'm leaving, don't worry."

He finally leaves, and I toss uncomfortably in bed. I know it's improbable that I'll be getting any sleep tonight and that fuels my restlessness. I debate the idea in my mind, but it doesn't take much time for me to come to a decision. I find myself walking to Charles's bed for the night. I knock gently on the door, peeking in through the tiny crack. He wakes with little hesitation.

"Maris, is everything alright?" he asks, looking concerned. "I didn't mean to bother you. If you're sleeping, I can go away." "I couldn't sleep anyway, to be honest," he tells me. "Come in, please."

I enter his room with as little sound as possible—I don't need Mother's bat ears and condemnatory voice. It'd be hypocritical. I'm sure she wouldn't waste any time if he showed the same interest in her. I can't imagine many women resisting. I perch at the foot of the bed. "It's hard sleeping with all this going on." "I can't find a way to get to sleep. I see him asking for me, and I'm not there."

"There's nothing you could've done," I reassure him, neglecting the fact that had he not been in my bed while his brother bled out and dehydrated in my cottage, or had Charles not drawn me to him at all, the boy would still very much be alive. I wouldn't be able to describe the thrill.

"Get in, it's cold," he says. He lifts up the edge of the quilt. "Is it always this cold in here? Our air-conditioner at home barely even runs at all anymore."

"My parents should probably come to terms with the fact that we don't need a freezer to keep cool. This is Seattle; nature does that for us at no cost." I climb into the sheets with him. My body buzzes when his arm brushes mine. It's the kind of giddiness I'd expected in middle school, only to be disappointed. I made up stories about my magical hookups with Hunter when the other girls fawned over their sloppy, truculent two-week boyfriends. The stars exploding in my body were about as realistic as the possibility of snow in Jamaica. I never felt tongue-tied like this.

"You have great parents, Maris. Your family is wonderful." He holds my hand in both of his.

"Only when they're not actually your family," I tell him. It comes out rueful. "I've seen Daddy more in the past few days than I have in the last year. Mother won't go away. I don't know which is worse."

"You look upset, I hate to see it." He reaches for my hand. His fingertips send currents of electricity through me. His eyes meet mine for a moment before he leans in to kiss me on the mouth. His lips are sweet and gentle, the sterility of the alcohol has evanesced any lingering trace of dinner. Something wells inside me, threatening to burst. I can't quite pinpoint it. I kiss him back, weaving my fingers through his. I hope he can't taste the bitterness of Hunter on me.

"I'm fine, I'm just fine." I think I mean it when I say it, surprised when a tear trickles down my cheek. I rush to wipe it away. "Honestly, I'm okay."

"You miss Carol, don't you?"

With that, expectation dwindles. I had built him up in my mind as a paragon of understanding, and it was silly. Why would this boy, as beautiful as he may be, happen to dramatically differ from the others? It was a fruitless hope to begin with, but I wanted to believe it. I wanted to believe maybe someone would decode me. A lousy pipedream indeed.

"Yeah, that's what it is," I say. I want to sob but I don't. I keep kissing him, down his neck and along his bare chest. I don't want him to speak anymore. He's surprised, but ready when I tug on the waistband of his boxers.

"Maris, you don't have to do this, you're upset."

"I know I don't have to do anything. Just lie back and enjoy, it'll keep our minds busy." I give him a hollow smile before I go down on him with enthusiasm I wouldn't usually fathom. The sole pleasure of another is not something I often set out to achieve, if ever, but the look on his face feels like a reward. I watch as he writhes, not in pain but in desire, another thing I wouldn't associate with a male and my happiness. His pretty eyes light up, his cheeks flush with color, and his grin is involuntary, showing teeth. His abdomen tightens under my palm, and I feel a strong, sudden twitch in his thigh.

"You're very good at that," he says finally, once his breath is no longer labored. "Incredible."

"Do you really think so?"

"I'd give up food for the rest of my life if I could get that once a day."

I laugh, surprising myself when the sound erupts from my chest. "If you play your cards right, I can be more generous than that. In the morning to wake you up and at night to help you sleep."

"You would be the most far-out girlfriend in the history of girlfriends," he tells me somberly. "Fuck, I sound like a twelve-year-old getting his first boner."

"Was that when you got your first boner?" I can't control my amusement.

"No, I think I was thirteen..." He pauses. "Actually, no, I do think it was when I was twelve."

"When did you lose your virginity?"

"Oh, this is embarrassing, really embarrassing. I was eighteen. I couldn't manage to lose it while I was still in high school. What about you?"

"I was...a lot younger than that, but it wasn't so much a choice per se."

"You don't mean rape, do you?" He looks alarmed. I find this endearing.

"No, I mean, I don't know. I wasn't as ready for it as I thought I was. It was all very quick. One minute I was watching a movie, the next I was bleeding."

"It sounds like the dude was a halfwit. Do you still speak to him?"

"It's Stephen." "That bastard."

"That's a kinder descriptor than I would've used." "If I can ask, why are you still friends with him?"

The trickle of tears turns into an unexpected, unwelcome flood. I'm bawling like a goddamn child. I feel my body shudder and become numb.

"I'm sorry, Maris, don't cry. What's wrong?"

"He took everything from me. He took everything, and I'm expected to be around him, smiling and happy. I can do it. I have done it. I've done it for years. Nobody would care enough to change a thing. I wasn't old enough. I didn't want it."

"Hey, come here," he says, holding me against his chest, his arms tight around my waist. "I care."

"Well, my parents don't. I told my mother, and she said I was lying, that I was an attention seeker. If I wanted attention it wouldn't be through something as humiliating as rape or whatever you want to call it."

"That's horrible. I can't believe she'd say that to you. Why would anybody lie about that?"

"I don't know, I never understood her reasoning. Looking at Stephen makes me feel sick. I think about the bloodstains on the bed."

"Trust me, he'll get his. I promise you, Maris, he will. He won't get away with all this."

"Please don't tell anyone what I've told you." "No, of course not. I won't say a thing."

"This is why I wouldn't put this recent stuff past him. Obviously, I can't announce it at the dinner table. Maybe he's escalated."

"The police won't do anything. We might have to do it ourselves," he tells me. The tone of his voice has changed, the undercurrent of malice is palpable.

"Honestly, I don't think it's time for vigilante justice yet. Hopefully, the pigs have an idea by now."

“They’re not going to do a thing. They’re clueless. We’d be doing them a favor,” he insists.

“Do you want a criminal record? I know Stephen. You’re not going to get a confession out of him.”

“I’m not interested in his confession. I want him to suffer.”

“He’s not worth it. He should rot in prison, not you.”

CHAPTER THIRTEEN

It's not a very long drive to Stephen's house. At an easy cruising speed of twenty-five miles an hour, I reach his driveway within ten minutes and park behind his embarrassing Mustang. A boy who looks like Stephen doesn't belong in a Mustang. I reapply a coat of lip gloss and adjust my mid-thigh length plaid skirt before climbing out of the car. I can hear The Spinners blasting from his radio. I ring his doorbell, waiting with patience for several moments before he gets to the door.

He's surprised, but it's to be expected. I didn't give him forewarning. "Hey, Maris, I didn't know you were dropping by. What's up?" His hair is wet and slicked back, presumably from a recent shower. He's haphazardly dressed in a white crew-neck t-shirt and tropical patterned shorts. There's a little disdain but also some excitement in his facial expression.

"I wanted to see you. We haven't had much time to catch up lately." I smile at him. "Am I allowed in?"

He steps back. "Of course. I'm sorry for being rude. Come on in. Do you want me to hang up your purse?"

"No, that's alright. Are your parents at home?"

"I think my mom is out getting her hair and shit done for the benefit your folks are throwing tonight. I don't know where Dad is."

I appraise him, apart from his clown shorts, he doesn't look too bad. "And Susannah, is she here?"

He laughs. "Why, are you getting bored of Hunter?" "Is she here?"

"She's not. Can I get you something to drink or eat?"

I adjust my skirt again, this time so he can see the lace band of my thigh-high stockings. "I'm not hungry, don't worry. Can we talk?"

When he realizes that he's been looking for too long, his eyes meet mine again. "Sure, come on up to my room."

I follow him up the stairs. While Hunter's room is meticulously clean and structured, Stephen's is in utter disarray. Hunter's compulsive in his cleanliness and is germophobic to a disturbing degree, but Stephen's gone too far in the opposite direction. I sit on the edge of his unmade bed, wondering how long it's been since he's changed his grubby-looking sheets. With reluctance, I place my purse on the carpet. "I really have missed you, Stephen. We've had no time to speak, at least not in private. It's terrible."

"I've missed you, too, Maris. I've heard some stuff, though. I don't know if it's true, but I wanted to give you the benefit of the doubt since I've known you so long. I didn't want to believe it."

"What have you heard, Stephen?"

"Some of our friends," he coughs, choking on his words, "have told me that you'd told them it was me who hurt Carol and the other girls."

"I hope you don't believe that, Stephen," I say, feigning shock. "I could never do that. All I said was that you knew some of the people, not that you'd been the one who hurt them."

"I didn't want to believe it. It didn't seem like something you would do. That's not the Maris I know."

"Who said it?" I ask. "If it was Hunter, I think it may be because I was complimenting you. You know how jealous he gets sometimes."

"I shouldn't say."

"Oh, come on, Stephen, we're closer than that, aren't we?" I place my hand on his when he sits beside me on the bed.

He studies my face and a smile appears. "We are. Yeah, it was Hunter."

"I think he knows I've always been a little interested in you. It upsets him. Don't get me wrong—I love Hunter. He means very much to me. But I've admired you too."

"Are you playing me, Maris? Look at you, why would you be interested in me? You have a perfect boyfriend."

"It sounds like you have more feelings for him than I do. Is there something you're not telling me? Don't tell me you've gone fruity."

"No, of course not," he says, flustered. "He's my friend and Susannah is yours."

"I don't know, Stephen, it sounds like you and Hunter have a little something going on," I joke, grinning. I edge a little closer, wishing I'd worn a lower cut top.

"I don't believe you'd want me while you have someone like Hunter."

"Maybe you're better looking than Hunter. Maybe you're smarter or funnier than Hunter. There are so many reasons. You'd see them if you stopped hating on yourself. I can't believe you haven't noticed that I'm sweet on you. What did you think was happening when we had sex last time?"

"I thought you were just angry at Hunter, and no one else was around."

"There's always someone else around." I take off my gloves, placing them on the matching purse. I grab him by the waist and pull him to me, kissing him. He doesn't resist. I lean back. "Does that seem like something I'd do if I didn't like you?"

His cheeks are red. "No."

He leans in this time, pushing me down onto the bed. "You're sure Susannah isn't coming over?" I ask.

"I'm meeting her there."

"Perfect," I say, trying not to tremble when his fingers trace along my inner thigh, the most ticklish spot on my body. "I like having you to myself."

He undresses me with extra care, relishing each second of it, and leaves my stockings on.

"Do you like them?" I ask.

"You have no idea how much." I do. It's why I wore them.

He kisses almost every square inch of my body with such vigour that I believe Susannah has been starving him of sex for an incredibly long time. I show the same enthusiasm, straddling him. He may be misogynistic in public, but in private he loves a woman being in control. "You're so perfect," I tell him with a smile.

"You're fucking with my head, Maris."

"I wouldn't do that to you. You know that." "You never show it in public."

"Do you want Susannah to punch me or Hunter to dump me?" "Well, maybe the latter."

"Just enjoy the moment, Stephen, don't make things complicated." I lean down and chew gently on his earlobe. I'm grateful he doesn't like to take control; I would get no satisfaction. He doesn't quite understand female anatomy, and last time it felt like he was furiously trying to press an elevator button. I don't orgasm, but he does.

"I'm actually pretty thirsty now. You've worn me out," I say. "Do you think you could grab me a Coke?"

"Yeah, of course. I'll go get one," he says, pulling his shorts back on.

"Thanks, sweetheart."

The second he disappears through the door, I rush to my bag, putting my gloves on. I place several Polaroids and Chris's keychain under the mattress of his bed, tucking them in safely so they can't slip if there's a little motion on the bed. I place the rest of the Polaroids and the cracked hyoid bone of one of the boys in the hidden cupboard within his unused window seat. I'd made sure to wipe my prints off each item, and I'm glad he didn't question my weather-inappropriate gloves. I wasn't going to undo all the work I'd put in with a little sloppiness. I take my gloves off as fast as I can and hop back into the bed. He comes in with a little glass bottle of Coke and a straw.

"Oh Stephen, you're a darling," I say, taking a sip. "I was parched. This is too much fun."

"If you actually are interested in me, have you considered breaking it off with Hunter?"

"Honey, you know I can't do that. I want to, but my family won't be having any of it. They've been planning this merger for a long time."

"But you said you wanted to be with me."

"I do, you have to believe me. I do want to be with you. I'll think about it, okay? I'll think about what I can do," I say, attempting to subdue my irritation. I start getting dressed.

"You're going already?" He looks like he's on the verge of tears.

"I have to go get my hair done for tonight. Can't be looking terrible."

He nods but doesn't say anything.

"Oh, and Stephen, don't mention a thing to Hunter, alright?"

I'm at the hairdresser Mother raves about to anyone who'll listen. I was only expecting it to be Millie and me, but she's forced her way in and deeming herself the queen of the Dead Girl Ball. She won't allow us to have a more elaborate hairstyle than hers. The fruit doing her hair doesn't stop chattering away, his high-pitched voice echoing painfully in my skull. He has hair so blonde it could pass for white and jeans that look like they belong on a small female child. Mother's getting an updo, a dramatic bouffant reminiscent of Brigitte Bardot. They share the same hair color, but Mother's is natural. I get a center part and wispy, feathered waves. Millie's hair is mostly down and straight, beneath a crown braid. I tell her she looks horrible for her own good. She sobs in the middle of the salon.

"Listen, Millie, I'm trying to help. Surely you want to have a boyfriend. Or you're well on your way to becoming a spinster."

"Millicent, you're going to ruin your face for makeup," adds Mother.

"I like it, and I'm going to keep it." Millie wipes away a tear. I roll my eyes and lean back in the chair as the assistant works the curling iron. "I don't want any missed strands," I tell her sharply, "I'm going to be photographed all evening."

"Don't you worry, darling, Jessy will make sure everything's perfect," he tells me, pointing to a small Asian woman who by no means looks like a "Jessy."

"Wonderful, thank you so much." I offer him a polite smile and return to the month-old copy of Vogue I've been flipping through.

"Maris, have you prepared your speech?" Mother turns to look at me, causing the hairdresser to tut under his breath.

"No, Mommy, I plan to embarrass myself on stage in front of 500 of our nearest and dearest."

She ignores the jibe. "Did you say 'Mommy'? I don't think

I've heard that from you since you were seven." She appears genuinely delighted.

"Maybe that was the last time you remember it." "Well, don't throw a snit about it," she retorts.

The absurdity of her childish response makes me laugh. For once it isn't choked or forced. I almost feel bad for the string of bruises along her dainty collarbone. I wonder how much makeup it'll take to cover them. "Oh, I do love you, Mother."

The dresses we're to choose from are all Halston and rather pretty. Had we more time, Mother would have personalized gowns made for us, but the dead girls and boys are piling up far too quickly. I've had enough of the colour purple. Carol may have loved it, but it does nothing for me. I have a red gown, not bright enough to be gauche, with slits in all the right places and a deep v-neckline, a small bow cinching in my waist. Millie is in royal blue, Mother in cobalt. I don't tell her, but I hope to look like my mother when I hit her age. There's hardly a wrinkle in sight. The worst marks on her are the ones given by Father, not nature. We aren't allowed to touch the gowns until our makeup is on and settled, tested by the tip of Mother's index finger. A speck of wet foundation will cause another minute of delay.

"Alright Maris, go get dressed," she tells me once she's run her cold finger down the center of my face.

"Glad to."

I slip into the gown and a pair of Manolo Blahnik stilettos. They're far from comfortable, but they look incredible. I was a bit late to jump onto the Manolo bandwagon, but his designs are gaining my loyalty. We're chauffeured to the hotel where Father is waiting. I have no doubt that there's a blonde tramp stumbling out of one of the staff entrances around the back. One glance at Mother tells me that she assumes the same. Her jaw is stiff as Father lends his hand to her, helping her step out of the car. Large standees and placards line the entryway announcing the gala. We're to pose in front of them as a family, first. Father thinks it's imperative for the journalists to know that. I suppose hosting the benefit in and of itself is too subtle, how is everyone going to know the Caldwells donated? I hold back vomit and wait patiently for Hunter, almost blinded by the incessant flashes of cameras. I smile as I see him walking toward me, looking as pretty as any ornamental accessory could aspire to be. He uses the attention from the media as an excuse to pull me to him, planting a kiss on my cheek. I won't deny that his natural scent, mingled delicately with a slight amount of Ralph Lauren Polo cologne gives me a headrush. I glance up at him—he'd look wonderful with a cyanotic hue. His hand travels instinctually to the small of my back as he leads me inside.

"You don't still have that creep here, do you?" His voice is hushed but terse. He fidgets with his bow tie, one I imagine he had his mother put on for him. He's always been inept with ties. "I saw him skulking around the neighborhood."

"Hunter, are we getting a little jealous?"

"Dream on, I'm more embarrassed that my girlfriend is entertaining the idea and parading him around."

"No, it's jealousy." I grin. "Don't be a spaz."

I hold him against me for support as cameras continue to flash, craving a poignant image of the philanthropists' children mourning their friends. I try not to react when I see the cause walking toward us. I'm aware that the Seattle Crime Prevention Advisory Committee had been invited to our shindig, but I wasn't entirely sure Theodore himself would make an appearance. I give him no sign of recognition, and he responds in kind, but there is piercing eye contact as he passes me. I have a copy of his rape prevention guide in my pocketbook. The irony is quite amusing, but who better to advise how not to become prey than a predator? Hunter is unmoved by Ted's entry and why wouldn't he be. As far as he's aware, he's just another good-looking well-wisher. I feel my stomach knot. "let's get some champagne," I say, grabbing onto his arm.

"Yeah, I'm too sober for this," he agrees. He falls into step with me and flags down a greasy-haired Latino waiter. "Two flutes, muchacho."

Even I find his lack of a "please" semi-offensive, but I'm glad to get some alcohol in my system. It both soothes and livens. "How are the others holding up?" I'm burning to remark on his snitching to Stephen. It's infuriating. "Are they doing any better?" "I haven't talked to anyone much," he says, as furtive as expected. "Jack is alright. He phoned a couple of times to shoot the breeze."

"What about Stephen?" I press.

"You're obsessed with Stephen, aren't you? Are you sweet on him?"

"Oh yes, you caught me, Hunter, I'm sweet on the guy whose freckles connect into a blistering rash after twelve seconds in the sun. I can't do any better than him," I say sarcastically, gesticulating to mock him. I roll my eyes with such force that I can almost feel them shift to the back of my skull.

"Alright, settle down. Jeez, did I hit a nerve?"

"You should feel that way if you think I'd be sweet on him while dating you. That'd make you on par with him, a solid two out of ten. You sound like a fucking twelve-year-old girl talking like that."

He laughs. "Carol would've loved that. She'd jump right in on the joke. She always did."

"She was the only intelligent one, the rest of you are dimwits." I let out a giggle to pretend I'm joking. They're not the brightest bunch, that's for sure. "I miss her. I miss her more every day."

An image of her fresh corpse flashes in my mind, Ted

hunching over it, startled when he realized he had company. It was July 16. The insects were yet to feast. The chief predator wasn't satiated with only life leaving the flesh. He needed her for more. The crack in her skull and her blood-streaked blonde hair were two mere appetizers. She was a vessel for pleasure and sadism, a garotte around her neck served to arouse him. For Ted, Carol's death wasn't her destination. Her body was ravaged sexually, pre and post-mortem, but he wasn't about to stop at round two. Unrestricted lust and rabid, beastly violence had taken over. He'd been startled when he heard my footsteps, as he should've been. The location wasn't exactly easy to stumble upon. I'm not sure which of us was more shocked. I tucked my father's trusty revolver into a holster on the belt of my jeans but panic still coursed through me. I could hear my blood thumping in my ears. Carol's legs were splayed, her bikini bottoms ripped viciously into three jagged segments. Ted was zipping up his corduroy pants before his ears picked up on my presence, one of his hands pressing on Carol's purpling chest to support his weight. Half of the seminal fluid was on her thigh, the rest on his.

He stared at me for almost a full minute, mouth partially agape. He was speechless. So was I. I didn't look away. I didn't know how to react. It was confronting, like a bullet to a gut that you only register once you fall. The other girl was a few yards away, congealed blood pooled around her abdomen. She was missing two forearms and a leg. Her eyes were open in the decapitated, semi-crushed skull. Adrenaline kicked in, forcing me out of my numbness. I held my hands up in surrender. He quickly finished zipping himself up. The girls' bodies were only a quarter of a mile from the body of one of my males.

"I haven't seen anything," I told him calmly. My voice was more strained than it should've been as if I'd escaped a chokehold. "I wasn't here, and you weren't here."

He was considering it, thinking it through in front of me. He didn't need a façade anymore. There was nothing to hide. He had two options: take my word for it, knowing how much I had to risk also, or execute a possible witness. It would've been impossible for him to miss the corpse of my doing. He was too skilled to not stake out the area. He would've known the hunting ground as well as I did.

"You've seen what I've done," I said. I gestured to the general area of where I'd discarded the body. "You know what would happen to me if I said anything." I reached for the back of my jeans anyway, just in case, my hands slow. He had no weapon on him, so I wasn't in direct danger, but I wasn't stupid enough not to recognize his ability to overpower me in a flash with his size. His legs were far more muscular than his corduroys cared to reveal. His arms were almost twice the size of mine. He was male; I was female. It wasn't a fair fight without a weapon or time on my side. I knew better than to be visibly panicked. "I'd incriminate myself. I don't want to be in prison."

"Do you know her?" He'd tilted his head toward Carol. "There are photos of both of you together in the newspaper."

"She's not important enough to risk incarceration." I was firm, believing it wholeheartedly. I loved Carol, but I wouldn't love dying or being thrown in jail. Her decomposing corpse made me want to heave, but her life wasn't as important as mine. "No one will know. I'm pushing for someone else to be made culpable."

"You know I'll find you if you try to do anything. You're the famous girl, getting to you won't be difficult," he'd sneered. His tone was as bitter and resentful as it was snide. He was pretending to be repulsed by it, to make a mockery of my position in society because he knew it was far above his, far above anything he could aspire to. It was then that my disgust kicked in. I had naturally what he craved and struggled for. I grew up in mansions and hotels. His low rent, middle-class family could only afford cheap cars and second-hand clothing. He could change the way he dressed, the way he styled his hair, and the manner in which he spoke, but he could never change his poor breeding and lack of pedigree. He had less value than the dirt at the bottom of my heels. His clipped accent could only give him so much. He begrudged his upbringing and took it out on the people he so desperately wanted to be in with or those he believed were easy targets. I found that pathetic. The victims he has sought over the past few months have all been petite women, lacking the physical ability to fight back. Women are smaller, more delicate, and easily overpowered. It wasn't a show of masculinity to subdue a human a foot shorter and fifty pounds lighter: it was cowardice. His ego was as fragile as their bodies.

"I believe you, Ted. I have nothing to gain." I'd said it through clenched teeth to avoid laughing, he wouldn't appreciate being mocked. No male does. "You could kill me, or I could go to jail. Only two options here."

"How do you know my name?"

I could've sworn it'd been another minute since he'd blinked. "You told me your name at Lake Sam. I was your target before you got to Carol." I was emboldened by the gun and lack of sleep. "You were going to take me up to Issaquah to get your sailboat. I assume this is what you actually had in mind."

"The things I would've done to you," he'd said, stepping toward me. "Or the first time, the weekend before."

I stepped back toward the safety of my car, but I could feel myself filling with rage. "If you know who I am, you know who my parents are. You're lucky you picked the wrong girl, or there'd be a lot more heat on you from the police, not to mention the media. Missing heiresses get a lot of airtime. People care."

"Well, aren't you a princess."

"No. I'm just not common," I said. "My absence would be noticed, trust me. I'm worth more to you alive than dead."

"A trustworthy woman." He tilted his head back and laughed a real loud belly laugh. "That's rare."

"Almost as rare as an intelligent man." I knew I was pushing it. It felt like a mask slipping, but it was comfortable, not unnerving. It wasn't that I was among peers—he wasn't what I'd call an equal, but there was a side to me that I couldn't reveal to others, one I felt was easy to share with him. "You won't hurt me; it'd be a silly strategy. It's something I'd expect from a normal man, but you're not normal, are you? Most guys like their women alive. Physically, at least."

"You've got a mouth on you, that's for sure." He was somewhere between livid and bemused, not knowing exactly what to do with himself.

"I'll leave you alone, Ted, but I know I'll see you around. Maybe we should get a drink together." I'd swelled with confidence by that point, obscene and obnoxious, even by my standards. I climbed into my car before he could respond, but he was left there just as he first noticed my presence, dumbfounded and mouth agape. The engine roared to life and I fled. I was annoyed that I was unable to finish my work, but it was safer to be there when he wasn't. I found Carol's decaying body a little bit of a downer too.

"Maris, are you alive in there?" Hunter's voice brings me back into the present. Realizing his thoughtlessness, he puts his hand over his mouth in concern. He sees me staring at Ted. "Do you know that guy?"

"Yes, he works at the crime prevention society. He's lovely. I should go say hello. He mentioned Carol in their latest bulletin."

He grabs me by the elbow. "Why are you always looking for a reason to get away from me?"

"Why don't you stop being a little whiny bitch? Come with me if you like," I snap. "That way, you might quit the paranoia."

I feel a sharp blow to my cheekbone, the pain searing as I fall to the ground. I look up and realize he's smacked me. The shock hits him when it hits me. I hear people rush, clicking heels on the marble floor. Hands on my arms, a set on my waist, lifting me up. "How dare you touch her," Mother screeches. She's echoed by Millie and Stephen. Ted is the one who brings me to my feet. The sting of humiliation is beyond me. I feel myself trembling.

"I'm so sorry, Maris. I didn't mean to—"

"To hit me or to be seen doing it?" I stare at him, nauseated. My cheek throbs and tears of rage threaten to stream down my face. I want to rip off his limbs one by one, douse him in gasoline and set him alight. This kind of indignity in public is unbearable, more so than any physical injury. "You don't feel satisfied enough hurting me and those poor girls in privacy?"

"What are you talking about?"

"You know what I'm talking about." I scream, "It's why we're here!" I gesture at the space. I feel the wheels churning in my mind. Maybe Stephen's not the right guy for this. Maybe it's the one standing in front of me, hand red from striking his gentle, vulnerable girlfriend.

"I think you should leave. It's never right to hit a woman." It's Ted's distinct voice. It's still amusing despite my burning face.

"This man's right," says my mother. She's firm, her voice cold. "You should leave, Hunter. I don't want to have to call security on you."

"Mrs. Caldwell, I'm sorry, it was a mistake. I don't know what happened."

"You attacked my daughter. That's what happened. I need you to leave."

"I didn't mean to...I'm so sorry. I just..."

"Please leave." She steps toward him as if she were about to usher him out with force far beyond the capacity of her five feet and eighty pounds.

"I haven't done anything like this before, I'm sorry," he says frantically. He's on the verge of tears, but no one shows him sympathy. Nobody should.

Hunter walks out, and I deflect the negative attention. I'll play the victim if I must, but I don't enjoy it. I smile at the onlookers to let them know I'll be alright, waiting for them to turn back to their drinks. Strong women don't gain much trust or sympathy. Everybody loves a damsel in distress. Vulnerability in women is second only to physical beauty in desirable traits. I wait it out a few moments, wiping a tear from my cheek, and then escape to the bathrooms. A line trails from the ladies' room.

"Say, Maris, what about that drink you wanted to get?"

Without turning to face him, I know it's Ted. I don't think it'll be easy for him to harm me in this setting, despite how adeptly he abducted two women from a police-infested lake amidst a crowd of 14,000 Seattleites. I'm too significant.

"I'd love one, Ted. Which did you have in mind?" "You look like a martini girl."

"Excellent guess. What tipped you off?"

"You're a classic beauty. Classic beauties are traditional."

"You're not wrong." I smile, letting him lead me to the bar. I'm bombarded with large images of Carol's face on banners around the room. I wonder if it's exciting him. She, too, was, in his words, a classic beauty.

His smile is warm, but it doesn't reach his eyes that stare through me, lifeless and disconnected. Unblinking. Maybe mine are like that too. I know mine are a better shade of blue, though. "Sit," he says, pulling out an oak chair for me. I do, not shifting my gaze from his hands. I'd rather not be roofied. “A martini and a double scotch on the rocks,” he tells the bartender.

“I see why you weren’t so fixed on the boyfriend idea,” he says to me.

“Well, that makes one person I know. My parents are gaga over him. Maybe that display will change their feelings.” I glance over at Mother, now happily chatting to a society lady. “Then again, maybe not.”

“Parents are useless anyway. Don’t worry about them.” “Now Ted, that’s what I always say. We sure do have a lot in common.” He sees me look up at Carol’s ten-foot face. “You’re very relaxed about everything.”

“Why wouldn’t I be? I’m sure the authorities are out there looking for the monster who hurt Carol. Maybe it’s the guy who smacked his girlfriend in public.” I take the martini from the bartender and have a sip.

He maintains eye contact and has a self-satisfied little smirk going on. “You’re right. I hope they find that monster.”

“He sure looks like that sketch, doesn’t he?” “Identical.” He clinks his glass against mine.

CHAPTER FOURTEEN

What do you think about getting out of here and finding somewhere private to talk," says Ted, slurring his words after gulping down his fourth scotch. "Maybe smoke some reefer."

"Listen, Ted, I'm interested, but I'm not an idiot." I speak low enough for the nosy bartender to not hear. "Carol and I aren't too different. I don't have any more strength than she does. Well, did."

"Do you think something's going to happen to you?"

"Maybe." I neglect to tell him about the weapons I have access to and how swiftly people would intervene to save me. "Imagine you were me. What would you be thinking?"

"I'd like the challenge."

"I have responsibilities here. I have to make a speech. How about I get you a key to the penthouse, and I'll meet you there in an hour. I don't have any weed, but I have plenty of alcohol."

"I have my girlfriend Beth here. I'll have to get rid of her."

"That mousy little brunette? Really? Come on, Theodore."

He laughs. "Theodore? That's bold of you."

"Is that not your name? Theodore Robert Bundy. Ted for short.

It was bold going by your real name."

"Nice one, Nancy Drew. Or do you prefer Maris Cordelia Caldwell? Maris for short. Unless you've managed to come up with a nickname because I, for the life of me, cannot figure one out for a name like that. How did your parents even come up with it?"

"The Virgin Mary, or short for Stella Maris. Jesus, don't you understand biblical mythology?"

"You do seem like a very holy girl, Maris," he scoffs. "Was knowing my name your trump card?"

"Damn, you sure caught me."

"And Millicent. Where did your parents get that from?"

"Still more creative than Linda and Glenn. I forget the rest.

It's like a clown car if you know what I mean. Are you sure you guys aren't Catholic?"

"You really do have a mouth on you." He drains the last of the scotch. I think at this point he's gulping air. His gaze is directly on my chest. "I'll get rid of Beth."

"I'll meet you at the lifts in an hour. Oh, and Ted, I'm never late. I hear you aren't either."

"See you in an hour. If you're not too afraid." He gives me a nod as he weaves through the crowd to find his insipid girlfriend. I see him in my mind, his hands around Carol's throat, her eyes devoid of light, and her body torn apart. I try to picture myself in her situation, but I can't. I'd never be a victim. Some people are born to suffer, and I'm not one of them.

I take the stage to applause, much of the crowd having witnessed me being assaulted by my boyfriend, thus amply softened. The burn of indignation is soothed by the compliance of the audience. I spout the same nonsense I've repeated a dozen times since the incident. It's become a script, well-rehearsed, well performed. Carol's unhinged mother is crying, dressed in a ratty, worn peach and gold gown that washes her out. Mother's watching me. The expression on her face could be mistaken for compassion to those who don't know any better. To the trained eye, it's contempt and humiliation. I should take my beatings in silence like her; it's less shameful. Unlike her, though, I won't roll over. I exit, down a flute of champagne, and head for the elevator when fewer eyes are upon me. I shirk out of Mother's cold grasp on my way. He's waiting for me, as promised. His hair has been re-coiffed, his suit fits perfectly, and his black patent leather shoes are gleaming.

"I can see why the girls are dying for you to take them out," I tell him, laughing at my own joke. I ought to be ashamed. "You're a clever girl," he says dryly.

"I have to be. I'm not exactly funny, am I? I've got to have something going for me." I half expect him to lunge at me with a homemade shiv.

"You're attractive, that's all a woman needs."

I neglect to tell him that his IQ would be about thirty points lower than mine and his life savings would amount to less than what I have in a purse at any one given point. Males aren't worth the effort of discussion: they don't have the intellect. Maybe they're defective or something, I don't know. I don't bother. "Let's go upstairs." I take his hand. His palms are slippery with sweat. Maybe he's more nervous than I am. I ignore the hammering in my chest. He glances down at our entwined hands, perplexed.

The elevator dings, and I lead him into the lush expanse of the penthouse. "I think we should talk, Ted." I dump some ice into a tumbler and pour scotch over it, sliding it across the counter to him. "Here. Drink."

"You don't need to get me drunk to talk," he says.

"Why didn't you take me instead, Ted? You let me escape. I know you were targeting me."

"You think very highly of yourself, don't you, Maris? How would Carol feel knowing you think she was second best?"

"I don't care about how she'd feel. It's acknowledging a fact. You approached me first. You lingered when I told you I had a boyfriend. If the timeline was right, and I know it to be, it took you another thirty minutes to secure Carol, and she's not a particularly difficult person to catch."

"I can't get into that right now. You can believe what you like." He takes a sip, settling into a soft burgundy wingchair. My control wanes, and I'm pulled onto his lap, my legs draped over the arm of the couch. I look into his pretty, hollow eyes and then lower my gaze to his mouth. I watch as his hands travel behind me, cradling my neck. I kiss him or he kisses me. I feel sick but not enough to stop. His lips are gentle, and his finger traces my collarbone, making me shiver. "Ted, we shouldn't," I tell him, not believing my own words. He doesn't either. He kisses my neck and my body trembles. I ease him out of his tuxedo jacket, pressing myself against his sinewy frame. The dress feels claustrophobic, the layers trapping heat, despite the coolness of the silken fabric. I keep it on, though. I haven't completely lost my mind yet.

"I'll say you're more beautiful, but that's all you'll get from me.

I'm not a fan of blondes. You're more my type."

"I was Miss Washington USA in '72. I would've won Miss USA if I hadn't needed to buckle down for med school. I'm everyone's type."

He eyes me, unblinking, like when he was on the prowl at Lake Sam. "I can tell."

I lean into him, running my fingers through his hair. "I've been trying to save you. Everyone that's, uh, disappeared, can be tied back to a friend of mine, Stephen Winthrop."

"Why would you do that for me?" He pulls back a little, but his hand now rests on my thigh.

"You're like me. It's rare." I neglect to mention that it gets me out of a bind, too, but I know he'd be aware. Men aren't as bright as women, but it's clear he's canny. Men are prime suspects; often, their biological samples from haphazard sexual attacks tarnish their victims. That's not something I have to fear as a woman. Maybe one day in the future they'll study vaginal fluids as well as they do semen, but I think that's quite far from current reality. Plus, which obese pig shoveling donuts into his mouth faster than the speed of light is going to have the foresight to suspect a delicate co-ed over the bogeyman?

"I'm not like you." He picks me up and lays me down on the pristine bed. He kneels over me. I feel the panic rise inside my chest as he watches me. He's easy to read. I know what he's thinking: he has the advantage. The more fearful I get, the more he'll get off. I try to stare back without wavering.

"Is this turning you on, Ted?" I lay still, even when he releases my arms, showing no struggle.

"Take off your dress," he orders. His face is only inches from mine.

"What's the point of you being here if I have to do that myself?

Don't tell me you like to watch."

"You know I do more than watch. How many pieces did they find of Carol?" He laughs. "She was fun."

"She wouldn't be better than me."

"You don't serve the same purpose. It's not a comparison I can make."

"What's my purpose, then?"

"Again, I can't get into that in any detail right now." He unzips me. The dress slips off, the extravagant lingerie doesn't. He takes in the image for a full minute or two.

"Am I not good enough for her—their fate?" I press. I stop his hand as it snakes behind me, making a sloppy, drunken unhooking of my three rung La Perla bra clasp. "Am I not better than your mousy girlfriend?"

"Maris, I don't want you that way. You don't understand. You won't." He withdraws from me. "You're a fucking princess. You're picture-perfect, delicate, untouchable. Made for that guy with the trust fund and multibillion dollar business in his grasp. Not for me. I couldn't fit in your world, just like I couldn't fit in Diane's." "You're kidding me, right? You're in my room right now, why would I bother if you were beneath me?" The sting of humiliation hits again when he starts re-buttoning his shirt. I reach for him, but he dodges my hand. Hot tears begin to well, seeping down my face one at a time as I close my eyes. I crumple on the bed. His disdain does little to comfort me. Maybe it's this fucking penthouse suite. First Charles, now Ted: two lower-class males. I don't know why it hits me so hard. I need them to want me. It physically hurts when they don't, no matter how much I try to rationalize it. "Get the fuck out, then, leave. Go or I'll have security throw you out," I screech.

He contains his rage as he combs his hair back into place.

I make myself a dry martini, using a chilled glass from the mini-fridge in the suite—one part vermouth, four parts gin. I guzzle it down, wiping my face with a hand towel. I know I'm drunk, but I have a level of mental clarity that would usually serve me well. I get dressed, touching up my makeup in the bathroom. Four minutes past 1 AM, the party would've well and truly disbanded by now, all the sympathy for the shattered lives packed into town cars and BMWs hurtling back toward the safety of Bellevue. I stay out of eyeline of the hotel security cameras, almost scaling the back wall to get down the fire escape. I hail a taxi back to the house, which is, unfortunately, still lit up.

I brace myself on the long path to the door. I'm greeted by Millie's lackluster smile as she steps back to let me in. A small mug of hot cocoa in one hand and swaddled in a thick Merino robe, she looks like she's a minute away from falling into a benzo-induced stupor. She'll be of no use to me.

"What happened to you?" she asks, probably seeing my puffy eyes.

"Nothing, move, I want to take a shower." My shoulder collides with hers as I push through.

"You disappeared for like, five hours," she tells me indignantly, rubbing her shoulder. "Where the hell did you go?"

I ignore her and take the stairs two at a time. Pangs of hunger gnaw at my stomach as I sit on the edge of the tub, turning on the bathwater. I dip my feet in as it fills, letting the scorching water burn my soles. Any kind of pain to distract myself from the humiliation is helpful. The rage and embarrassment weigh me down, and I want to scream. I scrub my skin raw with soap, wanting to throw the gown into the bin. I twist my hair into a makeshift updo so that it doesn't get wet. I won't have time to sit around drying it. I rid my body of any remnants of tonight and wrap myself with a towel. I dress quickly. A cowl-neck t-shirt and a leather miniskirt with platforms and baby blue eyeshadow.

"Fuck off, Millie," I say, seeing her figure in the doorframe as I try to exit. "I don't have time for you right now."

"What's wrong, Maris?" She seems genuinely concerned. "Seriously, Millie, ask me one more time, and I'll put your head through the wall." I walk past her, grabbing my car keys from the hook. I make my way to my car and toss my Balenciaga purse into the back. I drive to the only place I know will be populated at this time. The Velvet Elvis is a university nightclub that's never short of pretty boys trying to woo coeds till all hours of the night. I park a block away and my feet ache, but I'm restless. The first all-American blonde guy with a nice smile in my path is about to have the time of his life. It doesn't take very long to spot him. Sitting at the bar with a rum and coke in hand, gleaming white teeth, and the kind of hair that Clairol can't compete with. Slightly drunk and very attractive, still in his senses.

"Please tell me you're here alone," he says with a southern drawl. He pats the barstool next to him.

"I could be," I tell him with a grin. I slide into the seat with ease. My senses are heightened, and the familiar warmth rushes through me. "What's your name?"

"Eddie Salinger, what's yours, sugar?"

"Any relation to Jerome?" My sarcasm is finely veiled.

"Chicks love asking that. No, no one in my family wrote The Catcher in the Rye." He rolls his eyes. Hazel, I think, with brown flecks. "I'm sorry."

"Not even Franny and Zooey then, I'm assuming. That's a shame. You ought to buy me a drink to make up for the inconvenience."

He's taken aback and laughs. "Sure darlin', what're you having?"

I flag down the bartender. "A daiquiri please. Extra lime."

"And you, sir?" he asks of Eddie.

"I'm fine for now, bud, thanks."

"You seem like a bit of a lightweight." I gesture at his full glass.

"Darlin', I could drink Bukowski under the table."

His drawl is getting old, as are his tired literary references.

It's time for another funeral.

"Listen, I don't mean to be too forward or anything, it's just not like me, but I'm new to town, and I don't know anyone here...I just moved into a nice little place near Issaquah, I think you should come and check it out."

He processes it and nods. Confused but clearly interested.

"Sure thing, I haven't explored Issaquah yet either. I don't know how I'd get back to the city, though."

"I'll drop you off, no problem." I smile into my glass as I take a sip. "You might be worth the DUI."

"You've sold me. Are you sure you're new to town? I swear I've seen you somewhere."

"I doubt it unless you've been to New York recently. I only moved here for college. I used to model."

"Must've seen you on television then, I've never been to the Big Apple."

"You're missing out. This place has been pretty boring so far." "You've been hanging out with the wrong people then." He tilts his head back and drains his glass. "Let's go."

"Perfect." I take one more sip of my daiquiri and grab his hand. I take a quick look around to see if anyone's watching us, but it doesn't seem like anyone is. I'm beyond caring at this point, I feel the acute rage and humiliation bubbling up inside me, ready to erupt. Most eyewitness testimony falls through in trials anyway. I lead him to the Porsche, and he starts gushing about it; it's his dream car, apparently. He climbs in at the same time as me. "Oh shit, I'm a little drunk, could you get those?" I ask after dropping the keys on his side. When he leans over for them, I reach for the crowbar in the back and smash it into his head. He keels, and I do his seatbelt up for him. The blow is to the back of his skull, so the blood will seep into the seat, but at least the wound will be hidden should I get randomly stopped by a rogue policeman. I drive him to the cottage and drag his unconscious body inside—it's more difficult than I anticipated: he's heavier than he looks. I handcuff him to the railing in the bathroom. He doesn't seem to be rousing, so I fill a cup with cold water and splash it on his face. He jolts awake, groggy and disoriented.

"Where am I?" he asks when he's finally able to string some words together.

"Issaquah."

His arm struggles when he realizes that he's cuffed. "What the fuck is this?"

"Darlin', I'm trying to spice things up a little," I say in his hideous southern drawl. "Am I hanging out with the right people yet?"

"I don't understand," he babbles. "I thought—"

"You thought you were going to get laid. You were very confident about it."

"Listen, girlie, I didn't mean to offend you. I'm sorry, let me go and I'll drop it, I'll never mention this happened."

"You didn't offend me, I thought we could have a little fun together."

"What do you mean? Please, just uncuff me."

I pull the revolver from the vanity "Now why would I do that?" I shoot his left thigh. His scream is so loud and shrill that it reverberates in my head. "Sorry, you're a large dude, I need to incapacitate you, so you don't do anything silly." I shoot his other thigh and perch myself on the edge of the tub.

"I'm begging you, let me go. I won't tell anybody. Nobody will know."

"You'll run right to the cops." I laugh, then glance down at his bleeding legs. "Oh, well I suppose running's out of the picture for a while."

"I won't tell the police."

"No, you won't," I agree. I walk to the kitchen and pull my favorite knife out of the butcher's block. When I return, I show it to Eddie. "This'll make sure you're not able to speak at all."

"Please," he sobs, tears dribbling. "I'll do anything."

Ted's face flashes in my mind, the hot prod of indignity burning itself into my memory. The suite, Hunter's hand striking me, Charles pulling away. Using all my strength, I stab the knife into the male's chest, twisting it until the nerves sever. I pull it out and go again, this time in the sinewy shoulder. He's screeching in agony, and I force the knife into the gunshot wound on his thigh. I run the blade down the length of his body, cutting only gently before driving it into his abdomen. I play around with it, pulling it out and shoving it back in. His cries give me serenity, the anger slowly trickling out of me. I slap him repeatedly across the face and then gouge out his right eye. His speech becomes slurred, and I see his limbs going limp. I wring his neck, my fingers crushing his throat with such force that it almost collapses. I suffocate him until he's unconscious, then wait for him to come back to me. The look of terror in his remaining eye gives me a thrill. I leave him in the bathroom and wash my hands to make a peanut butter and banana sandwich. I switch on the TV and settle for Little House on the Prairie.

Just as the show wraps up, I polish off the last of my food and go back to the bathroom. He's still alive, barely. Not feeling as much anger, I decide to put him out of his misery. I slit his throat and let him bleed out peacefully into death. I take the ring from his forefinger and slip it into the pocket of my skirt. Gone with my rage is my energy. Just looking at the gore is exhausting. The scrubbing that'll need to be done to get his blood off the floor and walls is something that I wouldn't even want to put our Hispanic maids through. I scrub with a rag and some Clorox, only managing to get the tub clean. It's nearing 5 AM, and my eyes are bleary with sleep, for once not aided by benzos or dolls. I go to the bed, turn down the sheets and slip in, pulling my t-shirt (now splattered bright red) off over my head. I nestle into the pillow, my last view the skulls surrounding me.

It's gloomy and gray when I wake up, true to Seattle's reputation. I glance over at the bedside clock—2 PM. I haven't had this long of a sleep since I was fifteen. I feel refreshed and at ease, a sense of comfort settling into me, unfamiliar but warm. There's minimal food in this house. It's not livable, per se. I find what I can from the wardrobe and get dressed in a loose-fitting green tunic. I brush my teeth in the kitchen, avoiding glancing at the carnage in the bathroom. I assess the car for damage—less than I thought. Other than a damp, dark spot in the passenger seat, it's relatively clean. I drive past a Hardee's and pick up a cheeseburger with fries and a strawberry shake. I wolf the food down, satiating my hunger. I love Hardee's. So much value for seventy-nine cents. I drive the familiar highway back to Bellevue, listening to Paul Anka. I pull into the winding driveway, not surprised when Mother appears at the door in less than a millisecond, prepared. I'm a little disturbed when she opens her arms to me.

"Maris, sweetheart, are you alright?" Her concern seems genuine but confusing.

"I'm fine, Mother. Why?"

"You've been gone for the better part of a day. Listen, sweetie, there's someone here to see you. I know you're angry. I am, too, but everyone makes mistakes." She grabs my arm, pulling me in. I know who it is before I even look past her into the foyer.

"Hello, Hunter," I say coolly. I sip on the last of the strawberry milkshake. "How can I help you? Do you want the other side of my face this time?"

"Maris, I'm so sorry. Please. You have to forgive me." He looks like he's about to cry.

"I have to go work out. I think you should leave."

"Please, Maris, listen to me. I'm asking for a minute of your time."

"You've had five. Go home, Hunter."

"No, I want to make things right. I don't want you to hate me. It was a mistake. I'll always regret it. I can't believe it happened."

"Hunter, go home. When I'm ready to talk, I'll call you."

"Maris." My mother's voice is stern. "Talk to Hunter. Take him to your room and talk to him. He deserves the benefit of the doubt. He has been your boyfriend since you were ten."

I glare at the dumb bitch. While she may be moronic enough to believe my father when he tells her it won't happen again after each beating, I'm not.

"You win, Hunter. You can assault me, and my mother still thinks I should be speaking to you. Come on in, maybe I'll get another slap or two," I say, my voice harsh. I turn to my Judas mother. "You'd like that, wouldn't you? It'll remind you of your fond times with Daddy."

Her face is pinched when I turn my back to her. Hunter follows me up the stairs in silence. In my room, he breaks. He kneels at my feet, wrapping his arms around my hips, his face burrowed into my thighs. "I'm sorry, Maris. I'm so sorry. You have to believe me."

"Alright, relax. Just get up." By this point he ought to know when I'm lying, but he doesn't. He lifts up my tunic and starts kissing my legs and my stomach, his hands working their way across my body. His distress appears honest as he clings to me, almost sobbing.

He stands up, now towering over me. I look up to him. "It's alright, Hunter, we all make mistakes." I curl my arms around him, burying my face in his chest. I take Eddie's ring and slip it into Hunter's side pocket. "I'm tired. I'll call you later, alright?"

"So, you'll forgive me?"

"Maybe. I don't know. Give me a day to think about it. You're always suffocating me. You never give me space."

"I love you so much, and you ignore me. You treat me like shit in front of everyone. It's hard, Maris. You've always been the girl I knew I'd marry."

"Do you think that's the way to get me to marry you? To

beat me and humiliate me in public? I can endure what you put me through in private, but this was outrageous. I thought even you would be above it."

"It was the biggest mistake I've made in my life. You're everything to me, Maris. I love you. I'll do anything to make up for it, to be a better boyfriend and eventual husband," he tells me theatrically.

My leg is in prime position to knee him in the crotch, but I control myself. I level my voice. "Hunter, I have a lot of studying to do. Can you go home so I can have a little time to myself? I will call you."

"Please let me stay, just for a few hours."

The phone in my room starts ringing, and my mother screams up at me from the base of the staircase to tell me it's for me, but she doesn't recognize the voice. I hold my finger up to Hunter to silence him and pick up the receiver. The other side is slightly muffled and unclear. I hear my mother hang up once I say hello.

"Maris."

My face grows hot. "How did you get my number?"

"It wasn't particularly difficult. You should hire better staff.

Are you alone?" "No."

"I want to speak to you in person. Meet me at Mama Barone's tonight at seven." It's not a question.

"Alright. Goodbye." I place the phone back in its cradle, trying not to grimace at the thought of the greasy Italian fare. I turn to Hunter before he gets a chance to answer. "It was a reporter. I don't know how he got my number." I shrug. He wouldn't know Ted anyway.

"Where was he calling from?"

"KPLZ radio station. One of the chicks used to work there.

The ski reporter or something." "What did he want from you?"

"God, I don't know, Hunter! He asked if I wanted to comment on this bullshit." I turn to the window, my face in my hands.

"Hey, come here." He hugs me from behind. "It's alright."

"I love you, Hunter," I tell him instead of letting him know how much I'd like to pour gasoline on him and set him on fire or cut off his leg and feed it to him. "I need to get some stuff done. Why don't we go to Le Cirque tonight for a late dinner around nine?"

"Okay, fine. Can you wear that little black miniskirt I love?" "Sure, of course. Thanks for being so understanding. I'm really tired right now." I turn to him, reach up on my toes and peck him on his unnervingly smooth, chap-free lips. "Have you been using my ChapStick?"

He grins. "No, I bought some. It's flavorless." He's very proud of himself, like a six-year-old winning a putt-putt golf game.

I give him a thumbs-up and mocking smile. "Good work, champ!"

"Thanks, babe." He kisses me on the cheek. "I'll pick you up at eight forty-five."

"Alright, cool." I quash the urge to tell him that it takes far longer than fifteen minutes to reach the restaurant from my place. "See you then."

As soon as he leaves, I head for the shower. I need to wash the stench of him away.

CHAPTER FIFTEEN

Millie

I stand outside Maris's ensuite, hearing the torrent of water beating down on the floor. Her bathroom has more amenities than mine, including far better shower pressure. I wait for her, as instructed, but my body is trembling. I don't know what she has planned for me. Whenever she calls for me, I feel a pit of despair in my gut. I shouldn't be afraid of her; she's my twin sister. She's the only one I have on my side, but the sound of her voice terrifies me. I love my sister very much. It's not her fault that I do things wrong sometimes. She's only helping me. She wants the best for me, and it's only fair that I help her when she needs me. Any good sister would, right?

I wait dutifully for her, holding a heated towel. She reaches her hand out and snatches it from me. She opens the door once she's wrapped the towel around herself. She's standing on the bathmat as a bead of water trickles down her leg. She's very big on etiquette. Mom always told us to never let a drop of water hit the floor after a bath or shower, and Maris stringently abides by that rule.

"Did you borrow my Valentino skirt?" she asks. She's looking at the mirror, combing her hair.

"No, I haven't borrowed anything."

She turns to me. "Don't fucking lie to me, Millie. I know you have."

"Honestly, I haven't." I feel myself shake when she takes a step toward me.

She starts laughing. "I'm kidding, sooky sook. Relax." She gives me a Chanel bodywash-infused hug. She's radiant, even without makeup. It's what she uses to get her work done. Her turquoise doe eyes can enchant when she needs them to. If that doesn't get them, her smile and slender, hourglass figure will. Only a few see the lack of life, the cold gaze, and affect when the show's over. No one knows her better than me.

"You said you needed help. What do you want me to do?"

"Jeez, Millie, simmer down. You look like you're about to have a goddamn coronary. I need you to drop a few things off at Hunter's house for me."

I exhale a breath I didn't think I was holding. "I have plans with Susannah...I'm meant to meet her in half an hour."

"Well, are you planning to spend the night with her or something? I wanted you to go around seven or eight, not right now."

"Why, where are you going?"

"I'm meeting a friend." She crosses her arms over her chest. "Is that alright, Mother?"

"Charles?" I know I'm pushing my luck. Maris isn't fond of questions unless she's the one firing them.

"If you absolutely must know, yes." Her voice is cold and harsh. "I'm seeing Charles."

I know she's lying. Charles is back in Ellensburg with his

grieving mother and sister. He called earlier, and I answered the phone—he thought he was speaking to her. I don't blame him, even our parents can't distinguish between us on the telephone. They can barely tell us apart in person.

"Alright. What do you want me to drop off?"

"Well, when I say 'drop off,' I mean I want you to go inside his room, hang out for a little while, real casual and all, and then put a couple of the items in his bedside cupboard and in his bookshelf when he undoubtedly takes his bathroom break. That boy has the bladder of a ninety-year-old woman. Make sure he doesn't see you."

"Maris, seriously? I can't do that. I've helped you enough, even when I've been sick or tired. Why can't you go?"

"I just told you I have plans. Just fucking do it." She drops her towel on the floor of her walk-in wardrobe and puts on a red three-piece lingerie set. Over it, she pulls on a white minidress with a sweetheart neckline. I think it's my dress, but I don't say anything.

"Fine, I'll do it. You owe me for this. I was going to the movies." "The stuff's on the bed," she says. She pulls out a small bag of coke and does half a line. "Make sure you follow all my instructions, alright?"

"Are you ever sober anymore?"

She looks like she's been slapped. "Listen, Millie, you should be happy I'm even talking to you after the stunt you pulled. Quit whining and do as you're told." She gets closer to me, her index finger two inches from my face. "Don't you dare talk to Mother." She stares at me through the mirror, eventually breaking out into a derisive grin. "Millie, it's not brain surgery. You can leave now." "Yeah, of course." I fight back tears, swallowing hard to keep my voice even.

I walk out of her room, but I don't return to mine. Moving two doors down, I slip into the library, nestling myself into a chesterfield by the immaculately preserved first edition classic novels. There's only so much Maris can get away with. I'm not far off my mother in my hearing ability, and I keep myself still and quiet to ensure I can hear everything from Maris's room. I wait for her light footsteps on the carpet and then follow moments after, exclusively holding my weight in my toes—the one decent thing I learned from ten years of forced ballet training—making sure I can't be heard. She's always been a little paranoid, so I expect it when her gaze darts across the room as she slips her hand into the key bowl for her car keys. I hold my breath and duck behind the credenza. Once satisfied that she's alone, she steps outside and climbs into her car. I wait again, less patiently this time. I want to know what she's up to. Something has been very off about her lately, more so than usual. Not only evasive, she's been blatantly lying to me, something that she never did before. To Mom and Dad, sure but never to me. I tail her in Mom's old Aston Martin, the one she dented and then relegated to the back of the garage. I doubt Maris has seen it in years. I keep myself two cars behind her, but she's speeding maniacally, slipping through red lights, and swerving in front of oncoming traffic. I lose her for a few moments, but I left a paint drip in her trunk. She wouldn't notice it, but I see the sickly orange paint cementing the roads. She veers into the parking lot for a trashy Italian diner, Mama Barone's, and I almost rear-end the car in front of me.

Maris is very picky with what she eats, and she despises Italian food. She either eats fast food or fine French food with very little in between. I park on the street leading into the restaurant and watch her fiddle with her hair and retouch her lip gloss in the car while she waits. Another vehicle enters the parking lot, a beat-up '60s Volkswagen beetle. It's shabby and gross, so I'm a little surprised when its owner hops out with perfectly coiffed hair and glossy patent leather shoes. He walks to my sister, opens her door for her, and offers his arm for support, which she takes. He looks familiar, but I can't place him. I'm only good with my ears, Maris has the eyes. I sink down into my seat, hoping she doesn't glance back. She doesn't. She's fixated on him and it's mutual.

He leads her inside, and they're seated in a booth by the window. I take the risk, driving into the lot and parking for a better view. Usually guys slobber over her (and me), taking every opportunity to touch her or get closer to her, but this dude is keeping his distance, despite the staring. He sits stiffly on his side of the table, perusing the menu. He rebuffs her advances when she tries to make contact. Panic races through me when I think she sees me, but I know she can't in the dim light.

I look down at the trail of bruises from the last time I had a confrontation with her. I miss my sister. I want her back. She's never been like this to me. She's had her temper tantrums and lashed out, but she's not this cruel. I don't know what's happened to her. She doesn't tell me anything anymore, she just yells and hits me. It honestly frightens me to see how similar she's becoming to Dad. He's a sadistic bastard. The brutality he inflicts on Mom is inhumane. Maris is the only one who can sway him. She's managed to wrap him around her little finger. Even then, a self-centered jerk isn't easy to deal with. He's never hurt her—not that I'm aware of, anyway, but Mom and I haven't been lucky enough to elude his abuse. I watch this guy. He's self-conscious. I see him pat down his hair four times. They seem to be in deep discussion, which is quite odd because she never engages males in conversations beyond surface level. She guzzles down her drink but his remains untouched. I feel like one of those Peeping Toms who sits around watching women in stages of undress. This time, I don't look away. I wish I had a listening device or could at least do a vague lip-read. I stare at the man's face, scrutinizing what little I can see. I know it from somewhere, it's ringing a bell, but my mind is foggy. I don't know for sure from this distance, but he doesn't seem to be blinking very often. It's kind of creepy. I'm restless in my car—I glance down at my Piaget every few minutes. The lot is getting busier, working-class families piling in for their weekly fancy meal.

They finally finish. The dude pays the bill, almost pushing Maris's hand away when she offers her (or probably Dad's) Amex. He leads her out, and they both smoke a cigarette in front of his car. I finally get a better look at his face. It's very angular with sharp cheekbones and a fine, pointed nose. It hits me like a ton of bricks. It was a little while ago, July 7 after I'd gotten my nails done. I get my nails done on the seventh and the twenty-first of every month, like clockwork. It was an extremely hot day, and I hadn't had any real plans, so I drove out to Lake Sam for a dip. Unlike Maris, I prefer oceans and rivers to our utilitarian 200 – foot lap pool. I had on this cute red bikini and a white miniskirt coverup. I'd staked out a little area for myself and put down a picnic blanket, a copy of Breakfast at Tiffany's, and my bottle of suntan lotion. He'd sat down next to me, and he was attractive, so I wasn't too bothered. He didn't seem creepy or anything. I felt him staring at me, but every time I turned and tried to catch him, he looked away. He was pretending to read Gatsby. I was going to speak, but he beat me to it.

"I, uh, I read that a while ago. I really liked it," he said, gesturing towards my paperback.

"Yeah, I love Truman Capote. I was studying his work in my literature class." I smiled at him. "F. Scott Fitzgerald is great too." "Oh, uh, right. Yeah, I like Capote's work." He was nervous when he talked, and he mispronounced Capote. He was smartly dressed, very dapper, but also incredibly awkward. He had a slight stutter and an accent, maybe Canadian. "Do you live around here?"

"I live in Bellevue. I'm not too far from here."

We made small talk, discussing topics he feigned to understand. He cut to the point within about five minutes.

"Look, uh, I, uh, don't normally do this, but you're absolutely beautiful. Would you like to, uh, get a drink with me tonight?"

I could see sweat trickling down the side of his forehead—probably only partially from the heat. "Listen, I'd love to, but I have a boyfriend. I am very flattered," I told him. He was too shifty, too self-conscious. My non-existent boyfriend deserved more attention than he did. He didn't take it too badly, and I didn't think twice about it, leaving my spot to go for a quick swim to cool off. When I got back, he was gone. I stayed for a couple of hours, reading, and then I drove home. I'm not trying to act like I'm a wonderfully good-looking person but, more often than not, I get guys hitting on me and trying to take me out. He wasn't especially memorable. Yes, he was nice-looking and had decent facial features, but so do a lot of boys. I didn't talk to him again. I went home, where Charles was. This boy is by far the most attractive person I've ever seen. I'm entirely confident about that. The day Maris brought him to the house, I struggled to keep my composure, feeling like I was going to have a stroke. I'm not a sicko, I don't want to share a boy with my sister, but I knew I was going to struggle to avoid him. I'd never felt like that about anyone. I could see Mom fawning over him, Dad becoming livid to see the effect he had on women. Charles has these blue eyes and dimples that make me buckle at the knees, as cheesy and gross as that sounds. Maris had her claws in very deep. I didn't know where she found him, but he was just another plaything for her. She's not capable of any true emotion, so it's unfair of her to hoard him when she can easily draw someone else in. If I'd mentioned it to her, she wouldn't have been cruel about it, despite her general sadism, she would've played nice and backed off slightly, gifting him to me as it were. But she would've lorded it over my head for the rest of my fucking life. So, I didn't tell her. I went into Charles's room, and he knew I wasn't Maris, that was only a mistake he could make over the phone, not in person. I was sitting there on the bed with him, my voice raspy and my head spinning, absolutely overwhelmed. I wasn't taking in a word he said. I wasn't taking in anything other than his beautiful face. He made Robert Redford look passe. I was wearing some lovely lingerie underneath my gown. He enjoyed it. I felt guilty about it, even more so when Maris eventually came in, drunk and wired. I pretended it didn't happen. He did, too, which hurt me more than it should've. I get attached. Not often, but when I do, it hits hard. Seeing him crawl back to Maris was brutal.

I watch Maris follow the well-dressed man's car in her Porsche, ten over the speed limit. I wait a couple of minutes before tailing her. She used to be fastidious, but now she's getting sloppy with her work, especially when she's intoxicated. The paint dripping from her car would've caught her eagle eye immediately a year ago. There have been so many "incidents"—as she calls them— in recent times that she's become disordered, leaving behind evidence, and missing obvious details. She always justifies the acts to me, and they make sense. I've never questioned or pushed against it because men do hurt women. Men hurt women all the time, without remorse, without guilt, without empathy, so why should we feel anything for them? I've watched my father abuse my mother all my life. I know what they're capable of. And there is no world in which I'd sell my sister down the river for hurting a man. I'm trying my best to be inconspicuous, but it's difficult once I see Maris driving down toward a secluded spot in Issaquah, a trail leading to Tiger Mountain. I stop the car well before I enter. I recognize her playground—it's only accessible by foot. My heart is racing. He's not a victim. Maybe she is. I don't know what to do. I keep myself hidden behind the interlacing, leafy trees, praying that the sound of the leaves crunching beneath my feet can't be heard by Maris or the man. There's the familiar smell of decay and the evening chill is kicking in, sending through me a violent shiver.

I see her. Nude and decomposing. A blonde with a striking resemblance to Carol.

They're standing a couple of feet away from her, chatting casually. Maris takes a cigarette out of her purse and lights it, taking several long drags. Spirals of smoke stream behind. I don't realize I'm sobbing until tears trickle down my chin, falling onto my chest. I'm overcome with the memories and feelings I've been unable to face. This girl reminds me that my sweet friend has been ravaged and ripped apart. She would lend me books and cheer me up every time Maris would make me cry when we were at school together. She made my life bearable when Dad would put out a cigarette on my skin or shatter a bone. She would come into the hospital with cards and violets, my favorite flower, and tell me about what stupid things Hunter did in class, to cheer me up. I adored her. I feel bile rising, and I fight it as hard as I can. Maris puts her foot on the girl's decapitated head, digging it deeper into the ground with her heel. When I look past her, I see a male corpse, not yet in the same stage of putrefaction. Blonde hair and green eyes. I can't hear what they're saying, but Maris collapses into a fit of giggles. I want to strangle her. She said violence against women was foul, something she'd never do, and I believed her. I can't handle anymore, but I can't risk them hearing me running.

I muffle my sobs with the back of my hand. I wish I'd done what she told me to. Hunter is comforting and kind, and she's wicked and callous. My legs feel as if they're about to give way, my head isn't far behind, and I feel dizzy and detached from my body. I have to believe I'm dreaming or imagining; this can't be my reality. I cry quietly, the way I learned to when Maris would injure me and then threaten to do worse if I ratted to Mom, wanting to throw up what I've eaten today—half a hamburger from McDonald's.

Minutes drag on like days, and I shake from the cold night air. My strength wanes, but I hold on until Maris finally turns to leave, laughing as she gives the head one last sickening kick. The man follows, hands stuffed into his pockets, and climbs into his car. Maris takes the lead, and the man's car trails her.

I let myself collapse onto the wet dirt and my vomiting follows. I need ample time for them to leave and make sure they don't come back and see me. I can't stop the tears, and my hands feel grubby when I try to wipe my face. When I can finally get myself together, I head back to my car—the walk feels like a marathon. I know the muck will follow me in, staining the seats. I'll need another carwash. I can't go home, not like this. I find myself driving instinctively to Hunter's house but not with the items Maris wanted me to take. It's late but he'll be awake. He doesn't go to bed until at least 3 AM. I hope Maris isn't there. She isn't someone I can face right now. I wish I could go to Charles, but he wouldn't have me instead of Maris.

"Hey, Millie, I didn't know you were coming over," he greets me, shirtless at the door. Normally, it'd be one of the maids answering this late at night. I'm grateful he recognizes that it's me. He's quite often mistaken me for Maris. She's trained me to speak like her, dress like her and, most importantly, flirt like her. He's a lot less observant than Charles.

"I know, I didn't plan to, but here I am." I stand in the doorway. "Well, can I come in?"

"Of course, you can. What happened to you?" He gestures at the dirt on my clothing.

"I'm a little bit drunk, and I had a tumble. I didn't want to go home like this. You know how my parents can be." I laugh.

"Quinn would be so stunned, I'm sure. Come on in, and I'll see if I can find any of Maris's clothes in my room. I'm bound to have something. That girl sheds clothes like a snake sheds skin." I roll my eyes and laugh, genuinely laugh, for the first time all day. He steers me up the stairs, to his floor. One of the benefits of being an only child, I suppose. His room is spotless, as always, methodically designed and maintained. He rifles through his wardrobe until he gets to a myriad of dresses, Halston, Chanel, and Valentino. I never cared very much about designer clothes, but Mom wouldn't have one of her daughters turning up to an event (or even lounging around the house) in a Sears outfit, and Maris wouldn't let me hear the end of it. I pick the least fancy, a sparkly lame gold minidress. "A little bit much, but it'll do, I suppose," I say, taking it off the rack. He looks away as I get changed and then asks me to toss over my dirty clothes.

"I'll get Larissa to wash them, and I'm sure Maris can bring them back to you."

"Thanks, you've always got my back."

"Of course. What happened, anyway? You'd have to be out drinking in the woods. Is there something you're hiding from us, Mill? You're not an alcoholic, are you?" He laughs.

"No, that's your girlfriend. I'm kidding, of course. Maris is a good girl. She wouldn't be a drunkard."

"Oh, come on, Millie, Maris is anything but good. I love her but, Jesus Christ, that girl is fucking crazy. That's usually the case with the really sexy ones. Not much up top." He taps his temple with his index finger. There's a little voice inside me that is pushing me to remind him that she's in med school, and he failed very basic arts units, and it takes a lot of effort to quash it. It's been programmed into me since I was tiny. Maris can't be insulted. I must react. A good sister always defends, explains away, deflects. "You, of all people, would know she's brainy. You deal with her the most."

"Well, not lately. I never get to see her anymore, she's always too busy. Tell me something, Millie. Is there something going on with her and that weird guy that's living in your house?" He pauses. "And why exactly is that guy living with you guys?"

"Hunter, I could really use a drink right now."

"Of course. I'm sorry for being rude. What would you like?" "A martini. Or a gin and tonic. Actually, anything with gin."

He stares at me and laughs again. "You're not doing a good job of convincing me you're not an alcoholic. I've got you, though, don't worry." He reaches for the telephone on his bedside table and asks one of the kitchen staff for a martini and a Diet Coke. "You have to level with me. You can't need alcohol unless it's something bad. Just tell me. Is Maris cheating on me?"

The names threaten to tumble out, all at once. Charles. Christopher. Jack. Stephen. Lilith. Heather. All the nameless boys too. I sit still and force myself to focus.

"You're my only close friend right now. Jack's gone AWOL after Carol. He is always crying. He feels so guilty about it. And Stephen's always busy."

Hunter doesn't realize why Jack feels guilty. It's not about Carol's disappearance, it's about the fact that he was about to leave her for Maris only days before the worst happened. He'd been sneaking around with her, thinking she'd dump Hunter for him too. He was misinformed. There was no chance of that happening. The merger of Hunter's family and ours is inevitable and the most profitable for her. Her side pieces would always remain that way, despite the glimmers of hope she gave them. Maris has been cheating on Hunter for about as long as they've been dating. I've never divulged that information to anyone. I've been sworn to secrecy. I don't want to end up bruised and bloodied. There's a knock on the door, and thankfully alcohol comes with it. I sip my martini, enjoying the little lemon twist Larissa added. "She's not cheating on you." I avoid his gaze.

"You're not a good liar."

He's wrong. I'm one of the best. I'm crafty. I've lied directly to him more times than I can count. It's just that I don't want to lie anymore. I don't want to protect someone this vile. Someone who could do this to someone she claimed to love. The image of her foot on the decapitated head makes me want to hurl. It keeps flashing in my mind. Maris laughing, Carol decaying.

"What do you want me to say?"

"I need the truth. Please. No one's talking to me right now." He sits down on his obsessive-compulsively made bed and pulls on a white polo shirt. I feel sorry for him, for the way he's been treated. His best friend, his girlfriend. The two people he should be able to trust the most. Maris enjoys putting him through the wringer. She knows he'll stay. She loves the slow torture, the mind control, keeping him on the hook. That's the way she is with men. She's on the mark with Hunter. She's always said he's slow, and he must be to not know how often she cheats on him. I mean, he'd have to be an imbecile. A complete imbecile. She does it so brazenly. She rubs his face in it. I think that's the only reason why she's keeping Charles at our house. He's her temporary plaything, but she knows how much it's bothering Hunter, so he's becoming more of a permanent fixture.

"I don't think it's Maris you need to talk to. I think you need a conversation with Jack."

"Jack's been avoiding me." He looks like he's about

to cry. I feel horrible. I don't understand Maris's motivation. I don't understand how things like this make her feel good. I give him a hug, and he rests his head against me. "Mill, you're truly the only person I can talk to. You've got to know something."

I wish I could tell him what was actually devastating. Cheating is one thing, but it doesn't compare to the heinous activity she's been involved in. Carol was her best friend, and she would've met the same fate as the blonde at Tiger Mountain. To degrade and humiliate her corpse, one would have to be dead inside or blackmailed for something worse. I can't give her up if she's doing it to hide her own murders, no matter how sick it makes me feel. I can, however, relieve my burden slightly by outing her infidelity. "She and Jack were sleeping together before Carol went missing," I blurt out. Color drains from his face. He really didn't know. He goes limp in my arms, so I pull away and sit beside him. I gulp down the remains of the martini and feel it churn in my stomach.

"I'm sorry I didn't tell you. She would kill me. I've felt so guilty about it."

I see a tear trickle down his cheek, but he quickly wipes it away, concentrating his stare on the carpet and sitting very still. It takes him a while to speak. "How long has it been going on?" "A while. Six months, maybe. He was going to dump Carol.

He thought Maris would dump you, but she never would." "Does she still love me?"

I don't think Maris is capable of loving anyone other than herself and me. I still answer. "Yes."

"Well, everyone slips up sometime, don't they?" he rationalizes.

A forlorn little boy.

"Yes, of course. I shouldn't have said anything. Maris will kill me. Jack will kill me."

"Did Jack talk to you about this?"

"No, he kept sneaking out. Maybe he forgets that my bedroom is right under Maris's and the staircase goes right past me. He hasn't come over in a week now." My throat is burning, and my mind is flooded with images of the blonde girl's severed head. I don't know how many drinks I'll need to make it all go away. One is not enough. I want to lie down on the floor and sleep, but I'm scared to close my eyes. I have night terrors already.

"I just...I don't know. I don't understand. I thought she was mad at me."

"Why would she be mad at you?" She treats him like an indentured servant. She's explained it to me, he hurt her when she was younger, so she has the right to hurt him now, for as long as she wishes to. She always makes him feel like he's done something wrong.

"I didn't take her to Swan Lake. She really wanted to go. I was sick."

"Look, I doubt she's upset that you missed the Seattle Opera once. It's not like she hasn't seen Swan Lake before a gazillion times."

"She blew me off right after that too. Told me she was sick that time. I know Maris. That's exactly the type of thing she would do to get back at me. And then within about ten minutes, she and this Charles weirdo are glued at the hip. I'd made a reservation at her favorite place. The guy threw a snit about it being so last minute too."

"I don't know what to tell you, Hunter. Your girlfriend is a problem. None of us understand her." I don't want to either. I don't want to get inside that mind. Maris has many filters, so I can only imagine how dark it'd be in there without them. I wonder how her psychiatrist sleeps.

"I don't think she'd cheat on me, honestly. She can be a bit shifty, but she's not a liar or a cheat," he says with false resolve.

Carol's face flashes again. "Hunter, I think I'm going to be sick." I run to the bathroom and keel over the sink. He follows, handing me a Kleenex box. He holds my hair as I heave. "I'm sorry," I say. "I'm really sorry."

"Relax, Millie. It's alright. Nothing I haven't seen before." He strokes the top of my head.

"Larissa will clean it up."

"You're so sweet, Hunter." I wipe my mouth with the Kleenex. I feel grateful for his company. While a bit ditzy, he's truly sweet, kinder than Maris deserves. He gives me a hug, the awkward kind that platonic males and females give to one another. He doesn't realize that we've been a lot more intimate than this, and for that I'm glad. Maris wanted to keep it under wraps. It was a ploy.

"I think you need to lay off the drink for tonight."

"I think so too. I want another martini, but I don't want to mess up your floor." My hands are too clammy to handle glass. I turn on the tap and tilt my head under it, rinsing out my mouth before gargling a shot of his Listerine. I wash my face and wipe it off with a hand towel. I'm unsteady as I walk back to my seat.

"Can I get you some water? You're a bit pale. I'm glad you care.

At least one of the Caldwell girls does."

Does he think I'm this upset about Maris cheating on him? It's fine if he does. I wouldn't be able to explain the real reason anyway, not without Maris being arrested. I can't do that to her. Not even if my stomach twists in agony, and I must spend days hunched over a toilet bowl. At least I'll never have to diet. "No, I'm okay, thank you, though."

"Come on, sit down. Don't go falling over again." He guides me back to my seat.

"I thought you'd be angrier," I tell him. "You don't deserve to be treated like that."

"Well, there's no point being angry at you. You didn't do anything. I mean, you could've told me earlier, and I thought you would, but at least I know now."

"He's not the only one, Hunter," I say quietly. My will buckles.

I hadn't planned to tell him any of this. "What do you mean?"

"You can never tell her that I told you." "Millie, we're beyond that." He steels himself.

It's the one that'll hurt him the most. "Stephen."

He laughs for what seems like a minute straight. "Now I know you're fucking with me. Not Stephen, she wouldn't."

"I guess Stephen was studying physiology with Maris in her room, must be why his clothes were in our hamper. Isn't he majoring in engineering, though?"

I want him to feel the same rage I do. I want him to hate her as much as I do. I want her to face consequences for what she's done. This is the only way I can do it. I'm in agony. Carol deserved better. They all did. I did.

I startle when he smashes his nightstand lamp against the wall. "Jesus, what the fuck, Hunter? You're going to wake everyone up."

"No, my room's soundproof. You know that." He looks down at a shard of glass in his palm. It's pierced through his skin, forming an unsightly tear.

"I shouldn't have said anything."

"No, you should have. You should've done it a hell of a lot sooner. I can't believe you would hide this from me." He shakes his head. "No, I'm sorry. I know Maris, she'd murder you."

I feel sick again when I hear the word. I wish I were him. I wish I could be ignorant, raging about my wholesome little girlfriend cheating on me, not being aware of things that matter. He's thinking about her perfect body and her glorious, innocent-devil face, wondering why it doesn't belong to him alone. I'm thinking of my best friend being decapitated. Tears start flowing again, but he of course thinks it's about him and his relationship.

"It's okay, Millie. I'm sorry for snapping at you. It's not your fault," he reassures me.

I want to run away, go back to our villa in Barcelona and lie on the daybed in the sun, weeping in the fetal position, as far as I can be from Maris geographically. I can't face Carol's mother. Mrs. Greene's agony has been unmissable, and I'd had no idea what was going on—it was bad enough then. Now that I do know, I won't be able to be in the same room with her without cracking, which will make Maris crack my skull open. I seek refuge in Hunter's arms, in his fastidiously tidy room, in his oblivious friendship.

"I'm sorry, Hunter. I really am. I wish I could tell you everything."

"Is there more?" He pales.

I stare down at the floor. I can't talk anymore without dissolving into absolute hysteria. I could write him a list on his monogrammed stationery, but even I know it wouldn't be comprehensive. Maris claims to show me one hundred percent of her life, but I find it impossible to believe. She would hide plenty from me too. The notches in her bedpost are more plentiful in her knowledge than mine. She'd hide them like she hides her (infrequent but very real) D grades. She can't ruin her chaste, straight-A image. She can't be a known bisexual. She only studies, exercises and has sex within her monogamous ten-year relationship. Nobody would even believe me if I told them the truth. She is much better with her words than I am. She can enchant, her compliments spiraling through people until they radiate sunshine, until they feel infallible. I don't have that kind of charm on my side. I'm blunt. I strive to be honest in all situations that don't involve her. I don't flatter people for favors, I physically cannot. My brain freezes, my mouth jams. Unless she's with me, prodding me, or has sent me on a job, I stay silent and observant. I'm either with her or I'm thinking about her. I could confidently say that about everyone that is in her orbit, but it's not all adulation like she believes.

Hunter wipes the gash on his hand, using a tissue in the place of a Band-Aid.

"Oh, Hunter, come here. You're going to hurt yourself." Maris is the doctor of the family, but I'm the one that took the MCAT for her, not that she'll ever admit it. She begged me for days, then resorted to threats. I put pressure on the wound, which soon soaks through the tissue. "Jesus."

"I'm fine," he tells me, clearly choking back tears of pain. "It's just a little cut."

"Where's the Dettol?"

"In the bathroom vanity. I don't need it."

"Yes, you do. Here, press on this while I get some." I move his fingers to where mine had been. I force them down and slide open the vanity. I find a small bottle of antiseptic behind a stash of barbiturates and Motrin. My eyes catch a glimpse of gold. I dig a little deeper. I see Carol's amethyst and white-gold birthstone ring hiding in a little nook. I have no doubt Maris is the one that stripped it off her friend's cold, dead finger to hide in her boyfriend's bathroom. I don't know why, though. I leave it untouched and return to Hunter.

His bleeding has subsided, but he winces when I dab some of the Dettol on the cut. "Fuck, Mill. I know it's not your fault. I shouldn't blow up at you."

"It's alright, don't worry about it. I'd probably react the same way."

"I know what'll cheer us up. I recorded a couple of episodes of Mary. I know how much you love her."

Maris and I always cuddle up on the sofa-bed to watch

Mary together. It's the only thing that can calm me down when I'm panicking, and it soothes her too. That or The Brady Bunch. I love Marcia. It's a sister thing, though. It's something I only do with Maris, and we never let anyone invade our private hobby. I'm not about to start now. Besides, I hardly think a television show will help ease his mind: he knows his girlfriend is cheating on him with not one but several of his own friends.

"I'd love to watch a movie. Do you have Valley of the Dolls?" It's the perfect movie to zone out to and worry about Sharon Tate's woes rather than your own. Surely, nothing's worse than getting your breasts cut off when they're your only redeeming quality.

"Yes, I do. Maris loves it." He opens the cupboard under the television and quickly scans the expansive list of titles. He pulls it out with precision. The other videos remain neat and stacked. He presses play and the VCR whirrs. "Come here, it's a lot more comfortable," he tells me when he climbs back on to his bed, patting the spot next to him.

Well, I have nothing to lose now. I sit beside him. Burrow into him. I can't derive strength from him, but at least I can distract myself. Maybe that's why Maris keeps him around. To bring her back in from the lip of the peril she enjoys so much. The opening scenes are warm and familiar. I know first-hand how much Maris loves this movie.

"Why do you stay with her, Hunter?" It's something I've always wanted to know but have never had the nerve to ask. He hardly has the motives of someone like Mom, who relies on Dad's status, wealth, and the public image she must wear, all of which, to her, outweigh the bruises on her body and the decades of mental trauma.

He is silent for a while, the only voice in the room is Barbara Parkins's. He turns to me. "She's the only person who makes me truly happy."

It's not the answer I expected. The usual answer is how pretty she is, how fun she is. Her charm can only be spread so far, fleeting in nature, and when it wears off, brutality can result. Ten years would certainly do it.

"I mean, obviously she's an absolute knockout. You've seen her. You've seen how guys act around her. But it's more than that. I couldn't live without her. She has so much more to her than just that face." He breaks out into a goofy grin. "You're a pal, Mill, and I know you're identical, but there's something special about her. That's how I know it's not about looks. There's a connection I could never have with anyone else."

I don't know if I should feel insulted or yell at him—that's how she makes everyone feel. He's not special to her.

"That's why I'm devastated. I can't imagine her with someone else or anyone putting their hands on her. She's the most valuable thing in my life. The happiest I'll ever be is at our wedding."

I'm tempted to buy a bottle of bleach and take away any resemblance I share. Maybe get a piercing on my tongue, tattoo my forehead, see a plastic surgeon like a D-list celebrity. Instead, I move toward Hunter, place my hand on the back of his neck and kiss him. I wait for him to recoil, but he doesn't. I want to mark Maris's territory as my own, to defy her and hold it over her head for the rest of her life. Hunter's arm twists around my waist, and he pulls me into him. I can feel his taut abdomen against mine and his lips are soft, probably due to the ChapStick he claims to not use. I'm crossing a boundary now. I feel wonderful, rebellious. It's not quite the revenge Carol deserves, but it's a minor victory. I can taste his minty toothpaste, smell the faint scent of his aftershave. His hair is freshly washed and almost glossier than mine. I let the lust and rage flood through me as I pull off his shirt.

"Millie, we probably shouldn't do this," he tells me,

unzipping my—her—dress. He kisses my neck, along my collarbone and then down my chest. "You're so beautiful, Maris."

I pretend I don't hear him calling my sister's name. He is lying to himself, pretending he's with her. I'm not selfish like Maris. I know that her sexual conquests are only of interest to her when she's the one being pleasured. I've heard all the gory details; I've seen them. She's proactive with her victims, not her lovers. This is where she and I differ, and I'm going to show Hunter that. I let him undress me and stare.

His fingers trace down the center of my body to my navel. It's undiscovered and familiar terrain all at once for him. "Keep going," I tell him as he slips my underwear off. "Please." It's not a word I often have to use in this context, but the desire pecks away at my will and pride, about to consume me whole. I want to feel him. I want him to drive the pain out. His mouth travels to my hips and between, and I wrap my legs around him. I hold him in close. I lose myself in the pleasure, grabbing the headboard to keep steady. I hear the moans, almost secondhand, as I drift from my body toward paradise. He doesn't rush, and I climax sooner than I usually do (if I do at all). The tingles radiate down my legs continually afterwards. I'm soon breathless, and I can't offer any more than a simple thanks. Instead, I stay quiet. It's my turn to take care of him. To allow him to see what he deserves and what he's been doing without. His body is wonderful: tanned, lean and just the right amount of muscular. My heart races, and I know my face is an embarrassing shade of red. I didn't expect it to feel this way.

I don't usually engage in casual sex. It's never been right for me. I've always found the buildup more rewarding, memorizing someone's reactions and cravings and letting them discover you. I need sex to be in the confines of a relationship, preferably monogamous, as lame as that sounds in the era of "free love" and second-wave feminist promiscuity. I feel flustered but excited as this isn't as transactional as I'd imagined. He props himself up on his forearms and fishes in the bedside drawer for a condom. The palatial door to his room opens, and I spring up, my heart racing. Mrs. Carlyle, or Camille as she insists on me calling her, walks in. Her strawberry-blonde hair is coiffed into a painful-looking French pleat, and she has on a full face of makeup but only a silk bathrobe instead of one of her traditional Chanel dresses.

"Oh dear, I'm so sorry," she says with a visual flinch. "Hunter, I came in to let you know Maris is at the door." Initially, she covers her eyes with the back of her hand, then she narrows in on me. The realization soon kicks in. "What on earth are you doing with Millicent?" It comes out as a shriek. "Your girlfriend is downstairs."

"Mom, you should knock. I'd get smacked if I barged in on you and Dad," he deflects.

"I can't believe you would do this to your girlfriend." She turns to look at me again. "Or your sister. Absolutely disgusting." I can't seem to formulate a sentence, so I lay silently, wishing I could pull the covers over my face and disappear the way I used to believe possible at age four. I stare at the wall because I can't meet her condemnatory glare.

"The sweet girl is in the foyer. What do you want me to do about this, Hunter?" She can demand an answer from him. He's blood, I'm not. I'm nothing.

"Can you keep her busy for five minutes. Just let Millie get dressed."

"Keep her busy? She's not a child, Hunter. This is disgraceful. Put on some clothes and go downstairs to meet your girlfriend." She gives me another mordacious look. "I suggest you get dressed in the meantime—I would say take the back exit, but I'm sure she's seen the car. Lord, what would Quinn say?"

Maybe Mother would let her know what lovely Maris is like without an audience, but I don't say it. "Yes, Mrs. Carlyle. Please don't mention this to my mother. It was an accident."

"I'd prefer it if you didn't come back to our home for some time, I'm so disappointed in you. I'd always thought you were such a lovely girl."

"I am, I haven't changed, Mrs. Carlyle. I'm sorry." "It's not me you need to apologize to."

"Lay off her, Mom," snaps Hunter. "Get out of my room." He's irritated but elated at the thought of Maris here. I can see he's struggling to contain his happiness. My soul is being eviscerated. Everything from tonight comes flooding back. I want to cry. I wish I hadn't seen it. I wish I'd driven the car off the side of a cliff. She's calm but forceful, which propels Hunter to his feet. He awkwardly threads his arm through his t-shirt. She leaves and closes the door behind her.

"Hunter, you can't tell Maris," I tell him, blinking back tears. "About any of it. I wasn't here, we weren't in bed, and you don't know that she's seen Jack or Stephen. Please, Hunter."

"I won't tell her, don't worry. You know my mom. She's probably had enough Percocet to forget this conversation tomorrow. Just get dressed." He smooths down the bed. I put on the overly dramatic dress. I anticipate a barrage of questions about why I'm in possession of it. I shift to the wingback chair, not wanting to re-rumple the sheets on the bed. Maris glides in on six-inch platforms. The gauzy material of her skirt trails behind her.

"What are you doing here?" she asks, first curious, then suspicious. "In my dress."

"Well, we didn't want to spoil the surprise about planning a birthday getaway for you," says Hunter. He manages to not fumble. I don't think I could say the same about myself.

"In my dress?" "That's a long story."

She smiles at me, the smile reserved for when she's furious but is pretending not to be. She glances down at the white-gold Piaget (identical to mine) on her delicate wrist. "You know what, darling? I've got time," she tells me, plonking herself down onto the bed. My leg breaks into a nervous twitch. The hawk eyes zero in on it right away.

"Hunter and I got a little drunk at Dante's, and I took a tumble and ruined my outfit. I didn't want Mom to see, of course."

She stares at me and then breaks. "It's not a shock, Millie, you've always been a bit of a klutz. Remember when you had that obsession with roller skating and fell into a trashcan in Central Park? That was a hoot!"

It's not the best of memories, so I don't try to recall it often, but I laugh with her. "I had those hotpants Mom said belonged on a streetwalker on the Lower East Side."

"Daddy still has them in his home office. On the bottom shelf next to his little booze stash."

"My hotpants?"

"No, you ninny, those roller skates. What kind of a person would keep their teenage daughter's fashion crimes on hand?"

"Of course. Anyway, I should get going. If Mom asks, I've been at a party."

"Wait, I'll come with you. I only came by to say hello to my boyfriend since he thinks I'm avoiding him," she says pointedly, glaring at him. Under recent circumstances, I can see why he flinches.

"Can't you stay the night?" He sounds like he's about to start bawling.

"No, you know I can't get a good night's sleep with someone else in my bed. We can get breakfast in the morning."

Hunter snorts. The likelihood of catching Maris awake before eleven is incredibly low, even for people she lives with. An outsider has no chance. "Just call me when you get up, and I'll pick you up for waffles."

CHAPTER SIXTEEN

Millie

I reach the house about ten minutes after Maris, despite leaving at approximately the same time. I didn't have the energy to continue driving like a lunatic to keep up with her. Besides, I feel like I'd be dead by now if I started taking the reckless turns she does. She's waiting for me in the foyer, dangling her bare feet off the edge of the three-person stool.

"Is there something you want to tell me, Millie?" She reaches her hand out to steady me as I try to slip off my shoes. "Is it normal to find your sister at your boyfriend's place this late at night?"

"It's been alright every time it's been your idea. Suddenly, it's not when it's mine."

Her laugh is ominous. "You clearly have something to say. Let's talk in my room." She looks around expectantly as if Mom will pop out of the shadows. She drops her purse on the floor and takes the stairs two at a time. I find myself following unconsciously.

I vow to stay silent, to not mention a thing. I'll keep it a secret, pretend I didn't see anything. Fight the nausea, fight the voice in my head. It's not worth the consequences. I steel myself as she sits down on her little Chesterfield loveseat and pulls me into her lap. She plays with my hair and kisses my cheek. "What's going on with you?" Her voice is gentle, sweet. My skin crawls, and my resolve lasts for all of three point four seconds.

"I saw you."

She stares at me. "You saw me what?"

I pull away from her and choose to sit on the end of the bed. I don't want her touching me. It's not even fear anymore; it's genuine revulsion. "I fucking saw you, Maris. Tonight."

"You're going to have to elaborate," she tells me calmly. "With Carol."

"Carol's dead, Millie. What are you talking about?"

I feel the tears gushing down my face. "You killed her. You killed your own best friend."

"Millie, are you huffing glue? I'm asking in all seriousness. You must be on something."

"I saw you with her and that guy at Tiger Mountain. I saw the decapitated head."

She flounders to maintain her composure. Her skin pales. "I knew someone was tailing me. I'm such a moron."

"Why did you do it?"

"Oh, get a grip, for fuck's sake. I didn't kill little Carol. I don't much care for hurting women."

"I'm going to see that girl's beheaded body for the rest of my life. Carol must've looked exactly the same. She wouldn't have been spared. You can do a little better than swearing and deflecting," I shout.

"Millicent, be quiet. You're going to wake the bitch," she hisses at me. "I didn't kill Carol. Ted did."

"Bullshit he did. You're a liar. You're pathetic. I don't

know how you can live with yourself. You can't keep your lies straight or your legs closed."

"Says the girl trying to fuck my boyfriend. Honestly, if that boring dud makes you happy, you can go for it. I have a new toy three bedrooms down."

"You killed your best friend. You are scum."

"How many times do you want me to repeat myself? I didn't kill her."

"Did she rape and amputate herself?"

"Women can't rape. That was a male designed crime. I don't have the necessary appendage for that, you know? Kind of hard to grow a penis and produce semen overnight. Stop shooting yourself in the foot. Rub those two brain cells together and think about it for a second."

"So, you didn't rape her. That doesn't mean you didn't kill her or at least help the man who did."

"Why would I do that?" Her expression is devoid of emotion.

It makes me want to rip her throat out.

"Oh, I don't know, Maris, all you do is cause misery. You should be dead. Not Carol."

"Boy, that was a logically sound, utterly compelling theory, how on earth will I defend myself against that one, Sherlock?" She yawns for effect. "Are you done yet? I need some sleep."

I reach under her bed for her penknife before I can stop myself. I look directly at Maris, pin her down and hold it against her neck. She doesn't even flinch. She pauses for a second and then grins. She grabs my wrist and twists it sharply until I hear a crack and feel searing pain down my arm. Maris may not let me live through the night.

"If I can take down men who are double my weight, do you think you'd be a challenge?" Her voice drifts down from above me. I can't move my hand.

"You always need my help," I tell her through clenched teeth, tears streaming down my face. "Every male." I've endured her abuse for years. I've developed a tolerance for pain, but this is a particularly bad injury. She's broken my wrist. I try to pull away from her, but she grabs the Bible she keeps on her nightstand and slams it down on my hand. I let out a scream and double over. She kicks me in the gut and then steps on my face with considerable force.

"Don't you dare try to claim victory for any of my achievements."

I lay on the floor crying and shaking. She watches me, evidently disgusted.

"Boy, you're pathetic, you really are," she says. "I can't believe I'm related to you."

"Maris, you broke my wrist. I need to go to the hospital. Please." I know I should bolt, but my entire body feels numb, heavy.

"I'm going to watch Mary first. You'll survive." She settles into her bed, reaches over for the television remote and turns the volume of the set up to drown out my whimpers. "Jesus, Millie, it's a wrist. Dial it down a notch."

Mary's voice is normally a solace, comforting and sweet, but I can't focus on it through the pain. I stay on the floor and try to quieten down. If I anger Maris, this could get brutal. I don't know what else she could do to me today. Better a broken wrist than a broken hyoid bone. Mary is talking to the annoying new character Sue Ann Nevins, and Maris laughs when she hears that Sue Ann would rather flush her veal down the toilet than serve it reheated. Tears are still pricking at my eyes. I struggle in pain. If I try to get to Mom for help...I always had faith in Maris to not hurt me, but if she could violate Carol that way, I'd end up similarly. Normally, Maris would not strike my face—that would leave bruises. I try not to speculate how Carol had been murdered, what she would've endured, how she was callously desecrated. She was such a gentle, sweet girl. I'm not going to let her die in vain. I need to survive and not set Maris off. I can't be of much use from a grave. I'm patient. I wait for the twenty-two minutes of the show and eight minutes of commercials to pass. I ask her again, softer. "Maris, can you please take me to the hospital?"

She sighs, terribly inconvenienced. "Yes, alright, Millie. I'm not sticking around, though. I need to get some sleep. I'm very tired."

"You can just drop me off," I agree weakly. I'm bleeding from my cheek. "Outside, even, if you want."

She rolls her eyes at me. "Oh, thank you, your grace. How kind." She grabs a light coat from her wardrobe and pulls it on. She helps lift me, propping me up against her side. I lean on her for support when walking down the staircase. She's gentle as she tucks me into the passenger seat of her car and straps on my seatbelt. "I'm sorry," she tells me quietly before climbing into her seat. "I snapped. I didn't mean to hurt you. I couldn't believe you'd claim I'd do those things to Carol, of all people, and then you pulled a knife on me. I don't know how you think I could hurt her. I had nothing to do with it."

I'm timid but I try. "Why were you there?"

"Look, Ted knows some things that I can't afford for him to know. I have to play along so that I don't get caught out. I would think you'd understand that."

"How long have you known about Carol?" I wince as the pain flares up. I'm desperate for an opiate hit.

"He tried to pick me up that day, at Lake Sam. Ted. He pulled a phony ruse to get me to his car to do something dumb, to help unload a sailboat or some other bullshit like that. I thought it was ridiculous how he was asking women to help out with manual labor. I told him Hunter was waiting for me because I knew that he was lying, especially when there wasn't a boat—that beat-up little Beetle could barely drag along a bicycle for god's sake! It was a garbage rouse, terrible, but he was pretty darn attractive with those baby blues. You've seen him. Well, anyway, when Carol went off, I didn't realize he'd managed to fool her, so I genuinely had no clue about where she was. I went to visit one of my toys, the blonde college dude, in the bush, and Ted was there, and so was Carol, but I couldn't do anything—he would've murdered me. I struck up a bit of a friendship so that he knew I wasn't a threat. I can't tell the police and, clearly, I couldn't tell you either by the way you're reacting now. It was an unhappy coincidence. I didn't know other people visited there. It's not exactly the most popular hiking trail. If it were, I wouldn't be using it."

"You go to dinner with him as a friend?"

"Only twice now. I've got to keep up my end of the bargain." "You know, he tried to pick me up too."

She looks at me incredulously. "No, he didn't. You weren't there."

"Not on the fourteenth. The week before. He sat down next to me. He was reading a book and then asked if I'd go to dinner with him. I told him no and he left. I didn't think about it at all until I saw you with him at Mama Barone's."

"You're fucking with me."

"No, Maris, I'm not." I hold my wrist in place and my teeth grind involuntarily from the agony. I'm confused, I don't understand why this is making her angry. Does she think it makes her less special that he approached me too? "I'm not fucking with you. He asked me too."

She brakes the car to a sudden halt in front of the hospital's emergency department, jerking me forward in my seat.

I break into a nervous sweat seeing the gray linoleum floors and bleak bare concrete walls. I panic at the sight of hospitals—the flashbacks of bones breaking, bruises on my body, contusions to my head, from before I could read, at the hands of my father and then my mother, and eventually my sister. I recall all the tears that I shed alone in the private rooms when my parents were too busy to visit me and would have the nanny attend with a homecooked meal so that I wouldn't have to eat mystery meatloaf and stale mashed potatoes because "Caldwells never consume hospital food." My solitary consolation would be a visit from Carol or Mrs. Greene. They'd bring games and toys and books that would be read out to me in the most soothing of tones. Mrs. Greene would hug me (if I wasn't nursing a shattered bone) and her perfume would be warm and wonderful. Hunter would occasionally drop by with some candy and Stephen if he weren't too busy sulking about his own life. When Maris came, my body would shudder involuntarily, flinching at the thought of another injury, but she was never mean to me in public. She'd sit with me like any good, loyal sister would and, in front of the doctors, she'd always help feed me and comb my hair, often using her own hair ribbons to make beautiful bows on my plaits. I dread hospitals. I feel nauseated, reluctant to leave the car but frightened of spending more time with Maris. She has her sweet moments—she would take care of me when I got home, fixing me large bowls of ice cream and sneaking in Godiva gems, telling god-awful jokes that'd make me laugh out of sheer embarrassment, and that's the Maris that I try to remember, but recently there's been no trace of her.

My lip trembles. The tears begin to drip again, my body seizing with fear.

"You are such a fucking baby, stop crying and go inside. They'll patch you up and send you on your way within an hour, tops." She offers a cruel smile, revealing the inner sadist as she does every so often. "You're kind of a VIP now, aren't you? They should give you a loyalty card and a stamp every time you visit." I open the car door with my good hand, and she gives my shoulder a little shove, pushing me out. I let out a little yelp, and she laughs. I walk in through the familiar sliding entrance for what feels like the thousandth time. Maris soon follows, which is unexpected. I thought she'd dump me outside as per usual.

"You're coming in?"

"You act like I'm some kind of a monster, Millicent. You're hurt, of course I'm going to help you in. I'm your sister."

My heart is racing, and I want to run away, but I'm in too much pain to put up a fight. Maris strides confidently to the reception and triage, walking straight past the people in the queue. The nurse looks up at her, confused.

"Hi, I'm Maris Caldwell. My sister fell down some stairs, and she must be looked at urgently." She gives the people waiting a disparaging look when they try to speak up. She drums her manicured nails against the countertop. "Is Dr. Islington in? He knows our family very well."

"Yes, he is. I'm afraid she's going to have to fill out some forms and wait. There's a backlog tonight."

"Oh, I think you're a little bit confused, my darling." She glances down at her name badge. "Glenda, right? I'd page Dr. Islington right now if I were you and needed to keep my job." She smiles.

The nurse appears defiant but gets elbowed in the rib by the woman next to her, one whom I vaguely recognize as one of my previous nurses. "Just do it," she whispers.

"Let me see what I can do," Glenda responds tersely. She glares first at Maris and then at me but stands up and reaches for a wheelchair. I offer her an apologetic look. "You can sit down, dear."

"Thanks, Glenda, I really appreciate you taking care of my sister," says Maris. "Do you need me to wheel her in or are you capable of handling that job all by yourself?"

I'm angry at Maris but nearly giggle at her condescension. She's not wrong. Glenda probably would get fired—Dr. Islington is the head physician of the emergency department and is a very good friend of Dad's, as is the chairman of the hospital, Dr. Leonards. Maris loves toying with her inferiors.

"I can handle it, young lady. Perhaps you ought to go home to bed," she snaps.

"I think I'll stay here with my sister. Is it illegal to spend time with an injured sibling? I'm very concerned for her welfare. Quite frankly, you would've left her to wait hours and even I, with only a partial medical degree, can tell you that a broken wrist and facial welts can be quite serious and could worsen with a wait. Maybe we should call Dr. Leonards and see what he thinks."

"We'll get her admitted and into an x-ray right away, Miss Caldwell," says the other nurse, bouncing off her stool as quickly as humanly possible, ushering me into the chair. "We have your insurance details on file."

"Thank you very much, my dear. My family will most certainly appreciate your help. What was your name again?"

"It's Simone, Miss Caldwell. Simone Beckett."

"Excellent, thank you, Simone. I'll come inside with Millie to help her get settled. Nobody likes going to a hospital alone, least of all my sister."

Glenda looks on in disgust, but I've come to agree with Maris. Without her, I would've been waiting for hours. I'm not strong enough to do what Maris does. I'd be too afraid of the judgment from people talking about me and wondering what they're thinking. I would accept my fate and endure the hours in an uncomfortable bucket chair in the waiting room. I don't use our name as an express pass through life. They wheel me into a private room with the same bland plastic curtains and squeaky floors. Another nurse greets us, and both she and Simone lift me into the bed. They're stronger than they seem. Maris gets ready to leave as soon as I'm tucked in under a stiff cotton sheet.

"I'll tell Mother to come and get you in the morning or call me if they let you out early. I might be awake," she tells me as she heads out the door. I don't know if I'm happy or sad to see her go.

"I'm in a lot of pain," I tell the new nurse. I can cry now. "I know, honey. What happened to you?"

"I fell down the stairs. I think my wrist is broken. My face hurts."

"I don't think you fell down any stairs. Are you protecting someone? A boyfriend, maybe?"

"No. I fell down some stairs." My head feels fuzzy. I don't know if I'm concussed or still drunk. "Can I please get some painkillers?"

"Of course, honey. I can get a line in you, and then we'll bring in a doctor to chart some pain relief. Would you like to talk to somebody? We have a counselor here 24/7."

"No, just some painkillers, please."

She nods but still appears concerned. I probably would, too, if I had someone like me come in. She misses a vein twice. Maris would be ideal for this job, being good with handling needles. When the nurse finally connects an IV, she calls in a doctor, and soon the morphine floods my body, wrapping me into a cloud of comfort and steering me into a deep sleep.

I wake up groggy and disoriented. It takes me several minutes to realize where I am and why. My wrist is stiff, and when I look down, I notice that it's been wound into a tight plaster-cast. There's an IV in my forearm, and I feel sickly. I reach for the assigned bag and vomit out what feels like my entire stomach and intestines.

I try to sit up, but I feel too queasy. I wipe my mouth with a tissue and sob. My entire body is wracked with pain. There's a sharp stinging on my face, where Maris stood on me, and my abdomen is raw and bruised. I don't know what time it is, but there is a pool of pale light streaming in from the gap in the curtain—possibly dawn. I feel helpless. I have nobody to call. Mom wouldn't be awake, and she certainly would not make the trip down. I don't know if Dad is even in town. Maris will be asleep, so will Hunter and Jack. Carol would've come and stayed with me, day or night. I miss her soothing touch, her kind voice. I sob silently. My body is weak. I'm scared of the repercussions of going home.

I know I need to tell Mom what's happened when I get back. I need to make sure Maris isn't in the house—she can't know I've said anything. Mom would be horrified if she knew Maris played a part in Carol's abduction. I don't believe Maris at all—knowing her, she would've assisted Ted. She would have no regard for the safety or life of Carol, especially not if hers was at stake. Hell, she would give Carol up for a line of coke or a couple of Quaaludes. She would do anything to save her own hide and continue killing boys for sport.

There was something between her and Ted in those woods. She was in awe of him. The vibe between them was very disturbing. I fear for the missing girls. They must've suffered the same fate as Carol. Raped, mutilated, murdered, and desecrated. The pain and horror they endured are unfathomable—their lives were inconsequential, less important than a sole man's psychological gratification, and Maris is aiding and abetting this! She almost became a victim. I almost became a victim. We would've been dumped at Taylor Mountain with Ted violating our decapitated bodies. He is a rabid animal, attacking at any cost. Beautiful, intelligent, unique women who were now nothing more than faceless corpses.

I wish I could go to Mrs. Greene and tell her what had happened to her baby. She deserves to know that her grief is justified—Carol was not safe, and she has been the victim of a voracious predator. I want her spared the details. I don't want her to have the same imagery of a decapitated head, with a missing eye, in her mind for the rest of her life. That's something that I will have to live with. She deserves better. I could never subject her to that trauma. The police will be kind to Mrs. Greene. They'll tell her no more than the bare minimum. I buzz for a nurse. The pain is overwhelming, and I'd rather the nauseous opiates and a few more hours of hazy sleep. She relents without much fight, injecting another dose of morphine and handing over a few pills of Motrin. I reject the latter. I know I'll throw them right back up.

When I wake up, Mom is sitting primly in one of the stiff hospital chairs beside my bed. It's an unfamiliar sight. She fears hospitals almost more than I do, and she's never once picked me up. I'm tender and woozy.

"They're happy to send you home now, Millicent. They gave me a call at six this morning. Your wrist is fractured in three places but, otherwise, you're alright. My poor darling, what happened to you?"

"Maris," I say. It's all the explanation she needs. She's used to the drill.

"I'll need to talk to her when we get home. She's only just gone to bed."

"No, Mom, please. You can't talk to her. Please. I don't know what else she'll do to me."

My mother sighs, fiddling with her opal and pearl necklace. "I don't know what we're going to do with that girl."

"Nothing, please. Just leave it alone."

"She can't keep getting away with this. She's out of control. I won't have that in my house," she tells me firmly. "Now get dressed so we can get you home. This place gives me the shivers. I've brought you a freshly ironed dress from the laundry. I didn't want to go through your wardrobe at this ungodly hour."

"Mom, I need a little bit of help to get the hospital gown off. My arm is killing me."

She finally pushes her huge, round sunglasses to the top of her head, revealing her vivid honey eyes and the dark circles beneath them. There is light bruising on the top of her right cheekbone. "Millie, I'm far too tired. Call the nurse."

I buzz for the nurse again, and she shows me the maternal nurturing I'll never experience from Mom. I don't think Mom even wanted kids, and I think she regrets having Maris and me. It was Dad who wanted children to carry on his legacy and company. I can't imagine what she would've been like during her pregnancy. Motherhood is meant to be joyful, but it's been far from that for her. The nurse gently slips off the gown and helps me into the rigid floral frock Mom brought for me. I don't think it's even mine, or if it is, I haven't seen it in about a decade.

"Can I do anything else to help, Miss Caldwell?" the nurse asks, her tone soothing and sweet. I don't know how she can manage to be so chipper after pulling a night shift, but I appreciate it more than she can imagine. I wish I could curl up into her arms and have her stroke my hair, the way I always wished Mother would have when I was little and lonely.

"No, that's all, thank you," I tell her, still groggy. My voice croaks. I want to spend the day in the safe cocoon of my bed, my door locked so no one can come in to drag me back into reality.

"Alright now, you wait here, and I'll bring the wheelchair." "I'm okay to walk," I say, but I'm unsure. I feel like my legs will give way, but I find wheelchairs terribly embarrassing. I didn't come in needing a wheelchair, and I don't think I need one to leave.

"It's hospital policy. I won't be a moment."

My mother watches her with suspicion and envy. That

caring and protective instinct isn't something she's ever had, and I think she wonders how others experience it. She was more than happy to dump us on a new nanny every few months when the previous one would run away. When alone with Maris and me, she did the bare minimum to care for us. Canned soups and messily braided hair. Her mother is sweet and affectionate, but I guess it missed a generation, or my mother was resentful for being forced into parenthood.

I get wheeled out to the exit, and I shiver in the frigid morning air. Mom is bundled into a butter-soft cashmere coat and long Chanel pants. It would've been great if she'd had the insight to bring me something warm. She helps me into the car and waits until I'm buckled in before driving.

"I'm going to take the scenic route, and you're going to tell me what happened to you," she says, reaching over to turn on the heater. I'm grateful for the warmth. "Maris isn't here, so you can talk freely for once." She's the most authoritative I've ever heard her. Normally it's Dad who carries that power.

I hesitate to speak. My throat is sore, and my cheek is aching. I don't think I could tell her without breaking down. The horror playing out is more than I can bear. "Nothing happened, mom. It's one of those scuffles with Maris."

"It looks like a little more than that, Millie. I will not drive home until you tell me, and I don't think either of us wants to stay in here any longer than we have to."

"I don't know where to begin."

"Maris is involved with what happened to Carol, isn't she?" Her gaze sears holes into the side of my face, and I'm stunned into silence. That isn't at all what I was expecting. I've never known her to be involved with or have any knowledge of Maris's activities.

"Why do you think that?"

"I'm not as oblivious as she thinks I am. I don't think it was a coincidence that she was around when Carol disappeared. I know what that girl is capable of. She is a heinous creature. There has always been something wrong with her."

"She says she didn't do anything to Carol. She was there, but she didn't do anything."

"You know I don't appreciate liars."

"Mom, I've had a lot of morphine, and I'm about a minute from puking. I don't want to discuss this right now."

"We're not going home until you tell me."

I've never seen her dig her heels in this intensely. She's not often a stubborn person, despite what Maris says. She's finicky and a perfectionist about jobs needing to be completed, but she never offers ultimatums. I want to tell her so I can go home and lie in my own bed, but I also don't want to tell her because Maris will kill me, maybe literally. The beatings at her hands are getting more severe by the day, and the drugs aren't helping. She's been more volatile than I've ever seen.

"What do you want to know?"

"First, what she's done to you and then what she's done to Carol. I know she's involved, and I will know if you're lying."

"Listen, I'm sick of being everyone's punching bag. I hear crap from her and from Dad, and now you're being horrible to me too. I've been in hospital all night. I don't want to be spoken to like this. I'm sore and unwell. Please talk to me calmly. I'm not the criminal."

"Alright, I apologize if I sounded rude. I'm frustrated with the situation, not you."

"It's fine." I press the gauze against my lacerated cheek. "How much do you know?"

"I know that she's hurt quite a few boys, and that she's out most of the night, every night, doing god knows what with god knows who."

I decide to omit specificities and focus on Maris's recent activity because it's mostly what Mom is concerned with.

She's attached to Carol, almost more than she is to Maris and me.

"She says she didn't kill Carol. She wanted me to plant some evidence on Hunter. I'm not sure exactly what it was because I didn't take the keepsakes and Polaroids. I followed her because I was suspicious of what she was doing. You know when Hunter hit her at the ball and that nice-looking guy picked her up? Well, she went to dinner with him."

"That lovely Ted? He was delightful to speak with. He didn't look like Maris's type at all. A little bit on the older side. He looked more your speed. I had half a mind to organize a date for the both of you."

"As much as I'd appreciate that Mom, he'd already tried well before then. Dating wasn't on his mind. Ted killed Carol. He tried to pick me up the week before that, then he tried to pick up Maris an hour before Carol disappeared. Like I was saying, she went to Mama Barone's, and he met her there. I thought it was fishy. I hid in the car, and I don't think either of them saw me. I followed them. They both drove to Tiger Mountain...where Maris goes to do certain things that I won't get into now."

"Tiger Mountain? The hiking track Maris and your Father use?" "Yes, you have to park down at the bottom and walk up. I don't think you've been there." Mom's as unathletic as me. Maris and Dad are the fitness fanatics. I couldn't imagine anything worse than hiking on a Sunday. I'm only there for familial obligations. "What was Maris doing there at night? I knew she was involved."

"She said she had nothing to do with it, but I saw her and that other blonde girl's head."

"What do you mean 'the blonde girl's head'—you don't..." "She was decapitated. Maris had a foot on her head. It was already decomposing, but I knew it was her, and Maris admitted it was."

"I think I'm going to be ill," Mom tells me. Her small hands are trembling on the steering wheel.

"You're lucky you didn't have to see it. I can't stop thinking about her. I close my eyes and it's there, again and again. Maris was laughing, too, like Ted was telling her witty jokes or something."

"Did she see you there? Did he?"

"No, they didn't see me, but I told her I was there, that I saw it all. That's how I ended up in the hospital. I'm scared, Mom. I've never been this scared. You can't tell her about it. I don't know what she'll do to me. She's getting more violent every time. I'm in so much pain." I inadvertently start crying again.

It's hitting me again as the morphine wears off. The realization of what I've just admitted to my mother. It's like taking a nightlight away from a kid, forcing them to acknowledge the darkness whether they're ready or not. I prefer ignorance. Mom ends up driving to the mouth of Lake Washington and does an abysmal parking job across two spaces. She leans forward against the steering wheel, placing her arms over the back of her head. I hear a few sobs. She looks even smaller than usual, her compact frame fitting neatly into the seat. Locks of her hair tumble out of her loose ballerina bun. She slips her sunglasses back on. She doesn't like to be seen crying. Dad hates weakness and, though it took time, Mom's learned the stronger she looks, the less likely she is to be beaten or hurt. "My daughter," is all she says. I don't think she's been this devastated since the first time Maris killed. "I'm a failure."

"Mom, please promise you won't tell her. I'm begging you." "I have to tell Henry. I can't handle this on my own. He will protect us. We will be okay."

"He won't believe us. Maris will come up with a story. The last time I told him, he went straight to her. She split my lip, and my arms were bruised for a week." I'm nearing the stage of hyperventilation. If Maris finds out I've talked, she'll make sure no one will hear me again. If I go to the police, my parents will go to any length to protect her and the family name. Nothing is more important than our name and reputation. A serial killer daughter involved with the Ted killings would unquestionably cause a significant drop in bookings in our hotels and a damaged profit margin. Our board of directors is quite conservative, but even the most liberal of people would be disgusted.

It's not like I'm entirely innocent either. Maris could implicate me without any trouble. I participated in her crimes. I helped her clean up. I feigned naiveté when people questioned me. I hold her secrets. It's what family does, but I know Mom will think less of me for not having the integrity or courage to stand up to Maris. Each killing made me sick, and the victims piled up in my head, always watching me, forcing me to concede the atrocities committed against them. I remember them every night before I sleep. Their cries for help are burned into my memory. If I hadn't have helped, Maris wouldn't have been able to carry out most of the crimes. I could've saved dozens of lives. She claims that she's done many without me, but I find it doubtful. If she has, she has more reasons for Saint Peter to keep the gates shut. I've accepted my fate; I deserve brimstone and fire. Maris understands the concepts of guilt and culpability on a cerebral level, but she can't process it physically like the rest of us. She doesn't feel the same kick in the gut, the nightmares, and nausea. I can't say the same about myself. For me, it's crippling, no matter how hard I work to justify it. The cognitive dissonance is all-consuming.

"Millicent, you need to stay strong and have faith in me. I'm your mother. I will protect you. Nothing will be done to you. I'll have her put in jail if I must. She will not lay another finger on you, my precious girl. I've let you down before, I know, but I'll be better this time." She reaches over to hug me, and I try to nestle into her bony shoulder. It seems foreign and wrong. As a child, I'd have the warm embrace of chubby nannies who cared for me as if I were their own. This cold, emaciated woman feels unnatural, despite our mirror-image visage. I extricate myself from her arms and try to control the avalanche of emotions threatening my sanity.

"Please, Mom. You don't know what she'll do to me."

"Just trust me. You will be fine. We all will. She needs to face justice for what she's doing. What did she do to you last night?" "She socked me in the stomach, stood on my face, and broke my wrist. Well, fractured it. I don't know, it hurts all the same.

I deserved to be punished for what I did, but Carol didn't do anything."

"What did you do? Honey, you can't blame yourself for what Maris does."

"I can't tell you. It's so humiliating."

She shakes her head. "Your sister is involved in murders. There isn't much you can do to compete. I've already failed as a mother, and this is how I'm being punished for not wanting children."

She's never admitted it before. I don't know how to react. "Can we go home?" I can't tell her about Hunter.

"Yes. Avoid Maris until I tell you it's alright to speak to her. Barricade yourself in your room if you must. I need to talk to Henry. You'll be okay, Millicent. She can't do anything to you if we're around, and we will be."

If Maris were controlled that easily, we wouldn't have a serial killer in the family. My tremors get worse the closer we get to the house. I can imagine her in her bedroom. Inert but awake, watching television, bingeing or starving—whatever suits her at the present stage. She could be asleep, but she rarely sleeps for more than three or four hours at any one stretch. The Benzedrine keeps her awake and productive if she doesn't have coke, and the benzodiazepines help her sleep. I always thought the lack of a conscience would help her sleep easy. I guess not. The dread fills the pit of my stomach and slowly spreads throughout my body until I'm almost paralyzed as we pull into the driveway.

"Remember what I've told you," Mom says, quiet and stern. She sets her purse down on the table on the foyer, despite never allowing me to do so ("It's so uncouth!") and calls for my father. It's not a surprise that he's not home. He's never home.

"Go to your room. Stay there."

I climb the stairs cautiously, making as little sound as possible. I feel settled when I don't hear her television, but the despair soon returns when I realize she could be reading or studying for exams she doesn't need to take for another three months unless she wants to continue her string of Ds. I want her asleep, benumbed by downers. I lock the door immediately when I get into my room. Mom's words lend me no sense of security.

I'm happy to remain imprisoned in my little suite. I have candy bars and television. It's comfortable as far as prisons go and a small price to pay for safety. My heart is still pounding in my chest, and the memories of Carol are making the nausea unbearable. I keep a bucket by my bed and curl up with one of my plush teddy bears. I've had it since I was five. It was my substitute for a security blanket. Maris has a matching one with a navy-blue bow tie. Whenever we were subjected to physical mistreatment, we'd get new teddy bears, but I threw out every bear other than this one. It's been in all the bedrooms I've occupied over the last seventeen years. My room feels like a haven. It's perfectly designed and about the size of a small house. I have an unobstructed view of the immaculate gardens, tennis court, and the Olympic pool. When I need some time away but don't want to go too far, I take the pool house. It's on the far side of the pool, so it feels like it's a suburb away. When it was first built, Mom and I would escape together. While she'd never been truly maternal, sometimes she and I would share chocolate-coated almonds and read Roald Dahl storybooks, like we were in our own world. She would have her own bruises while mine were healing. Dad was too smart to bring his whores home, but Mom would know. She'd confront him each time, never taking into account the history of slaps and punches she'd received. She was brave in her own way. If I knew confronting him would result in a concussion or broken collarbone, I'd retreat into my own space and stay there.

She had the temper to rival him, but she was small and weak. She had no chance. She always refused refuge back in our grandparents' house in England. Her father was even richer than ours and always offered to get her out of the toxic relationship, but she loved Dad more than anyone could understand. Certainly, more than I could understand. I would've left him after the first slap.

As his daughter, I didn't have the same freedom. I couldn't just leave. I was a child, vulnerable. I didn't have a choice, but she did. If she'd left, I could've had a real childhood, not one filled with abuse. I had glamour and luxury but none of the love of a regular home. I've never experienced middle-class life, so I can't speak to it, but I believe I'd prefer a home in which I was cherished than one in which I was rewarded with opulent cars and handbags for my silence during abuse. I don't think nannies and trips to Paris can take the place of doting parents. Hell, I'd be happy with mild affection. It would be strange, but it would mean something. I've never felt wanted by my family, but I suppose not everyone has the freedom to reach into their wallet and take out a limitless credit card. I can fly to any city in the world and my parents would be none the wiser.

You'd have to care about someone to wonder why they're not around, and I'm in no danger of that. Perhaps Maris cares: we do have a bond, and she needs me to run errands for her. It's a bleak existence, but one day soon I'll be my own woman. I'll go back to university and study child psychology, have my own practice. Fix the broken kids. Maris is going to run the hotel business anyway. Our dad would never trust me with it. I remember writing him a letter when I was ten, for Father's Day—I told him that he was my inspiration, that I'd be good like him and wanted to achieve the greatness he had. I found the letter crumpled in the bin of his home office.

I glance out the window. The sun has made an appearance, and the skies are clear of any of Seattle's usual clouds. It's 10 AM. Mom had either picked me up a lot later than I thought, or we had spent a very long time in the car. I lie on my side and watch the dappled, glittering water of the pool. It is still and calming, without the waves of the ocean or water lapping in a lake. It's an arm's reach away, and it looks like the perfect escape. I wrap the cool, beige silk sheets around me, using two pillows to support my aching body. I wish I could talk to Carol about this, or the only other person who brings me comfort lately—Charles. Both are out of reach, held hostage by the same insatiable person.

There hasn't been a time Maris has "allowed" me to keep a boyfriend or girlfriend. I used to date Connor (a nickname for Cornelius, which he loathed) Wilton, a sophomore at UW, for a year and a half. I saw a future with him, despite how corny that sounds, despite his questionable involvement with Phi Beta Kappa, and despite how much Maris hated him. She enjoyed having unfettered access to me, and he was getting in the way of that, so he had to go. She made sure of it. She told him that I was cheating on him, which I'd never do, and shattered his self-esteem every time he came to the house for dinner. She always let him know he wasn't good enough to be a part of this crappy family. She made it seem like we were the Kennedys or the Rothchilds, for god's sake. He started to doubt himself and our relationship— he genuinely began to believe he wasn't good enough, despite his family's investment banking background. His insecurities got the better of him, after enough Maris's irritating jabs. She chipped away at his ability to trust me, and soon enough the relationship collapsed. She put her own relationships on hold to ensure mine dissipated.

Her determination makes her an indomitable force. I'm her property, with no more sentience or will than one of her purses. The only difference is that she'd never damage a purse. Humans are disposable to Maris, bags aren't. She isolated me from all my friends as the only ones I have now are ones we share. Carol was the one exception, one friend I had a genuine connection with outside of Maris. She had to steal her, too, to prove she will always have the upper hand. She says she wants what's best for me, and the answer is her. I've never known anyone as cruel or as kind as her.

I spend two hours in silence, staring at the pool before I get the courage to turn on the television. I freeze when I hear footsteps on the stairs. I'm grateful when they continue right past me. I know what I've got to do. I can't rely on my mom's words to ensure my safety or that of anyone else's. Maris on her own is enough of a terror to society. I don't know how much worse it'll get now that she's working with someone potentially more malicious than her. Leaking information is something that no one in the family will approve of, but it needs to be done. This matter needs to be handled by someone outside the family, not biased by the charm or ire of Maris or having to maintain the reputation of our brand. Mom says she'll have Maris put behind bars, but she's nothing but talk. She will never be able to convince Dad to punish her properly, to let the families of her victims know their loved ones aren't coming home. She'll still torture, maim and dismember in peace. I don't think Mom understands the extent of the crimes. I'm not sure if Dad does either. I call the only person I can trust. Elaine, Carol's mom.

CHAPTER SEVENTEEN

Millie

I've been staring at the ringing phone in my room for the last fifty-one seconds. My hand trembles as I reach for it. I'm still reeling from my conversation with Elaine. I feel my throat tensing, my words choked when I answer. "Hello?"

"Millie, it's your father. Quinn came to the hotel to let me know what's been happening. I know you're scared, but it'll be alright. I can help you. I didn't know how bad the situation had become," he tells me, his voice tranquil and smooth. "I have back-to-back meetings until seven tonight, so I can't see you until after. Please come to my office at eight, so we can decide what to do together."

I consider it for a moment. I'm supposed to be meeting Mrs. Greene at her house. She needs to get her closure. What's being done to her is atrocious. "I don't think I can. Can we talk about it tomorrow?"

"Tomorrow?" he asks incredulously. "This is rather time-sensitive, Millicent. We need something done as soon as possible. If Asahi Takahashi and his partners hadn't flown in from Tokyo to discuss a merger, I'd come home right now. We need a plan. We're in the middle of an emergency. You need to be here at eight."

There's no arguing with my father. Once he's decided something, there's no room for discussion. I've learned this several ways. Mrs. Greene will understand that I'll have to tell her all I know afterwards. She's waited months to hear the fate of her daughter. A couple of hours is better than never knowing. There's only so much you can say over the phone. I felt my heart shatter when I told her the bare minimum—seeing her in person is going to break me. I've cried more in the past few days than I have for most of my life. "That's fine, Dad. I'll be there at eight," I acquiesce. "I'm worried that she'll see me leaving."

"Maris said she will be out with Hunter tonight. She won't be there when you leave. You're safe, I promise. It will just be you, me, and your mother."

"Alright, I'll see you at eight. Love you, Dad." "See you then, pumpkin."

It's rare for my father to use nicknames. Neither of my parents cares for them. All our interactions are sterile and lack emotion, so I feel a bit of warmth when I hear it. Mom's word in the house doesn't count for a lot, but Dad's does. He has the utmost authority and with his presence and reach in the community, he probably has figured something out, maybe a punishment for Maris that won't drag our name through the mud or affect sales with the hotels. He's a very logical problem solver. He doesn't care much for emotions and focuses on outcomes and resolutions. It's one of the reasons he's managed to expand the business around the world. There are few major cities that are without a staple of Caldwell Hotels spread across them. He did inherit the chain, but he's taken it to levels that Grandfather wouldn't have dreamed of. Maybe he's at his wits end with Maris too. He's a man with great power, but everybody has their limits. He's spent a decade protecting her; I've spent the better part of my life backing her up. Maybe it's finally my turn to experience the spotlight and have a safety net.

I feel horrible about delaying my talk with Mrs. Greene, but it comes as somewhat of a relief as I don't know how I'll tell her the details without collapsing in on myself. I've had a day to process it, and she's had half an hour to process the partial gore I shared with her, but time doesn't heal the merciless cruelty of the situation. When we were younger, Maris managed to skirt the lines of justice, but I have no idea if it'd be possible to avoid the current grave that she's dug for herself, even with the help of money and influence. I don't know how to tell Mrs. Greene that the little girl who spent the majority of her childhood with her daughter had such an influence on her demise. Her rage would be tenfold to mine, her grief even more. If I were her, I'd get a gun and a shovel and meet Maris and Ted in a forest, alerting the police to follow close behind. One is bound to act in violence, and the other one would most certainly snitch to save their own hide. I feel the nausea rise every time I think about Carol's decaying head, her gorgeous face disfigured and her joyful existence sucked out by unfeeling sociopaths. Beauty and trust served to be her downfall. I wish I could trade places with her.

I'm sickened knowing I actively helped someone who was destroying families, snuffing out lives for no reason other than pleasure. I believed Maris about men causing harm, but her crimes had nothing to do with that—she's not a feminist. She doesn't want justice for women. She wants to prove that she's stronger, tougher, and better than men. She wants to prove herself as a woman in a world she knows is run by men. She wants to beat them at their own game. I believe Hunter did sexually assault her like she said. If she wanted her retribution, she could harm him and be done with it. She may not be able to rape organically, lacking a penis, as she puts it, but plenty of people can get around that issue with an inanimate object, one that can cause irreparable damage. Maris's access to weapons is close to limitless. Or she could dump him.

I lay in my silk nest reading Nancy comics from 1951—the year I was born. There's something about the strips that settles me. They're wholesome and sweet, a fleeting idyllic escape. The evil in my world is absent in Nancy, Sluggo, and Aunt Fritzi's. I wait for as long as I can before I have to get ready. I'm fearing every minute of the rest of the evening: seeing Dad, explaining things to him. Mom's frantic hysteria if she's there. The consequences of possibly turning in my twin. Telling Elaine where her daughter is, how badly her spirit has been defiled. Facing Maris eventually, her wrath. Maybe another night in the hospital. My body is screaming at me, fighting me, telling me not to go. I try to convince myself that if Dad says I'm safe, I'm safe. He can keep Maris at bay, I chant repeatedly to myself, as my limbs defy me. I feel my skin crawl, my stomach sink. I focus on breathing, in and out, slowly, to drown out my racing mind. I'll need more than Valium to keep myself calm. I wear my faded Lee bell-bottoms and a long-sleeved floral turtleneck (that Maris hates) with patent leather purple Mary Jane-style heels. I don't know how to dress for an occasion as macabre as this. Carol's mom is very conservative, and I want to be as innocuous as possible to allow her to focus on the facts. I don't think I'll be very coherent after the first few minutes. I struggle to get dressed with the cast on. Sharp jabs of pain shoot up my arm.

My driving is a lot slower than it should be. Unconsciously, I've been going ten under the limit. I'm jerked out of my stupor when I get honked at by a grandma in a hideous brown Buick Electra. She overtakes me, giving me a dirty look when she drives past. I honk back at her and then pick up the speed. The hotel is not very far from the house, and my father has the most opulent room as his office. It's the second most frequented hotel for him, the first being New York. His expansion to Utah and Colorado is, quite frankly, a bit stupid when he's already in the prime cities of the US. Seattle is crappy enough.

I get onto the 520 instead of the I-90 and get stuck in traffic that shouldn't exist at this hour. When I get into the hotel, I let the valet handle the parking. I give him the only cash in my purse, a five-dollar bill as a tip. He usually expects a lot more, so he's visibly disappointed.

"I'm sorry, Javier, I only have that much on me. I'll make it up to you on my way down."

He smiles and nods, taking the keys. "No problem, Miss Caldwell. Cheer up, you look sad."

"Oh, I'm fine. Thank you."

I take the lift into the granite lobby and feel at ease in the crowd. The din of the people is soothing. I feel reassured by their voices, by their presence. No longer trapped in the house of loneliness, possibly free to step out of Maris's shadow. There's still something tugging at me, trying to pull me back as I walk to Dad's office. I'm cold, but beads of sweat trickle down the base of my neck. He normally has a personal assistant who sits outside his door, but she's absent today. The mahogany doors are imposing, as is the bold lettering in gold: Henry Lloyd Caldwell, Chief Executive Officer. I step in hesitantly.

"Millicent, wonderful. Thank you for getting here on time." He offers me a smile, something rather unfamiliar.

"It's fine, Dad."

"Your mother was quite upset this afternoon when she

came in. She's upstairs in the penthouse suite. I gave her some Ativan and put her straight to bed. let's go and check in on her," he says, standing up before I get a chance to take a seat. "I'm a little bit concerned."

"Mom's here? Is she alright?"

"She should be fine, let's go up." He leads the way to the private elevator that opens directly into the penthouse. It takes an eternity to ascend the levels. I've always been afraid of heights, so the penthouse doesn't appeal to me. I'm unfamiliar with it, but I sit on the Prussian-blue chaise longue, which is more comfortable than it looks. "Where's Mom?"

"She's in the master. Would you like something to drink?" He stands behind the large bar.

I sit, bewildered, looking at him. This is a man who never lifts a finger around the house. He is waited on hand and foot. He doesn't make his own drinks, let alone anyone else's. He delegates, he orders, he demands. I'm caught off guard, not knowing how to respond.

"Well?"

My mouth must be agape, but I manage to form words. "Y-yes, please. Is there any iced tea? Even lemonade, I'm not fussy."

"There's iced tea. Lemon iced tea, actually."

"Oh great, thank you." I'm awkward. I don't spend much time with my father. Family brunches once a week are our only real interactions, but he's barely around for any of them. Outside of that, I only get the privilege of speaking to him if I'm in trouble and he's dishing out a particularly caustic lecture. "Should I check on Mom?"

"Just give it a minute." He comes and sits across from me. "We need to talk about this. It can't go on." He gestures at the bruised face and arm. "Your mother came to me very distressed after she picked you up from the hospital."

"What did she say?"

"She tells me Maris has been terrorizing you, and that she has been involved in Carol's murder. There are things your mother doesn't know about Maris, and the things you two partake in together. I will have to tell her. Quinn needs to know. I'll be frank here. I know Maris is a murderer. I know about her little house and the skulls and all the paraphernalia. I also know that you've been participating in nearly all her crimes."

"Not willingly. I don't want to go out killing guys who've done nothing wrong to me. It's not fair. She says they deserve it, Dad, but she's sick...she's trying to justify things that cannot be justified. I helped because I'm her sister, and I believed her. I love Maris but, when it came to Carol, I couldn't do it anymore."

"I'm aware. I heard your call to Elaine. I've had your phone tapped since you last told me about what Maris had been up to. I already knew, but I wanted to see if you'd say something. When you did, it became obvious that I needed to take extra precautionary measures."

"Precautionary measures against me? You tapped my phone? I'm not the one who was doing something wrong. I told you in confidence, I told Mom in confidence. I thought you could help Maris. The psychiatrist thing was obviously doing nothing. I don't understand."

"That's where you should've left it, Millicent. You should've informed only me and your mother. This is not a matter for outsiders."

"She's not an outsider. She's Carol's mom! You threw a ball to raise money to find Carol's killer. Mom says Elaine's like a sister to her. She deserves to know. It was almost going to be me or Maris. She's allied with a psychopath. Ted's a predator—he shouldn't be out on the streets."

"You're not the arbiter of justice. You're letting out information that will incriminate your sister and land both of you in jail, dragging our name through the mud on your way." His jaw stiffens the way it usually does when he attempts to swallow a bout of rage. He takes a deep breath and unclenches. He dips under the counter to get the pitcher of lemon iced tea. He pours me a glass, stirs it, and places it beside me. He drinks his usual: scotch, neat. My throat is raw and dry, so I take a long swig to ease it. I'm lost for words. I don't understand how anyone can think that family reputation is more important than someone's life. I wish I were in a dream, away from this carnage and indifference. His face is apathetic. It's like he's discussing what to have for dinner.

"You were equally responsible for a large number of the crimes if we're talking in a legal sense. Now, Millie, I care very much for you. You are my daughter. I may not express my feelings often because I wasn't raised that way, but you must know you mean the world to me. I'm sorry to see the pressure you've been under and the pain you've felt. It must have been immense for you to reach out to someone other than your parents. I wish I'd known what was going on in your mind. Maris is easier for me to read, but I rely on Quinn to relay your thoughts to me. I've told you many times that it's important to be discreet about everything that goes on in our family. We have legal teams and public relations managers for a reason."

"Do you care more about profit margins than your own daughters, Dad?" My lip trembles, but I keep my composure. "What about Carol? What would you have done if you saw her decapitated body in a forest where you go on hikes every weekend? The girl you and Mom claimed as your own so publicly? What if Ted took one of us? I don't understand your priorities, Dad, I really don't."

He watches me for a few seconds, wistful. "I'm sorry I've failed you. I would've done anything to protect my girls. I'm sad for Carol. She was a wonderful, sweet girl. What you've done is put us in a very compromising situation. You understand that the first call Elaine made after receiving yours was to the police, right? You did everything but name Maris, but Maris will be linked immediately to the scene, and you know why. They'll say my daughter is deranged, perverted. Sick. I can't have that. I won't allow my Maris to be tarnished. What she's done is horrible, she doesn't deserve sympathy, but she cannot go to jail. My power only goes so far. It's not about profit margins, and I can't believe that's what you're reducing it to."

"What about me, Dad? Do I not matter to you?" I feel something inside me shatter.

"You matter very much to me, Millicent. But you've taken this matter out of my hands. I can't do anything to protect you."

"I don't need protection. I need help. I need justice. I'm not saying Maris should be given a life sentence, but she's done so many horrible things. You should've seen her there with the corpse, laughing, happy. I couldn't face it. Then she came home and broke my wrist. She beats me senseless so often now that I don't even remember how critical the injuries are until people point them out to me, like the valet. Dad, look at this bruise. Look at this cast. Please don't let me down."

He freezes, his tumbler of scotch in mid-air. "The valet saw you? Which one and what did he say?"

"Why does it matter?" I ask, puzzled. "He asked me why I looked so sad and why I was bruised. Don't worry, I didn't tell him anything. I'm keeping it in the family."

"That's the problem, my darling, you're not." He takes a sip. His other hand balls into a fist. It shakes. "Everybody knows now. They know everything. You're a troubled girl. You've hurt yourself before, and you could do it again."

"What are you talking about? I'm not troubled. I tried to

kill myself after Maris's more gruesome murders. I couldn't handle seeing them crying in pain every time I tried to sleep. It was too much for me. I've been okay since then. I haven't harmed myself." "You've made significant allegations against your sister to Mrs.

Greene, and she's relayed that to the police. You've told her that Maris was involved in the murders of the young men, and also that of Carol and the other young lady from Lake Sammamish. There's a witness who can identify Maris and ensure she gets jail time. Several, in fact. Our family reputation is on the line. Maris's freedom has been jeopardized. Carol is the least of our concerns, currently. Her demise was unfortunate. She was a very pleasant girl. I can't comprehend why she's taken priority over your twin. Why would you threaten us this way? Haven't I made it clear to you by now? I shouldn't be surprised, but I am." He paces the room, his blue eyes cold, his brow furrowed. He walks to the door and double locks it, then slings a chain across it to disable the elevator. He reaches into the pocket of his suit jacket and pulls out a small pistol, directing it at me. I freeze. Fear courses through me. I stare at him. This can't be right. This can't be happening. This is my father. My dad. He's supposed to protect me.

"I need you to do something for me, Millie. I need you to do this for our family." He closes his eyes for a minute, then pinches the bridge of his nose with his thumb and forefinger. His hand shakes when he grabs my arm. He drags me to the office-style desk. The gold and white monogrammed blank stationery for Caldwell Hotels lays atop it with an uncapped pen.

"Daddy, please, I don't understand," I sob. I feel sick. I could never have imagined anything like this. I've been a lamb willingly led to my own slaughter. "Please don't hurt me." My pleas are eerily familiar—the same as each one I've heard from the boys Maris killed.

"Millie, I need you to write out a confession letter."

"And a suicide note. You've tried before, but now you'll finally be successful at something," says Maris. Her voice lilts in from behind me, a delicate whisper that freezes my core. It feels like my heart has stopped. My chest aches for oxygen.

"Daddy," I plead, tears pouring. My hand is too shaky to write anything. The walls are closing in on me. I struggle to see straight. My body can't process any of it. I don't dare to turn my head toward Maris. "Why are you doing this to me?"

It's sinking in. If I don't get out now, I won't get out at all. "I'll write it, please, Daddy, put the gun away. Please don't hurt me."

"I don't want to hurt you, Millicent. I never wanted to. You haven't given us a choice. Write a confession letter. You murdered the boys. You were raped. We tried to help you, but you wanted to end your own life. You planted evidence on your sister and Hunter and Stephen."

I write the letter. My hand trembles as I cry. He holds me at gunpoint the entire time. Maris stays where I can't see. I hear the crumpling of a chip packet and a yawn. I write the lies they want me to. I confess to crimes I didn't commit. I tell the intended audience that I'm miserable in my existence, that I feel trapped in my body, and I want to be released into death peacefully. I apologize for the murders, for being an accomplice to the murder of my friend. I sob and I shudder, the finality settling into me, cold and vicious.

Maris grabs my hand and forces it down on the paper. "Gotta leave some fingerprints, you know, to make it genuine," she explains casually. "I'm sorry, Mill. I tried to give you a chance to stop. You should've seen this coming. I wish we had worked it out."

"We still can, Maris. I'm sorry. I beg you. Please. Please don't kill me. I'm your sister. We only have each other. We always have relied on only each other."

I try to figure out how quickly I can get to the door. People are around. If I can get out, I'll be okay. It's about fifteen feet away. I can make it if I can convince my father to drop the gun. When I try to move my hand, I realize I can't. My limbs are paralyzed. I'm trapped. Maris stands in front of me, wearing my purple Diane von Furstenberg wrap dress and knee-high suede boots. She doesn't look overly happy, but she's committed. She's not going to back down. Neither of them will. My body quakes as I plead for my life. My father lowers the gun from my temple, pulling it away from me entirely. The weight lifts off my shoulders. I've been given mercy.

Before I have a chance to think, I feel a bag being placed over my head, narrowing around my neck. I gasp for air, but all I get is plastic. My heart races, I sweat. I can't move. I'm frantic and scream for Mom. My voice is muffled, but I screech again and again. My throat and chest burn as my body struggles for oxygen. The tears are constant, and my lungs are desperate.

My father settles himself beside Maris, slightly more affected than she is. He watches as I thrash in agony, fighting fervidly for my life. The two of them stand in solidarity. There is only one other person who could be holding the plastic bag around my head. One person I've always had the most faith in to save me.

"Mommy, please," I whisper, tired. I feel myself fading. Blackness is setting in before my eyes, but I get flashes of me and Maris in our matching frocks on our fifth birthday, of my mother braiding my hair when I was very little, in the ski lodge in Colorado. I think of Carol discarded as trash. I think of us posing as a family, of sitting on Dad's leg in a Christmas photo. Playing with Maris and watching Mary, cuddled up together, cozy, secure. I see Charles, Connor, Hunter, and Jack. I think of my mother hugging me this morning, reassuring me that I was safe. I let out whimpers when I can't get any more air. "Please Mommy, please don't do this to me, I'll be good. I promise. I love you, Mommy, please. I'll be good. I'll be good." It's the same thing I would say to her when I was little, and I angered her into beating me, with whatever instrument of torture she had on hand. She would stop hurting me. I never thought I'd be saying it to keep her from taking my life. Every inch of me fights. "Please."

"I'm so sorry, baby." My mother's voice drifts. "Please forgive me. You won't be in any pain anymore." I can hear her crying.

My last glimmer of hope dwindles. The darkness consumes me. My body gives in.

EPILOGUE

Maris—January 5, 1975

I can't say it was easy to lose my twin. She was an assistant, a confidante, a shoulder to lean on. The only real semblance of a family vanished soon after she did. We keep up appearances.

I mean, it's pretty horrific when you have to explain to people that it was your sister who murdered those poor boys (and some of the girls) and then went on to kill herself. Her funeral was small, not attended by many, and held in a small church in Redmond. After being associated with the murders of upwards of thirty attendees, people weren't exactly jumping up and down to celebrate her life and mourn her. The Seattle Times published the entirety (or close to it) of her suicide note, issuing a moral condemnation that swept the population. Hunter, Carol's mother, and that weirdo Connor were the only ones to join us in the service. The tears I shed were genuine, but I had time to process her absence.

It had been planned over two months—primarily as a contingency plan, but I knew it would come to it. She was under the impression that she could outplay a puppet-master as skilled as our father. As always, she was wrong. I think about her every now and then. I feel bad that it had to get to that stage, but she needed to be stopped. Once she was gone, Seattle could again sleep easy—the killer had moved on to another realm. It was a foolproof plan: Millie was going to crumble either way because I'd been dumb enough to involve her, and then she stumbled upon Ted's site and thought I'd done something to Carol, so Daddy took it into his own capable hands. He wouldn't have his daughter in prison. Not his heiress. He'd rather a dead condemned daughter to an incarcerated princess. He did it begrudgingly, but it had to be done. Mother didn't have a say in the matter, but Daddy talked sense into her, and she played her part. Very convincingly, at that. Collecting her from the hospital was a nice finishing touch.

I've always been a good actress. It's not difficult to act horrified when people ask if I knew what she'd been up to. By god, I was as shocked as them! How someone could hide a secret that earth-shattering, I would never know. I'm getting used to being an only child. King County is a distant memory.

Behind me is 1974, and I have no intention of dwelling on the past. I spent New Year's Eve with Hunter in New York. We got very drunk, had terrible sex, and he proposed to me. I said yes. It's all part of the plan my father has set in place. Caldwell and Carlyle must merge, not only in the business world. I let him head off to Gstaad for a month to ski with Jack (they patched up their differences—Millie was a liar, there had never been an affair between me and Jack) and promised I'd be there to greet him as soon as he returned to SEA-TAC airport.

While Switzerland would've been pleasant, my current plans are far more exciting. I'm bundled up in a figure-hugging white sweater-dress, with matching gloves and a cute little beret. My Wolford pantyhose is about as close to my skin colour as possible, giving me the sex appeal while keeping me very warm. While my thigh-high suede boots aren't quite appropriate for the snow, they do wonders for my legs, long and slender, just as my date likes. I've kept our dalliance a secret; we're both attached, after all. I'd contemplated driving, taking in the scenery and the alone time, but the thought of eighteen hours in a car made me want to blow my brains out. Plus, Idaho and Utah are basically a waste of space on a map. If I wanted to see toothless hillbillies or inbred Mormons, I'd visit Carol's extended family. I made the sane decision to fly, and I'm a little bit too excited when I see Ted at the arrivals hall in Aspen. He's wearing a turtleneck the same color as my dress, with corduroys, a thick wool coat, and shiny patent leather shoes. I throw myself into his waiting arms. He's certainly grown fonder of public affection since moving three states away from his "homely geriatric" girlfriend.

"You look just terrible, truly. Look at you." He grins at me and reaches immediately for my suitcase to carry to the car.

"I've missed you," I whisper into his ear. I run the back of my hand along his well-defined cheekbone.

"I didn't expect you to come, I thought you'd be spending the start of the year with your fiancé."

"And I thought you'd be with that little girlfriend of yours, but clearly we both had better plans. I can't think of anything better than getting into the suite's hot tub with a bottle of your favorite— Mickey's Big Mouth beer. You'll need it after having been in Utah for so long," I tell him as I follow him to his bug. He can chug the beer while I'll sip on some very fine Krug with a bowl of strawberries and cream. The Caldwell Palace in downtown Aspen has a penthouse suite to die for, and I made sure to book it out for the entire week. Daddy's in Salt Lake, and Mother's back in Seattle, so I don't need to dodge any pop-ins, stares, or interrogations. I'm sure she can finally enjoy Elaine's company again, now that they both have a dead daughter, common ground. No more jealousy and resentment. Ted's passenger seat is often absent but, in anticipation of my visit, it's made a return.

"Let's get ripped, those sonuvabitches in Salt Lake get off on nothing but prayer," he agrees, and laughs as he rolls down his side window. He has a penchant for marijuana, which I've come to tolerate over time, but I'll never partake in it myself. I don't need that stench on me or the inertia in my body. I need to be active, hungry, ready to strike. Usually men don't seek status in women, but Ted sure does. While initially hostile about the differences in our upbringing, he's warmed to the idea of me being able to show him the finer things in life—things he could never access on his own. Caviar service, first-class trains and planes, penthouse suites, and finely tailored designer clothing. It's all within Ted Bundy's reach now, thanks to me. He tells me I remind him of Diane, his very first girlfriend, the one who shattered his heart. She was wealthy, with good breeding and incredibly sophisticated, I'm told, but when I see photos, I resent the comparison. Boy, was she hideous, and a giraffe, at that. Six feet is no height for a woman—and she was no former Miss Washington. Ted's not nearly as handsome as Charles but, since all that's occurred in the past year, I haven't seen him too often, and being with him gives me none of the thrills that being with Ted does. We have more personal things to discuss, things that Charles could never relate to. Ted's stutter pisses me off, especially all the "uh" and "um" nonsense, but when it comes down to it, his conversational ability is impressive. The things he says are mostly pseudo-intellectual, with no scientific backing, but the conviction with which he says them is laudable.

"Don't worry, I'm well-stocked," I say, my hand on his leg.

"Even the crap you like."

He looks thrilled when he hands the keys to the valet. I believe he used to work as one, and now he's finally able to have one. His status in society has finally elevated being in my presence. He seemed to think it did when he was in the Republican party, being surrounded by rich politicos and helping with their campaigns, but he doesn't understand that people in our social strata only humor those around us—they are never truly equal to us. Dating me is a glimpse into the high life, but as long as he dresses the part, no one will be able to tell. I've helped mold him. Though, I must say, a lot of his new wardrobe has developed from his shoplifting habit. Initially, it was difficult to reconcile finding him sexually attractive after seeing him satisfying himself with Carol's corpse, but he has a certain charm about him that puts me at ease. It's probably how he got so many women to trust him, especially with his poorly thought out ruses. It took him time to be less suspicious of me, to open up to me. I'm sure glad he did. I check into the hotel under my name. Millie can no longer take the blame, unfortunately. It was much easier to check into a penthouse suite under the guise of being her so Daddy would yell at her and not me. It's a loss I can manage.

"Miss Caldwell, it's a pleasure to see you," says the blue-uniformed concierge woman, her blonde hair pulled so tightly into a ponytail that I feel pain seeing it.

"Thank you. Is the room ready? I called this morning before I left Seattle."

"Yes, it's ready. There's a note here about a particular brand of beer, so we've ensured there is a six-pack in the fridge," she tells me dutifully.

"And the '55 Krug?"

"Absolutely." She hands me the key. I hand her a fifty-dollar note. She lights up like a Christmas tree.

"Please send up some strawberries and cream too," I say with a polite smile.

"No problem." She clicks her fingers and another employee appears beside me with a golden trolley. "Benjamin, can you take Miss Caldwell up to her room?"

"Right this way, Miss Caldwell. Have you been to this particular hotel before?" he asks me.

"Only briefly. I've booked for longer this time. You guys were far too kind to me! I needed to visit again."

He offers a courteous chuckle to my unfunny joke. He joins Ted and me in the elevator, and we all stand in silence until we reach the top floor. I tip the bellboy, and he leaves.

"You guys sure have a lot of Negroes working for you," Ted comments, and slips off his shoes.

"Is that an issue?" I scoff. I head straight for the beer—I pour him a glass and drop the empty bottle into the trash. I don't drink any myself. I intend to keep my figure. Mother always said that ladies don't drink beer, so I use that as an excuse, but I have indulged in a few Coors while in Colorado. We don't get it in Washington.

"No, I love them. Good vibes, you know?" He takes a sip. "Copacetic. My parents used to hate them. I brought this one kid home from school to get a rise out of them, it was really something."

I wait for the strawberries and eat them greedily when they arrive. I dip them into the cream, ignoring the calorie count. I feed some to Ted, but I feel strange. This isn't my usual dynamic. I'm not the caring housewife sort. I never dreamed of this domesticity, sitting in a man's lap feeding him berries. But Ted isn't like other men. He isn't the Wall Street type or someone like my father. Nor is he the mild-mannered "nice guy" accountant. He's volatile, feral almost. I can't predict what he'll do and it's exhilarating. I'm fine with being the wife when the husband opens all the doors, extends all courtesy and chivalry to me, and then surprises me with debauched actions even I can't foresee. I enjoy talking to him, letting him ramble on about things he doesn't quite comprehend, and then hearing him explain what he does in his secret life (in great detail) without missing a beat. We have a lot in common, except that I have a high IQ.

"Tell me more about your parents," I say, and sip the champagne slowly. I want to hold my liquor. "Or what you were like as a kid. I want to know."

"I don't know who my father was, but my mom was great. Very intelligent. Too poor to go to school, some rich girl got the scholarship she wanted. Married this simple guy, and when I say simple, I mean it. Couldn't possibly be smarter than a gnome. Drove these huge, terrible cars. I was a good kid, probably like you were." The last bit is sarcastic, and he jabs me in the side with his elbow. I giggle but let him continue. "They didn't have the money to get me involved in sports, and I was too little anyway. I loved lying in bed in the sixth grade listening to Meet the Press on the radio. Yours must've been like walking on rose petals."

"Well, we certainly didn't struggle to pay for sports uniforms or hobbies. Mother made my sister and me take piano, French, ballet, violin, tennis, racquetball, cooking classes, deportment classes. As long as we were out of her hair, she was happy. We had a new nanny every couple of months. Occasionally, a nanny would stick around for a year. Those were impressive. Daddy beat the hell out of Mother, Mother beat the hell out of me and Mill. Told me how I wasn't thin enough, not ladylike, not elegant enough. Not a daughter she could be proud of. You met her, she's the shrill little blonde."

"I also saw your house, you had everything you wanted. I went out and got everything I wanted. There was this little Sony television set I had my eye on a little while ago, out at Northgate. I stared at it forever and went home. I had a couple of beers. You know that stuff makes me nasty, and I decided to go and get that damn television. I parked close to the store, walked right in, picked it up, and walked out. It was brilliant! I felt terrific. Who's going to question you when you walk into a display window? I just had to be brazen."

"Jesus, that is bold. The most I've done is take some lingerie. I could've paid for it but, really, I couldn't be bothered, so I left it on underneath and walked out." I'm disappointed with my rather tame retaliation.

"It's kind of like that with girls. I go out and see one that I want, and I take her. Just like the television, just like the Ficus tree and the expensive Navajo rugs from the hotel gift store. She's mine. I get to do what I want. From her being alive and kicking, rosy-cheeked to still and blue."

It's something I truly understand. Possession. "It's fun, isn't it? Owning someone entirely. Deciding what will happen to them, what won't, over whatever length of time suits you. It's funnier with men, Ted. The way they beg. Completely reliant on you, no macho left."

He stares at me in a peculiar way, somewhat wistful, somewhat agitated. "You know, you make me think of Diane. Both dark-haired versions of Grace Kelly. Sophisticated and intelligent, always wanting to be in charge. Rich and spoiled little princesses."

"And you can't control either of us. But, Ted, I don't look like her. She doesn't compare." I don't mention the crystalline blue eyes and perfect nose—hers requires the best plastic surgeon in the country, plus she could do with a visit to a proper hair salon. "And I wouldn't leave you." The latter isn't quite true. Ted is fascinating and consuming, but I'm not the kind of girl that gets attached. My infatuations are fleeting in nature. I don't know how long he'll hold my interest. I think that's the only commonality Diane and I have.

"I'll take your word for it." He takes another swig of his

beer. "I love what you did. Getting her to say yes to marriage and then dumping her via a telephone call. That was incredible." I'm onto my second flute, and I feel it coursing through me, stronger than a shot of morphine. The desire and the alcohol. I lean back.

He rolls a joint with the cherry-flavored paper he had in his pocket. He offers it to me, but I decline.

"I won't lie, I was pretty happy with myself. I think I was drunk that day. It was fun courting her, letting her fall into the lies like the fool she was."

"Tell me, Ted. If she hadn't done what she did, would you still have gone out and killed the girls?" I know I'm pushing it at this point, but I'm genuinely curious. "Was it her or was it that feeling of owning someone? Did you get off on the violence?" (I know I did).

"She contributed, but not in a major way. The violence was to...contain things. I didn't necessarily, uh, get off to it."

I could talk to him for hours at a stretch and not get bored. There's so much I want to know and so much I want to tell. But I want him. I want him so badly. More than I've wanted anyone. I want to taste him. It nearly brings me to tears. It's strange how my perception of him has changed so dramatically. His hand on my thigh sends a jolt of adrenaline through me. My heart races when his finger traces shapes on my skin.

"Show me what you've got on under that pretty little dress," he tells me as he feeds me the last strawberry. He's told me about his voyeurism, both past and present, so I've made sure to impress. I stand up, a little bit clumsy from the alcohol, and he watches with vigor as I slowly pull off my dress. Underneath, I have on a glorious three-piece Chantelle Paris black and gold lingerie set. It is the finest they had in stock, and the suspender links seamlessly to my thigh-high Wolford stockings. His reaction is one of pure joy and spurs me on. The first to come off is my bra, then the garter belt. It's not something I usually wear as I don't have fat to wrangle into submission around the midsection like most women, but it makes the outfit. If there's one thing I know how to do, it's to impress, visually. The way I dress, my makeup, the way my hips swing when I walk, my hair tumbling to my waist in silky waves. I need to look perfect, and it's paying off right now. His gaze is fixed on me, concentrated, and not wavering in the slightest. His mouth is faintly ajar. Darkness enters his eyes, making the crisp blue hazy, almost black. I am overcome with longing when I see this until I am physically struggling to resist him. Having seen him numerous weekends in Utah and Seattle (when he returned to see his parents), I know that he likes complete control when it comes to the bedroom.

He's gentle, which surprised me at first, but ardent. I'm usually in control, but I must let him have it if I want the pleasure that he's provided me in our recent trysts. I offer my hand to him, which he takes, pulling himself up onto unsteady feet.

His lust is all-consuming and infinite. He grabs for my panties, tearing them. It thrills me as much as it does him. I grin at him and catch his hand before it reaches my chest. I can feel his pulse in his wrist: rapid 110 BPM, as expected in high arousal. I sometimes wish I could forget what I learned from medical school. It takes the magic out of the moment.

I turn to walk to the master suite. I feel him close behind, his breath warm on my neck.

"Ted, what are you do—"